Praise for *Standing By*

"In Alison Buckholtz's beautifully written book *Standing By,* she shows us how love of country, love of family—and commitment to both—can sustain military families separated by war."

—TANYA BIANK, AUTHOR OF *ARMY WIVES* (BASIS FOR THE LIFETIME TELEVISION SERIES)

"As a father who waited up at night for those rare treasured calls from my Marine son at war in Afghanistan and Iraq, I not only understand this book but empathize so deeply as to have almost lived every story herein. The author does full justice to the story of those who wait, suffer, and long for the return of the loved one in uniform."

—FRANK SCHAEFFER, AUTHOR OF THE *NEW YORK TIMES* BESTSELLER *KEEPING FAITH: A FATHER-SON STORY ABOUT LOVE AND THE UNITED STATES MARINE CORPS*

"*Standing By* is full of heart, soul, joy, and anguish. What a great writer Alison Buckholtz is, at once intimate and literal, artless and elegant in style. I could read her anytime, on any subject. But no subjects are more urgent than the ones she addresses in her book: love, family, patriotism, heartbreak, joy, and ultimately hope. It will grab everyone's heart. It is a book to be celebrated."

—DA CHEN, AUTHOR OF *COLORS OF THE MOUNTAIN* AND *SOUNDS OF THE RIVER*

"This memoir by a Washingtonian about adjusting to life as a military wife is a touching account of giving up preconceptions and reaching out to others."

—*WASHINGTONIAN* MAGAZINE

"A vivid and sensitive account of the sacrifices made by families of military personnel in wartime."

—*LIBRARY JOURNAL*

"By recording her journey, *Standing By* expands ours as well. Buckholtz serves as an intermediary for the reader, guiding us through the intricacies of Navy family life as she is forced to learn them herself. Buckholtz laments the culture gap between the civilian population and the military and the American layman's narrow understanding of the institution that defends his way of life. Her memoir—insightful and self-aware . . . helps close that gap."

—*HADASSAH* MAGAZINE

"Remarkable . . . Buckholtz vividly and frankly writes about the poignant feelings of loneliness and love experienced by a military wife as she struggles to cope with her children and her own sense of the void in her life. . . . Her effective rendition of what it means to be a military wife offers special lessons for the general population who have not known compulsory military service for more than thirty-five years. . . . It deserves to be widely read."

—*THE JEWISH CHRONICLE*

"Alison Buckholtz's memoir is a universal story of friendship, family, and endurance that reveals the history of the American military spouse from Revolutionary War camp followers to her own experience as a Navy wife in the post–9/11 world. *Standing By* is sometimes funny, sometimes heartbreaking, but always a beautiful, honest book about the toil and triumph of modern military life."

—SIOBHAN FALLON, AUTHOR OF *YOU KNOW WHEN THE MEN ARE GONE*

"An inspirational but not sugarcoated account of military family life. The author tells her family's true stories in a way that will encourage and inspire."

—*STARS AND STRIPES*

"*Standing By* provides civilian America a glimpse into the inner workings of a military family. . . . It also allows military families a chance to realize that others have experiences similar to their own."

—AMERICAN FORCES PRESS SERVICE

"Everything about this book is unexpected. Although based on Alison Buckholtz's experiences as a military spouse, which is a life of quiet sacrifices and countless hardships, *Standing By* is a hysterically funny, deeply moving, and ultimately breathtaking book. Any husband or wife will draw inspiration and wisdom from this extraordinary story."

—ANDREW CARROLL, *NEW YORK TIMES*–BESTSELLING AUTHOR OF *WAR LETTERS* AND *BEHIND THE LINES*

"Alison Buckholtz has penned the reality of military marriage. . . . In *Standing By,* Buckholtz gives this perennial tale a fresh perspective and a healthy dose of historical grounding, highlighting the significant role of military spouses throughout America's history, beginning with Martha Washington and the camp followers of the Revolutionary War. Buckholtz also provides us with historical depth and insight into Navy traditions and practices, making the book educational for even the most seasoned military spouse. *Standing By* is both honest and compelling reading. With her civilian roots and candidly naive perspective of military life, Buckholtz evolves into an admittedly proud Navy wife on its pages. Her book will make veteran military spouses nod their heads in agreement and will mesmerize many civilian readers who want to learn more about the sacrifices, upheavals, and surprising pleasures in the daily life of the naval aviator's spouse."

—*PROCEEDINGS* MAGAZINE, U.S. NAVAL INSTITUTE

Standing By

THE MAKING OF
AN AMERICAN MILITARY FAMILY
IN A TIME OF WAR

Alison Buckholtz

JEREMY P. TARCHER/PENGUIN
a member of Penguin Group (USA) Inc.
NEW YORK

JEREMY P. TARCHER/PENGUIN
Published by the Penguin Group
Penguin Group (USA) Inc., 375 Hudson Street,
New York, New York 10014, USA

USA · Canada · UK · Ireland · Australia
New Zealand · India · South Africa · China

Penguin Books Ltd, Registered Offices:
80 Strand, London WC2R 0RL, England
For more information about the Penguin Group visit penguin.com

First trade paperback edition 2013
Copyright © 2009, 2013 by Alison Buckholtz

Pages 301–2 constitute an extension of this copyright page.

Most Tarcher/Penguin books are available at special quantity discounts for bulk purchase
for sales promotions, premiums, fund-raising, and educational needs. Special books or book
excerpts also can be created to fit specific needs. For details, write Penguin Group (USA) Inc.
Special Markets, 375 Hudson Street, New York, NY 10014.

The Library of Congress catalogued the hardcover edition as follows:

Buckholtz, Alison.
Standing by : the making of an American military family in a time of war /
Alison Buckholtz.
p.   cm.
ISBN 978-1-58542-695-9
1. Buckholtz, Alison.   2. Navy spouses—United States—Biography.
3. United States. Navy—Military life.   4. United States. Navy—Aviation—Anecdotes.
5. Naval Air Station Whidbey Island (Wash.)—Anecdotes.   I. Title.
V736.B835   2009   2008054634
359.0092—dc22
[B]

ISBN 978-0-399-16379-1 (paperback edition)

Printed in the United States of America
1 3 5 7 9 10 8 6 4 2

Book design by Jennifer Daddio

FOR THE AMERICAN MILITARY FAMILIES

WHO SHOW ME THE WAY, EVERY DAY

"Child, my heart feels nothing. I have no words, no questions. I cannot even look him in the eyes. If it really is Odysseus, and he is home, we will recognize each other well enough; there are secrets that we two know and no one else."

—The Odyssey, XXIII, 104–110. *Penelope is speaking to her son after seeing her husband, Odysseus, for the first time in twenty years. He has made his way home after fighting in the Trojan War.*

All the new thinking is about loss.
In this it resembles all the old thinking.

—*Robert Hass, "Meditation at Lagunitas"*

Contents

PART ONE

| Workups |

PART TWO

Deployment

PART THREE

Homecoming

Author's Note

When my family moved to Washington state during the summer of 2006, I had no inkling that I would write a book about our experience as a military family. Neither did the scores of new Navy friends who trusted me with their stories, or the spouses in our squadron who reached out for help. Within weeks of our relocation to Naval Air Station Whidbey Island, I obtained the most treasured security clearance of all: access into the lives of people who would come to mean a great deal to me. I heard their heartbreaks and triumphs in confidence, and to maintain that confidence I have changed names and significant identifying details of nearly all non–family members. In cases that required a greater level of sensitivity, composite characters and altered situations stand in for the real thing, though the essence remains intact. The only secrets revealed are my own.

So, first, a confession: I am not an expert on the military or even the Navy family. I read many books and articles on these subjects, and these texts tutored me in a heritage I am privileged to claim (though I alone am responsible for any errors in the telling). To gain the broadest understanding of the military-family experience, however, I talked to the people who constitute this extraordinary community. Many of the service members' spouses I have met since embarking on this unexpected path have traveled it much longer than I have, and their experiences are richer and more dramatic than my own. Learning of the far-flung places they have established their lives, and the hardships and losses they have endured, has humbled me. Their adventurous spirit has inspired me. They have taught me valuable lessons about the challenges and rewards of a military lifestyle, and I feel honored to transmit what I have learned from them—especially if I can bring these stories to a civilian population with a limited understanding of America's armed forces. But no one military spouse can represent another, and certainly not the entire group.

Finally, a note about the way I refer to military spouses. When discussing our squadron's officer families, I often write about "wives," and I use the pronoun *he* to refer to the married officers of our squadron. Although many officer spouse clubs include both men and women, ours was composed solely of women. Within the squadron, approximately one-fourth of the officers were women. While this is a larger proportion than in most similar units, the female officers were all single, so there were no men among the group of officer spouses. (There were several men among the enlisted spouses.)

I explain my use of pronouns in such detail because female members of the armed forces make up an ever-growing and important portion of the military's enlisted and officer ranks. Their sacrifices and their service cannot be overstated. I don't assume that all service members are male and that all spouses are female, because the reality is quite different. However, during the tour I describe in this book, my peers were fellow military wives, and my use of pronouns simply reflects the reality I lived at that time.

Introduction

A Navy wife should be proud of the Navy and her connection with it, and never by word or deed should she cast any discredit upon it. Times will be hard and separations will be long, but she should present to the world a cheerful agreeableness rather than a resigned stoicism. The Navy doesn't particularly care for a wife who is too *obviously* carrying her load. Take life as it comes in your stride, my dear, and you'll be loved all the more for it!

> —*The Navy Wife: What She Ought to Know*
> *About the Customs of the Service and the*
> *Management of a Navy Household* (1942)

Scott paced in front of me, back and forth, back and forth, silent. But I knew what he was thinking.

"This will never work," he finally said. "We need to break it off now before it becomes too painful. I've been in long-distance relationships before. They always go bad. I don't want that to happen to us."

He was breaking up with me, but it was hard to get upset. This was the third time he'd tried to call it quits, and we'd been dating less than a month. He was a nice guy—too nice—and though we both felt an intense bond immediately after we had met, he remained worried. The problem was obvious: We would have only another month to get to know each other before he moved from southern Maryland, where he was a Navy test pilot, to a base in

Whidbey Island, Washington, where he would undergo two months of flight training. After that, he was headed to a squadron in Japan for three years.

"I think we can make it work," I said, as gently as I could. After our two previous breakups, I saw how easily he could be persuaded. But I had a shred of dignity left, however tattered, and I refused to let him off easily again. Besides, this time, I had an inkling of what nagged at him. His sister, a high school friend of mine who had set us up, confessed that he feared I wouldn't make a good Navy wife.

I didn't want to dance around the issue any longer. I had already started to grow my hair long for our wedding. We needed to move on with this thing.

"Are you afraid I wouldn't make a good Navy wife?"

"I know you'd be good at it," he finessed. "I just think you would hate it. It's not for you. It's not who you are."

Scott counted all the things required of an officer's wife at his level: relocating frequently, involvement with the wives' club (the "knives club," as it is sometimes referred to), "mandatory fun" with people you hardly know, being left behind during long and frequent deployments, shouldering the problems of younger service members' wives, exposure to the ever-present possibility of death.

Carrier aviation, after all, is a dangerous business. Just a few months before we met, two friends from Scott's test-pilot school class had crashed while he was flying. He witnessed the event and the subsequent fire from his jet. He'd been close to the wife and girlfriend of both aviators who died; watching them at the funerals and helping establish scholarship funds for the children forced him to think practically about what he required of a girlfriend, even though we'd been dating for such a short time.

I understood why Scott believed military life wasn't for me. I loved my urban Washington, D.C., apartment. I loved my job handling communications for a national nonprofit association. I loved dining at the numerous ethnic restaurants within easy walking distance of my place. My parents lived twenty minutes away, and I visited them nearly every weekend. Two of my younger siblings rented nearby apartments, and the third was a short Amtrak ride up the Northeast corridor.

Most of my friends' lives mirrored mine. Like me, they were in their early thirties, with graduate-school degrees and jobs that promised either great riches or deep fulfillment (depending on the diploma). We read *The Washington Post* and *The New York Times* and *The New Yorker* and *Harper's*. We agreed on most issues and voted for the same political candidates. We commuted from condos within three subway stops of one another on the D.C. Metro's Red Line. We met for readings at Politics & Prose, a nearby bookstore-café. We scheduled brunches on Sundays. We dated one another. None of us had friends or relatives in the military.

Before I met Scott, I imagined service members to be well-intentioned robots, necessary to society but alien to my thirty-one-year experience of life in America. We began dating during the spring of 2001—before the attacks of September 11 and the subsequent war on terrorism brought faces in uniform to morning newspapers and evening broadcasts. So no military presence peopled my consciousness. I'd never heard of a wives' club, except maybe as the punch line to a joke. I didn't understand Scott's point when he referred to the responsibilities of an officer's wife or the ways the Navy consumes your personal life.

But none of that mattered to me in those early days. Since I'd never seen Scott in his flight suit or his uniform, just in the polo shirts and khaki pants he wore on our dates, it didn't really seem like he was in the Navy.

"I think we can make it work," I repeated.

I was falling in love, and I brushed away my fears. So we talked for hours, repeating ourselves, circling back to the same issues, until he said he couldn't take it anymore. He broke up with me anyway. But he was too tired to drive the two hours back to base, and he asked to sleep on my couch.

I undressed in my room, in the dark, and slid under my quilt. I lay awake, certain that Scott would knock lightly at any minute or just push the door open and proclaim that he was all wrong. He didn't. He slept on the couch. All night. And when I peeked out in the morning, he was gone.

By the end of that year, we were married.

I n the seven years since we stood under the wedding canopy, Scott and I have moved four times and have had two children: Ethan, who is now six, and Esther, who is four. After tours in Japan and Washington, D.C., we currently live in Anacortes, Washington, a friendly town of 16,000 tucked into the far northwest corner of the state. My husband is the commanding officer (CO, also known as Skipper) of a squadron of EA-6B Prowler jets at nearby Naval Air Station Whidbey Island, and I am the "wife of." Fortunately for me, many requirements for military spouses have changed over the decades, and expectations have shifted even further during the last few years. When Scott became skipper of his squadron, he offered me the opportunity to opt out of the responsibilities that are normally associated with being the CO's wife—those same challenges he counted on the fingers of both hands during that anguished night in my old apartment.

But our tour here is just three years, and a lot of good can be done in that time. I've seen firsthand how visiting an enlisted couple with a new baby can boost the morale of the whole squadron, simply by demonstrating that someone at the top of the food chain (however short and insignificant a chain it is) cares about them. I've witnessed how delivering a meal to a woman with sneezing kids, and a husband in Iraq, can transform her whole day. I've watched the way that the squadron's emotional support cheered a young mom who took her toddler to the base hospital for a bruise and was wrongly accused of child abuse. And I've learned how potluck dinners, birthday celebrations, holiday parties, and afternoons at the bowling alley can make military families feel just a bit less alone during a long deployment.

For an institution that prides itself on following directives and procedures, it's interesting that no formal rules exist for spouses to organize, lead, or participate in these sorts of activities. As the skipper's wife (this is how I am known within the squadron), my level of involvement falls somewhere in the middle of the spectrum. Many spouses do much more; many do far less. Sometimes the end result is exactly the same.

A few items in the job description are critical. In naval aviation the CO's wife, with the help of the ombudsman (who works closely with family members, especially enlisted spouses), provides a continual flow of information to squadron families during deployment. If a jet crashes, if there is a terrorist incident or an emergency on the aircraft carrier, the CO's wife often hears it from her husband first. She or her husband notifies the ombudsman, activates a phone tree, and sends an e-mail message to families so that everyone receives accurate, current information. If serious illness strikes a family member at home or if a relative dies, she facilitates a call to the Red Cross, which is organized to handle emergencies for deployed service members, and coordinates support on the home front. (The Navy's Command Spouse Leadership Course, a one-week, full-time class, develops the facilitation skills of incoming CO's wives and trains them on Navy resources. Other branches of the military provide similar courses for senior service members' spouses and family readiness group leaders.)

As a neophyte to military culture—one who drank in feminism along with mother's milk—I was startled to hear that these kinds of responsibilities fall under the purview of the commanding officer's wife. But this tradition is as old as the military itself. The standard for volunteerism and general good works among officers' wives was set early on in America's history by Martha Washington, America's original First Lady. Before she became the wife of the President, she was the General's wife. During the frigid, deadly winter of 1777, some of our nation's first military wives followed their husbands to Valley Forge to support the Continental Army as it fought the Revolutionary War, and she was among them. Historians document that these "campfollowers" created the precedent for the millions of wives of enlisted troops and officers who would accompany their husbands to posts worldwide. In *Campfollowing: A History of the Military Wife*, the authors write movingly about how these women labored to maintain a semblance of domestic life for their families. Their contributions exceeded anyone's expectations. In addition to mundane tasks such as washing the camp's laundry, they nursed countless wounded soldiers back to health and even carried out dangerous espionage missions. In some cases, wives fought and fell in battle next to their husbands.

As General Washington's wife, Martha enjoyed a privileged position, but according to letters and accounts of the period, she never put on airs. She spent her time with the other officers' wives as they knitted socks, patched garments, sewed shirts for destitute soldiers, provided medical aid, comforted the dying men, and took widows under their wing. Leveraging her high-level contacts in the civilian community, Martha collected cash donated by upper-class women who supported the Revolutionary cause ("the offering of the Ladies"), and used it to purchase linen to make more than two thousand shirts for soldiers. Without knowing that the implications of her actions would resonate for hundreds of years, Martha created the prototype of the CO's wife as well as the great-great-grandmother version of today's wives' clubs and family services programs.

Military wives who followed their husbands from camp to camp looked out for each other because no one else did—certainly not the military, which in the early days could just barely clothe, feed, and arrange transportation for a force continually moving and expanding. As another campfollower, Elizabeth Bacon Custer, wife of General George Custer, wrote in her 1885 memoir *Boots and Saddles*:

> *It seemed very strange to me that with all the value that is set on the presence of the women of an officer's family at the frontier posts, the book of army regulations makes no provision for them, but in fact ignores them entirely! It entered into such minute detail in its instructions, even giving the number of hours that bean soup should boil, that it would be natural to suppose that a paragraph or two might be wasted on an officer's wife! The servants and the company laundresses are mentioned as being entitled to quarters and rations and the services of the surgeon. If an officer's wife falls ill she cannot claim the attention of the doctor, though it is almost unnecessary to say that she has it through his most urgent courtesy.*

Elizabeth Bacon Custer lived her long career as an officer's wife one hundred years after Martha Washington, but very little had changed for women by then. Martha, Elizabeth, and the other early officers' wives whose diaries and letters survive (historians have found nearly no recorded documents detailing the experience of enlisted wives) were industrious, supportive, and most of all flexible—qualities still required of military spouses, especially when confronted with frequent moves and even more frequent deployments.

Two hundred years after the earliest campfollowers sewed shirts for the regiment, expectations for American military wives finally started to shift. It was long overdue. Because starting with Martha Washington, who called herself "an old fashioned Virginia housewife, steady as a clock, busy as a bee, and cheerful as a cricket," a military system evolved that judged male officers' suitability for advancement partly on how well their wives fit this ideal. For decades, senior officers evaluating a subordinate for promotion would also assess his wife's fitness as a military spouse. This evolved from the idea, especially popular throughout the 1950s and 1960s, that military wives operate as unofficial ambassadors for American policy abroad, serving as soft-power resources in international relations. Therefore, this "two-for-one" theory goes, the military couple needed to be appraised as a team, and the ambassador-wives must therefore adhere to their own set of rules and regulations.

Formal judgment of a military wife's suitability for her husband's career has gone the way of engraved calling cards and white-gloved teas. Officially, advancement in today's military depends solely on merit. In the Navy, for example, selection boards are explicitly prohibited from considering the marital status of a service member or the employment, education, or volunteer service of a service member's spouse. The volunteerism I see appears to stem from a genuine desire to contribute to the military community. That's encouraging, because being an involved military spouse isn't a job that can be performed under duress or with half a heart. There are too many personal interactions, too many potential stressors, too many important causes, too many people in need. Simply put, there are too many opportunities to slip up.

Scott never asked me to take a role in our squadron wives' club or participate in the social side of his career. I chose to do so, though I also continued working (as a part-time communications consultant and a freelance writer) during most of this tour. I've increased my involvement in the squadron over time, as I felt the gratification that comes from building a community of families. I've also seen how happy it makes Scott to know that we are partners in the toughest job he's ever had.

But if it had been up to me—the person I used to be, that is—Scott never would have volunteered for military service. Because the person I was before my close-up with camouflage grossly mis-understood the essence of that service. Scott's job is difficult and demanding, but it's the path he chose, and he finds it meaningful and fulfilling. He set his sights on it long before he laid eyes on me—and long before the Iraq War, or what's known in the military as the Global War on Terrorism, was ever conceived.

The question that rushes from many people's lips when Scott tells them what he does for a living is not "How do you do it?" as I'm most often asked, but "How *can* you do it?" Sometimes the query remains unspoken, lingering in the eyes of a fellow parent at our children's school. Sometimes a civilian friend dances around the issue, mentioning a politician's name but refusing to voice what would force an inevitable change in the relationship. Complete strangers have no such worries. Scott has been accosted on the street while in uniform by people who demand to know how he can fight in America's current conflict. He engages each and every one with a respect and patience that, I suspect, mask his enthusiasm for de-bate. He starts off by explaining that when he joined the military, America was in the midst of a Cold War with the Soviet Union. He names each of the presidents who have recited the oath of office since then, and touches on the wildly diverse list of national pri-orities that have consumed the country at various points.

"Being a military pilot is my profession," he likes to say. After all, the Navy, unlike some of the other military branches, is a career force, with historically high rates of retention that reflect its need for specialists in a diverse array of fields. It would be impractical to change one's profession every four years solely in response to the political views of each U.S. president, or the actions taken by each Congress. He invokes the service member's oath of office, in which he or she swears to support and defend the Constitution—the entire machinery of government—rather than an individual elected of-ficial. He somehow manages to take the long view.

In the social history of our time, the military serves a proxy role in the culture wars, and keeping this in mind allows both of us to see his service in a broader context. So we are each engaged with our conscience but not in conflict with it. Supporting America as a military family has little to do with who sits in the Oval Office, which political party dominates Congress, or even how we feel about the Global War on Terrorism. I feel strongly that terms like "pro-war" and "antiwar" don't apply anymore because the complexity of the situation we find ourselves in as a country transcends pat positions.

My feelings about service members and their families, however, are not complicated. I have never met people who worked harder, spoke more earnestly, or internalized a stronger sense of responsibility toward their fellow citizens. Marrying into the military granted me a passport into an America I never knew existed, populated by a people whose overwhelming public silence masks lives lived at a level of intensity that would crush most mortals.

That relentless intensity has transformed me into a warrior on behalf of my family. One front is the battle to keep my kids psychologically healthy in the midst of an insane environment: A world where they can identify their dad's electronic attack jet flying overhead and track the progress of his aircraft carrier across foreign waters. My children live in a land without dads; many of their friends' fathers are deployed too.

I'm also pitching a battle to advance my own professional and personal goals as motherhood and the military threaten to engulf everything else I've dreamed of achieving for myself. Ever since I could write my name, I wrote it as a byline. I interviewed teachers for my elementary school's mimeographed newsletter. I staffed the newspapers and literary magazines of nearly every school I've attended. My first essay was published in *The Washington Post* eleven years ago, and the intoxication of seeing my name in print left me permanently hung over. Nevertheless, I've tried to stop writing many times, especially since I had kids and took on squadron responsibilities. I just couldn't afford the hours hunched over my laptop.

But now I have to write about our family's experience of wartime deployment, because it keeps me honest. During the course of Scott's tour, our military family was forged by the iron will to stay connected to each other despite long absences and impossible distances. To stay connected to Scott and the kids, I had to connect with myself. To do that, I wrote. And wrote. That's the only reason Scott, Ethan, Esther, and I survived the odyssey ahead. And that's why this book isn't about politics, but about particulars—the particulars of our family, as we grew to know each other in new and surprising ways, under conditions none of us would have wished for ourselves.

Several years ago, I visited a carrier and heard the intercom announcement, "Stand by for a word from the commanding officer." Activity on the boat froze as the crew awaited a message that might change their lives. In the universe of women and children where I now live, we wives spend our days standing by. We await critical information on our husbands' schedules, swapping rumors and scraps of data on carrier departures, tanker status, and flights from Bahrain as if we ourselves are the aviators.

I'm going to win this war. I don't yet know how, but I will. The future of our family depends on it.

| Standing By |

PART ONE

‖ Workups ‖

The high, emotional tension under which a flier's wife lives will eventually break her unless she is made of pretty stern stuff. . . . [So] be prepared to adjust your social and home life to the odd hours of your husband's vocation. All of these adjustments are vital and necessary to his flying, and, as the real Navy wife, early in your career you will find that they make for contentment and real happiness.

—*The Navy Wife*

Shock and Awe

It wasn't a covered-wagon journey with a caravan of campfollowers, but as Scott drove the kids and me from the airport in Seattle to our new house ninety miles away—which we rented months before, sight unseen—I reflected on military wives throughout history who had been escorted to homes not of their own choosing. To be precise, I wondered how many of them had been able to hide their tears, as I now struggled to do.

Anacortes, a cheerful postcard come to life, had nothing to do with it. In summertime, the town is a paradise, and on that August day a light breeze ribboned the waters of Fidalgo Bay. I glimpsed the length of Commercial Avenue, Anacortes's version of Main Street. Colorful, overflowing flower baskets hung from every lamppost; tasteful banners welcomed visitors to the weekend's arts festival. There wasn't a garish billboard or a chain restaurant in sight. I counted four traffic lights.

Anacortes isn't your typical military town. In fact, it's not a military town at all, especially when compared with places like Fayetteville, Pensacola, or Twentynine Palms. Scott's new base was located twenty miles away, but Anacortes beckons an ever-growing number of Navy families every year precisely because it's not a Navy community. Residents praise the well-run schools, the renovated library, the vibrant arts scene, and the carefully planned commercial area, purposefully devoid of Big Box stores. The proximity to several beaches and lakes doesn't hurt, either.

But my emotions swerved at every bend in the road. Scott turned right, and we drove past a row of rundown rural shacks; my heart fell. He turned left, and we passed a sweet Victorian with blooming gardens. I wiped my eyes and managed a smile. He turned right, and I spotted a barren patch of land with scrawny horses grazing. (Horses!) He turned left, and a small neighborhood of Arts and Crafts–style bungalows gazed back kindly at us.

"I think we're getting close," he mumbled to himself, studying the map.

More turns, more shacks, more farms, an out-of-nowhere hair salon, then a mobile-home park, a few cute cottages, and the last right turn—"We're here, honey," he said—into a newish neighborhood of Craftsman homes. I discovered later that locals call it Wisteria Lane. It certainly appeared perfect. That evening, teenagers rode their bikes in the cul-de-sac, looking after younger siblings playing catch with their friends. Doors swung wide open. The annual summer block party was scheduled for the very next night.

We pulled into the driveway. A wooden play set in the backyard beckoned Ethan and Esther, and both kids revived, curiosity pushing through their exhaustion. It had been an especially trying day of cross-country travel. We had arrived at Dulles Airport outside Washington, D.C., at sunrise; our kids, half asleep, still grasped their nighttime sippy cups of milk. As my father hugged us goodbye at the curb, we wondered why the check-in lines seemed so much longer than usual. Post-9/11 travel remained unpleasant, but the way the line snaked to the end of the terminal seemed excessive, even for Dulles. Word soon reached us that just a few hours before, authorities had uncovered a terrorist plot to use liquid explosives to bomb airplanes. Two and a half hours of line later, we checked our bags and carried our whimpering children to the security checkpoint. As instructed by increasingly frazzled security guards, we dumped the kids' apple juice boxes and milk bottles, the infant Tylenol, and their snacks. Trash barrels were already overflowing with other unfortunate passengers' water bottles, shampoo, perfume, toothpaste, and makeup.

Ethan, who had recently turned three, frowned as he watched his booty disappear. But when the security officer demanded he remove his shoes and walk through the X-ray machine alone, the insult was beyond a toddler's tolerance. He burst into tears. We had no choice. We pushed him forward, sobbing, without us.

I shouldn't have been surprised at being caught up in trickle-down terrorism. The milestones of our family life already read like a mini-history of the war. I had flown cross-country from D.C. to Seattle in the early-morning hours of September 11, 2001, to visit Scott, who had relocated to Whidbey Island earlier that summer. Halfway across the country, the seat belt sign flashed, and the pilot announced that we would be landing immediately because of a national security incident. We were near Minneapolis, the pilot continued in a voice that sounded distracted and distant, and he added that he had no information on when the plane might take off again. I looked up from my book in search of a conversation I might eavesdrop on. Generalized, dissatisfied grumbling wafted from one or two seats, but few of the other passengers exhibited any interest. One person announced that there must have been a backpack left somewhere.

When we touched down on the tarmac, I pulled out my cell phone and dialed my mother's number. She listened to NPR during her commute to work in downtown D.C., and would surely know how to translate the cryptic phrase "national security incident."

Her voice mail picked up. "Mom, I'm not sure what's going on, but we just landed in Minneapolis unexpectedly," I said. "I'll call you later." Cell phone lines went down soon after that.

I spent the next four days at a no-frills roadside motel, waiting for the airlines to resume scheduled flights. Though I knew a few people in Minneapolis, and friends from home fed me phone numbers of their own relatives in the area, I remained alone in my room, venturing out across the six-lane highway only to send e-mail from Kinko's and buy an occasional cheese sandwich and an apple from the deli in the strip mall next door. It seemed right, this frugal, isolated approach to life in the days immediately following the terrorist attacks; it was my penance for being on the right airplane that devastating day. The spareness of my room and the emptiness of my hours reminded me of my travels to a convent in the hills of Nazareth, many years before. During that trip I woke every morning to the slow, hollow ringing of bells. Existence at the convent was as mournful as the peal of those bells. No one smiled—not the nuns who pocketed my shekels and not the other guests, whose eyes reflected the dolor in the air. No one at my motel in Minneapolis smiled, either. The identical shock stamped on our faces wiped out our features, rendering us all related.

After several days at the motel, I finally joined Scott (who had awakened on an aircraft carrier off the coast of San Diego to news of the attack) for our long-planned vacation on Whidbey Island. But the phone rang at three a.m. the night after I arrived, with orders for him to report to his new squadron in Japan as soon as possible. We shared a few more days together as he finalized his paperwork and travel plans, and he proposed the night before he flew to Asia.

Once I returned to D.C., I rushed the wedding plans to coincide with Scott's Christmas leave. My best friend took the train down from Manhattan, and together we addressed and stamped two hundred invitations. But because of the anthrax poisoning at a post office in the city—the post office through which my mail was routed—more than half of the invitations came back destroyed. (Five people died in the anthrax attacks.) We got married as planned, and a year and a half later, after a move to and then back from Japan, a nurse wheeled me into my room at George Washington University Hospital after a last-minute C-section. Scott was then living on the USS *Kitty Hawk*, flying missions in the "Shock and Awe" campaign over Iraq. As our newborn son Ethan nursed, I reached for the television's remote control. The first image I saw was the statue of Saddam Hussein slamming to the ground in Baghdad's Firdas Square.

The conclusion of the initial phase of the air war coincided with the end of Scott's tour. He flew off the carrier to a base in Bahrain and boarded a commercial flight home just a few days later. He finally met Ethan in the International Arrivals terminal at Dulles Airport.

As a newcomer to the military, I am continually astonished by the way war's twists and turns affect the lives of individuals far removed from the actual conflict. Pulling into the driveway of our new home in Anacortes, I couldn't help but wonder what surprises loomed ahead.

Often, when I tell civilians that my husband is in the Navy, a faraway look in their eyes cues a long-ago recollection, and that's when I know I'm about to hear the Myth of the Military Wife. "It must be fun," they say wistfully, imagining a sisterhood of Sunday potlucks and shared babysitting duties.

I, too, had always heard that military wives form a strong, cohesive support group to keep each other going during their husbands' long hours at work and many absences. When in the past I heard "military wife" I would sometimes picture the wives of the Apollo astronauts, an elite sorority whose husbands transitioned from jobs as Navy and Air Force fighter pilots to NASA pilots—public service missions far more demanding than what the family originally signed up for. (Alan B. Shepard, the first American in space, was the first in a long list of astronauts who began their careers as naval aviators.)

I see those women in their careful 1960s hairdos and their linen shifts, eating, drinking, and smoking with each other, watching each other's children, and attending each other's funerals, as dramatized on PBS's *Race to the Moon* series. At the time Scott and I met, my viewing taste leaned more toward *Sex and the City* than documentaries on space missions, but during one of our first dates, Scott, smiling shyly, pulled the videos from his armoire. He'd viewed the series many times and was thrilled to be able to share it with me. It was the closest he could come, I think, to articulating his awe of flight and his own dreams for the future.

As often as Scott had watched the series, he had never slid episode five—"NASA Wives and Families"— into his VCR. As a single guy, he didn't find it relevant. All that was changing fast. So one Sunday afternoon, we propped up the pillows and settled in for the show.

It was probably not the friendliest introduction to the Myth of the Military Wife. But I could tell, if only from the hair and clothes on the NASA series, how outdated were the requirements of the wives to create a *Leave It to Beaver* household. Since Scott had begun introducing me to the wives and girlfriends of his colleagues, I saw quickly they were not cut from that mold. Friendly, smart, and funny, they looked like women I could have gone to college with. Something else made me pay attention too: a sympathetic, been-through-it-all look in their eyes that made me wonder if they knew what my future held. As it happened, they understood exactly what I was about to experience, including the highs, the lows, the lower lows, and the quick elevator trip back up to the penthouse. I'm sure I now scan other aviators' girlfriends with precisely the same look.

At the time I fixated on the question of how to find friends among military wives who shared my interests. It seemed critical to replicate the social circle I had emerged from, intellectual wannabes who gathered at museum lectures after work. When I mentioned it, Scott just shook his head, worried and serious.

"It's a question of finding people you can spend time with," he repeated over and over throughout our courtship. "In the military you don't get your choice of friends. You'll have to spend time with people you might not want to. But you will find someone you like. I promise."

He was halfway right. I didn't find people I liked. They found me.

O ur doorbell rang the first Saturday morning after our arrival in Anacortes, when boxes were still stacked high in every room. Scott, Ethan, and I looked at each other. Even Ethan understood that we could be expecting no one.

The woman at the door smiled. She held a small, potted orchid in one hand; in the other hand she grasped the handle of an infant carrier. I glimpsed the closed eyes of a newborn under the fleece blanket.

"Hi, I'm Martina," she said, thrusting the orchid forward. Mutual friends, she explained, already told her that our sons were the same age. We invited her in, and she rested the infant carrier on the rug. Ethan and Esther came out of hiding to peek at the baby.

Martina knew far more about us than we knew about her. I tried not to give her the third degree, but she didn't mind my questions. She and her husband had lived in Anacortes three years already, though he'd been away most of that time on deployment after deployment. He worked as an EOD officer. I didn't know it at the time, but EOD stands for "explosive ordnance disposal," and it's one of the most dangerous jobs in the Navy, especially in wartime. EOD technicians handle and analyze explosives, clear minefields, and execute missions that make me shudder with fear.

Martina and her family (a seven-year-old, four-year-old, two-year-old, and one-month-old) had been scheduled to leave Anacortes that summer, following the end of her husband's tour. Usually, deployments in the Navy alternate with staff tours or desk jobs known as "shore duty," so the officer can gain a broader base of experience. Shore duty is also widely recognized as an opportunity to catch up on important family time. In our case, we'd just completed Scott's shore duty tour at the Pentagon, which was why he was again preparing for deployment on a carrier.

But times are changing. The protracted wars in Iraq and Afghanistan have drained the military's personnel resources. EOD expertise, unfortunately, remains in demand. The military offers no career-path guarantees anymore and has erased the old, set way of doing things that families used to depend on. A "new normal" reigns, and it encompasses any change that the war demands. Instead of family time and a desk job following three years of frequent deployments, Martina's husband received orders to Iraq as an Individual Augmentee—an IA, as I learned to call it. He left before the baby's one-week birthday. Devout Catholics, Martina and her husband held the christening in their hospital room, with no other family present.

I had never heard of IAs before, though it became an abbreviation that soon flew off my tongue because so many people I knew were tapped for the same thing. When naval officers or sailors are sent on an IA, they go alone, deployed separately from their units, to supplement other military branches that need additional staffing on the ground. Though the naval personnel in our circles tapped for IAs are typically aviators, they do not go in a flying capacity, or even to a naval base. They usually work with other service branches in the most remote locations, including Iraq, Afghanistan, Guantánamo Bay, and the Horn of Africa, helping coordinate specific missions or large operations.

Sailors sent IA are always gone at least six months. Some require a full calendar year in theater, and this does not include lengthy predeployment training and mandatory repatriation periods. Army soldiers, Marines, and certain National Guard and Reserve units have been subject to repeated, punishing twelve-to-fifteen-month deployments since the Iraq war began, with some units extended to nineteen months away. My heart bleeds for those families. Such orders used to be more unusual for sailors and naval officers, who typically deployed six months at a time. That was changing fast, and no one was immune.

Scott and I had planned Esther's birth in 2005 while he was working at the Pentagon to assure he'd be around for the first year of her life. Since he had missed most of my pregnancy with Ethan, as well as the birth and the early days, we wanted to do whatever possible to make sure he witnessed her entrance into the world. Though we both understood that Scott would miss plenty of birthdays and holidays in the future, we thought an initial foundation to build on would help our family through the hard times to come. So as I saw the tiny face peeking out of the blanket, I could not fathom how Martina could be going it alone with four kids, one of then a newborn, and a husband who was searching for explosives in Iraq for a year.

But Martina looked happy. I guessed she was around my age, maybe a year or two younger, in her mid-thirties. In gentler times she would have been called an English rose; her porcelain skin and pink cheeks shone like a pretty doll. She appeared rested even without makeup, her naturally blond hair pulled back into a simple ponytail, and wearing skinny jeans that made it obvious she'd already lost the baby weight. Despite all that, I liked her immediately. I couldn't believe that in the midst of everything, she found the time to buy flowers for me and introduce herself.

Martina became my first friend in Anacortes, and I still feel lucky she rang my doorbell that morning. Throughout that first year, as I struggled to raise my kids alone, I remembered that Martina was doing something much harder. She and I talked on the phone at night after the kids went to bed and checked in on one another with two- or three-line e-mails during the day. I marked my mood much as she did, by the ups and downs our kids experienced with their dad away. The old adage that mothers are only as happy as their least happy child applied to both of us. She called me to whisper a sad confession, or to vent about the military health-care system, or to rant about her family's uncertain future. In other words, she was real, she was honest, and she was the first military wife I met who wasn't scared to say what irked her about the Navy.

I called her to ask questions or, to be more precise, one question: How do you manage life this way? After all, she had been married several years longer than I, and had once told me that the IA was no big deal, because her husband had been deployed for so long during his last tour. He'd been gone for most of the three older children's lives and, of course, all of the baby's life. She repeated the same line I heard from everyone else: "He's been away longer than he's been here."

I would make several good friends during our tour in Anacortes, and all of them surprised me. Because we often called on one another in a crisis—we had no choice, as our husbands and families were far away—we came to know each other quickly and often without pretense. I learned fast that Martina was no Barbie doll and that none of the spouses, no matter how perfect their lives looked from the outside, lived in a dream house.

2

Who by Water

I had one particularly pressing desire during the first few weeks of our new life in Anacortes: I needed to find a synagogue. As far as I could tell, there weren't any within a seventy-five-mile radius. I would have settled for a small local Jewish community but I couldn't find any of those, either.

It wasn't exactly a surprise to find ourselves in a minority. "Are there any other Jews in the military?" I had asked Scott, when we started talking seriously about marriage and a future family. "I mean, I know there have to be, statistically, but are there?" He didn't know. Although he is Jewish, at the time we got married his participation in religion added up to two events: our meeting with my family's rabbi to plan our wedding, and the marriage ceremony itself. Raising Jewish children has become a priority for him, and during his deployment, he would participate in far more Sabbath services and holiday events on the USS *Truman* than I did back home. (In fact, during Scott's cruise, the *Truman* dedicated a Torah scroll rescued from a Lithuanian synagogue during the Holocaust.) Gradually, services in the carrier's small chapel would become a comfort for him, a spiritual respite from battle.

But that evolved over time and would be a huge surprise to everyone—especially him.

In those early days when we were dating, I typed "Jewish" and "Navy" in my Internet search engine. The link at the top of my response page was a name: Rabbi Irving Elson, the Jewish chaplain at the U.S. Naval Academy, in Annapolis. So one morning at work, I snuck into the empty conference room and closed the door. I dialed the number listed for the chaplain's office.

"Rabbi Elson," he answered pleasantly.

I thought I'd reach a secretary or voice mail. I wasn't prepared. I hadn't decided what to say; after all, Scott and I weren't even engaged yet. I stuttered out an introduction, rambled on about my relationship, and stumbled to the embarrassing point.

"I was just wondering if it's possible to be Jewish in the military. I mean, is it done? Well, it must be done, because you're a rabbi, so you're Jewish, but is it easy? Not that being Jewish is ever easy, but is it an acceptable thing? Or just okay? With the other people? Like, the other military people?"

I was imagining a camouflage-and-combat-boots version of the hymn "Onward, Christian Soldiers," with ecstatic troops humming the triumphal song as they marched off to war. In the past few years, a few incidents of military officers proselytizing to and intimidating Jewish troops have made news, and this weighed heavily on my mind. It's embarrassing to admit now, partly because I have met so many Jewish families committed to careers in the military and partly because I have seen firsthand how good, smart people throughout the armed forces work hard to make everyone feel welcome.

I finally forced myself to stop talking. Rabbi Elson was upbeat, sincere, and positive. As the son of a retired Marine NCO who served during the Korean War, he had a wealth of military memories to draw from. He related many of his own naval adventures at home and abroad, and he gave me his wife's phone number so I could hear her perspective as well. Of course you can be Jewish, he said. No, it's not always easy, but you find a group of people to create a community with, and you cherish each other and the experiences you share.

We weren't on the phone for a long time, but it made a tremendous difference for me. And a half-dozen years later, when Rabbi Elson (who was by then a Navy captain and the chief chaplain to the commander of Naval Air Forces) flew out to the Persian Gulf to conduct the Passover seder for deployed service members on the USS *Truman*, Scott was among the first to greet him. They had never met or spoken before. As they shook hands, Scott held out a photo of Ethan and Esther, and told him, "You're the reason we got married."

Figures on Jews in the armed forces are hard to come by because the military does not routinely report statistics on service members' religious practices. According to rough estimates from the Department of Defense, there are currently 4,000 Jews in all of the services combined. A recent *Military Times* poll found that Jews make up about one percent of active-duty military members and just over two percent of the National Guard and Reserves.

This hasn't always been the case. During World War II, for example, Jewish military members served at rates consistent with their ratio to the total population: around 3.5 percent of the total armed forces during that conflict, with numbers reaching 550,000. Institutional support was also much higher: 311 Jewish chaplains served on active duty during World War II, whereas today only twenty Jewish chaplains have answered the call to active duty, and almost forty more serve through the Reserves or National Guard. Lower rates of Jewish participation in today's military reflect a documented trend in American society at large, sometimes called the "civil-military gap." This phenomenon describes a divergence in the demographic makeup of the U.S. military from the population at large. Some characterize this "gap" as a deep and corrosive drift between mainstream American culture and military culture, attributing this to the emergence of the all-volunteer-force policies that replaced the draft after its abolition in 1973.

The civil-military gap applies to American Jews as well, though Jewish service members have served the nation since the Revolutionary period and many have been recognized for their achievements and heroism. For example, Uriah P. Levy (1792–1862), a celebrated naval officer, rose to the rank of commodore, abolished the tradition of corporal punishment in the military, and later saved Thomas Jefferson's Monticello from destruction. In the last century, Admiral Hyman Rickover (born to a poor Jewish family in Poland) exploited the nascent power of nuclear technology to advance the Navy far beyond its goals of the period. He is now referred to as the "Father of the Nuclear Navy." Many other Jews have also served with distinction and received the services' highest decorations, including the Medal of Honor.

Today, estimating rates of service among Jews is difficult because almost 400,000 service members list no religion at all on official military forms. Among Jews, some may be concerned about being captured in an unfriendly country, where their dog tags would guarantee certain death; others may worry about anti-Semitism within the armed forces; some simply prefer privacy. For Scott, it was a combination of those reasons that led him to initially list "NRP"—no religious preference—on his dog tags and in his service records. For years, he was one of the many who would not have been counted in official statistics.

When I first asked him what it was like to be Jewish in the military, he just laughed. Now I understand his reaction, because in a military setting where commonality is assumed, conformity is cherished. Though neither of us had any particular desire to declare our uniqueness, being Jewish was just one more in a long list of things that made us different.

"And not different good," Scott said, grinning. "Different weird."

I soon understood what he meant. For one thing, I use my own last name (a decision I made when I was seven years old), which is unusual among military wives. For another, Scott and I married and had kids when we were in our thirties, whereas many of our military colleagues started families when they were significantly younger. But being Jewish in the Navy—semi-practicing Jews, at that—trumped all the other elements of our lives that made us "different weird," and I figured the Navy would not be a source of Jewish friends. (I was ultimately wrong about that, too—one more item in a long list of misconceptions.)

Perhaps, I thought, there was a civilian Jewish community in my part of Puget Sound—Fidalgo Island and north Whidbey Island— that had already organized itself. But my very first night in Anacortes convinced me that this part of the country was worlds away from what I had left behind. Scott had stayed with the kids in our hotel room during our first full day in town so I could supervise the movers as they carted furniture into our new home. They dragged the last box upstairs around ten p.m., and I spent another hour doing what I could to get organized. Then I called a taxi to bring me back to the hotel.

The cab driver was young, white, and chatty. His greasy, shoulder-length hair hung straight as a curtain. He was interested in what brought us to Anacortes and immediately took on the role of town tutor. Apparently he thought I needed advice about how to deal with the tourists that flood the area every summer; he seemed resentful he had to depend on them to make most of his money. He was an encyclopedia of xenophobia, ticking off on his fingers the hateful qualities of the Japanese, the Europeans, even the Mexican immigrants who lived in poor towns miles away but came to Anacortes on occasional Sunday afternoons to go fishing at Bowman Bay. Halfway to the hotel, his anger peaked. "They all just try to Jew you down," he raged. "Pennies here, nickels and dimes, just like the Jews."

I stayed quiet, wishing myself back at the hotel with Scott, wishing I was already laughing with him about the cabdriver, instead of being stuck in this car, in the dark, in a town whose name I could barely pronounce. The rigors of the day finally hit me. I was exhausted. But I was also furious. I believe in signs, and meeting an intolerant misanthrope my first night in Anacortes did not necessarily bode well for the next three years of my life. The more I thought about it, the angrier I became. *This* guy? *This* guy is going to mark the start of life in my new home? *This* guy is going to be what I remember about moving here, the symbol of all things Anacortes? Not this guy, I decided.

So when we finally pulled up in front of the hotel, I paid him the rate flashing on the meter, no more, no less. And then, in my calmest, most measured voice, I told him that his words were hurtful and ignorant. I told him that the kinds of things he said started wars and stirred up hate. My younger siblings have always insisted that my dry, boring lectures were worse than any punishment, so I tried, in my own small way, to inflict the most pain. He was immediately contrite, a shadow of his former Talk Radio self.

"You're Jewish?" he asked. (He had the same dazed-but-interested look on his face as that of a hairdresser I would meet later that year who discovered I was Jewish and started quizzing me about my belief in Christ. "I hope you don't mind if I ask you these things," she finally said. "It's not every day you meet a Jewish person.")

Suddenly, I wasn't angry anymore. The taxi driver looked smaller than ever, gazing up at me from his torn upholstered seat.

"Yes," I answered, feeling as closely observed as a butterfly pinned to a mat. "And I'm just asking you to be more careful from now on."

———

A few days later, I reprised the Internet search that years before landed me on the line with Rabbi Elson. This time, I typed in the words "Jewish" and "Anacortes," "Jewish" and "Puget Sound," "Jewish" and "Whidbey Island." But my search revealed no resources nearby—no synagogue, no Jewish community center, no local *chavurah* (friendship group)—though in town I had already noticed many churches. In Anacortes these places of worship are located in every direction the compass points: There are churches in homes, churches on the second floor of town buildings, churches on long stretches of road that otherwise seemed completely uninhabited, churches on every other corner. Congregants convene in libraries and at schools and even meet on the Anacortes waterfront.

In our remote corner of the country, many other (typically secular) businesses operate in a Christian context as well. The gym I belong to—a sleek, friendly, and well-run facility with an excellent children's room—was founded on Christian principles enumerated in its outreach materials. The only indoor play area in the county, a popular place for rainy days and birthday parties, is run by a church. I understand the appeal of religious communities well, and people with deep Christian faith have long been among my dearest friends and colleagues; I haven't run into any Elmer Gantrys or modern-day patriot pastors. Even when the etchings on our stained glass don't match, I find these friends to be so clear-eyed I can see nearly into their heart. In any case, I have long relished the comfort of belonging to a community within a community, and that's why I find reassurance in Jewish groups; it makes the world seem a little smaller, a bit less intimidating. So I never minded bumping up against overt evidence of Christianity in every corner. I simply wished that there were more options for my family and me.

In Anacortes, with the taxi driver's face still fresh in my mind, I craved that comfort more than ever. Something darker gnawed at the edges of my consciousness too. Now that we lived in an over-whelmingly Christian area, Scott and I knew our children would soon be made aware that they were different. He and I both re-member the taunts we endured during our own childhoods from kids who discovered we didn't celebrate Christmas and Easter or go to church on Sunday. It was bound to happen to Ethan and Esther as well. We always hoped Judaism would be a long-term positive force in their lives, a rock to rest on when those waves crashed upon the shore.

Finding a synagogue in Anacortes became especially important because of the fast-approaching Jewish festivals of Rosh Hashanah and Yom Kippur. For many Jews, including me, these holidays are devoted to soul-searching culminating in a spiritual new beginning. Rosh Hashanah and Yom Kippur are the holiest days on the Jewish calendar, and I cherish the opportunity they afford to think through my year and my relationships with others. Though many Jewish holidays pass me by, and most religious practices, like keeping ko-sher or abstaining from work on the Sabbath, do not resonate for me, the high holidays are a different story. Even during Scott's tour in Japan, we celebrated these holidays with a group of Jewish naval personnel. Judaism is a religion that greatly values community, and none of us wanted to go it alone. I didn't want to go it alone in Anacortes, especially when our family already felt isolated in so many other ways.

As we began to settle into our new home, I left messages at the two closest synagogues, both about an hour and a half away. I also called the chaplain's office at our naval base to ask about Jewish resources. Since there are Jews in all of the military branches, I figured some of them must have wandered out here.

"I know there are no synagogues nearby," I started to say to the sailor who picked up the phone in the chaplain's office.

"There is one," she interrupted, naming a yeshiva in Coupeville, about forty minutes away. For some reason I couldn't put my finger on, the yeshiva sounded suspicious. Yeshivas are religious schools—seminaries—and it didn't make sense that there would be one in Coupeville that I wouldn't have discovered in my research. A synagogue is not synonymous with a yeshiva, either. My instincts were confirmed when I discovered that it was actually a messianic synagogue.

Messianic Jews, as they refer to themselves, maintain a Christian worldview and theology, believing that Christ was the messiah. However, instead of aligning with a mainstream Christian denomination, messianic Jewish organizations combine selected Jewish practices with faith in "Yeshua," or Jesus. They are known for predatory recruitment tactics among Jews, and their presence on the resource list made it clear that someone intentionally misled the chaplain's office. (Later, I learned that messianic Jews are attempting to infiltrate the military in order to target Jewish personnel for evangelization, including efforts to integrate as military chaplains.)

Hearing this news, I felt like my head was exploding. I was horrified by the thought that other Jews who had called the base for help were directed to an organization whose primary goal is to convert them to Christianity. It's hard enough to be a practicing Jew in the military without finding oneself the target of sectarian outreach. When I called back our religious ministries office and explained the situation to one of the base chaplains—a Protestant minister and former Navy helicopter pilot—he was even more shaken than I. He did everything right: apologized profusely, explained how well he understood the gravity of the situation, and immediately struck the contact from his reference list. I was grateful for his responsiveness and his sense of urgency. He also happened to mention that the base had no Jewish lay leader. Even I, with my limited knowledge of Judaism, can do better than this, I thought, so I volunteered Scott and myself for the position.

While that process marched ahead, I told the chaplain that we would offer Jewish service members holiday meals at our home, and

he promised to give our number to sailors who called his office looking for referrals. Since the nearest synagogues were too far away for
us to make the trip, I had ulterior motives: I hoped to be able to
share a Rosh Hashanah dinner or a Yom Kippur break-the-fast with
other exiles. Though at the time it felt like we were the only Jews
in town, I knew that couldn't possibly be true. During my junior
year abroad in college, I lived in Dublin, Ireland, and discovered the
vibrant, established Jewish community there in my first few weeks.
Then, too, I was looking for a way to mark the upcoming high
holidays, and I wasn't disappointed. In Dublin, I found three synagogues, a Jewish museum, and even an Irish Jewish boyfriend.

I remembered the happy times I'd shared with Jewish friends
in Dublin as I shopped at the base commissary for our upcoming
Rosh Hashanah meal. I wasn't sure how many people would RSVP,
so I bought extra brisket, extra vegetables to blend into the matzo
ball soup (following my mom's recipe), and extra ingredients for
side dishes. I even special-ordered bottles of kosher wine from the
base liquor store, and asked the local bakery to bake round, braided
loaves of challah bread, traditional for the Jewish New Year.

But no one called. I checked in with the chaplain a few times
but finally stopped, embarrassed as a jilted bride. Worse news soon
rolled our way. Scott discovered he'd been scheduled for training on
an aircraft carrier offshore on Yom Kippur—the holiest day on the
Jewish calendar, traditionally marked by prayer and reflection.

So our small family dined alone on the eve of Rosh Hashanah.
For the kids' sake—mine too—I tried to make it special. I smoothed
out a white tablecloth on the dining room table, unpacked our china
and silver, baked the brisket and simmered the matzo ball soup.
When I finished setting the table, I looked around, satisfied. It mirrored the holiday table at which I had grown up, marking the
Sabbath and religious festivals with family and friends, food and
laughter.

Scott and I tried our best. We explained to the kids that the world celebrates a birthday, just as they do. The new year, we said, is a chance to do everything better, especially to be nicer to the people we love. Those unopened bottles of wine stood accusingly on the kitchen counter.

D uring the ten-day period between Rosh Hashanah and Yom Kippur, known to Jews as the Days of Awe, I walked around anything but awestruck. Instead of reflecting on how to become a better person in the year to come, I tried to tamp down dark feelings of sadness and regret related to our move.

"I'm panicked," I finally confessed to Scott. "The new year is going to come and go. This is a big time for us, the start of life in a new place."

"Are you worried about something in particular?" he asked.

"There are too many uncertainties to focus on one," I said. "I just need some way to gird myself for the challenges ahead, no matter what they are. I use this period to decide how to live my life. The holiday is symbolic for me, but it's an important symbol."

The missing element was not inspiration or revelation, or even the need for a place to pray. I long ago internalized philosopher Martin Buber's idea that God is "the mystery of the self-evident, nearer to me than my *I*." In Anacortes, I was just simply searching for some peace.

"Then let's find a way to do it," Scott replied, always the pragmatist. That is just one of the many things I love about him. He listens when he needs to, and he solves problems when they present themselves. This was one of those times I asked him to do both, and he came through. So later that week we hired a babysitter for the kids, and he and I took a long walk on one of the trails near our house. We held hands and talked about the past year: Ethan's toddlerhood, Esther's birth and infancy, our move, our extended families, our jobs. We talked at length about the responsibilities of his new position, and strategies to stay connected despite the intense pressures we were warned of. We both recalled an admonition from a senior officer at a precommand tour training: "What you're about to go through can make you stronger if you have a good marriage, and if you don't . . . well, it just might break you."

Scott and I had a great marriage, but the way that senior officer described the coming tour convinced me it would be even more difficult than I imagined. Only so much preparation lay in our hands, though. We outlined our goals for the year to come and shared our hopes. I told him I would be there for him, and he said the same thing to me. We walked in silence, and as the leaves crunched under our feet, I began to feel calmer.

A day or two later, when he packed his flight bag for the carrier, I was ready. We kissed good-bye on Yom Kippur morning, and I drove the kids to school. Back home, alone in the bedroom, I opened the prayer book to the Yom Kippur service. I sat at the windows overlooking our backyard, and every few moments I found myself lost in thought, staring at the wilting hydrangea. I froze for good at the Unetanah Tokef, a religious poem that is intended to prepare readers for the seriousness of the introspection required. It reads in part:

> *On Rosh Hashanah it is inscribed,*
> *And on Yom Kippur it is sealed.*
> *How many shall pass away and how many shall be born,*
> *Who shall live and who shall die,*
> *Who shall reach the end of his days and who shall not,*
> *Who by water and who by fire,*
> *Who by sword and who by wild beast,*
> *Who by famine and who by thirst,*
> *Who by earthquake and who by plague,*
> *Who by strangulation and who by stoning,*
> *Who shall have rest and who shall wander,*

Who shall be at peace and who shall be pursued,
Who shall be at rest and who shall be tormented,
Who shall be exalted and who shall be brought low,
Who shall become rich and who shall be impoverished.
But repentance, prayer and righteousness avert the severe
    decree.

I closed the prayer book and stared out the window. Scott's upcoming sea duty, requiring months of flying jets on and off aircraft carriers, weighed heavily on my mind, and the phrase "Who by water?" sounded unthinkably cruel.

3

Gone Mom

Early in our friendship Martina mentioned that she never thought she would marry into the military, either. She had been working long hours at an ad agency in San Diego, her first job after college, around the time she met her husband. She always referred to him by his last name, which fit her I'm-tougher-than-I-look persona.

"We were at a *concert* with a group of friends," she shrugged helplessly, stressing the word as if to say, *I had nothing to do with it.* "McGowan told me he was a naval officer, and he seemed so proud of it. I thought everyone in the Navy swabbed the decks, and that none of them went to college, and I had no idea what any of them did or what on earth he was so proud of. I was like, 'Yeah, what are you smiling about, buddy?' I felt sorry for him—that he felt it was so great to be in the military and that he had no other options and had to enlist to get ahead." I know something about this attitude.

But Martina learned a little more about the military, just as I did, and she and McGowan married a year later. At the time, he was a junior EOD officer who dreamed of one day becoming an admiral. Martina wasn't sure how an admiral stacked up against a corporal, a colonel, or a general—the only ranks she'd ever heard of—and that was only because she watched *M*A*S*H* in reruns throughout her latchkey childhood. She was born and raised in suburban Sacramento, the daughter of two successful entrepreneurs, and no one in her family had ever served in the armed forces. But McGowan's family—proud Irish-Americans from Boston's South Shore—lived a very different American dream.

"They are so gung-ho about the Navy," Martina complained as we stood in the cheerful foyer of her house. "Nothing makes his parents happier than telling their friends that he's in the military. Yellow ribbons around the tree, needlepoint flag pillows, God and country—the complete package."

My parents support the military too, but that hasn't always been the case. My mother pushed my stroller in scores of antiwar rallies at the University of Wisconsin throughout 1969 and 1970, years my father was finishing his Ph.D. research there. Black-and-white pictures in their albums capture her, a somewhat bewildered-looking woman with long blond hair, surrounded by hundreds of other students whose features were contorted by rage. All were yelling at police, who were roughing up the protesters. Banners in the background displayed antiwar slogans in Helvetica bold italics, proclaiming their fury louder than any voice.

Throughout the Iraq War, many dissenters have been careful to note their support for the troops, even if they don't support the war. That didn't seem to be an option for my parents' generation, who labeled each other peaceniks or patriots. During the Vietnam conflict, many protesters at places like the University of Wisconsin identified themselves as "antimilitarist" rather than simply "antiwar." Wisconsin students even staged an annual Antimilitary Ball to protest the school's ROTC dance. But the 1970 bombing of the Army Math Research Center at the university convinced my parents that the radical fringe that dominated the antiwar move-ment had gone too far. "The postdoc who died in the bombing was just like us," my father remembered. "He was married. He had little kids. The protesters said they wanted to stop the killing in Vietnam, but they killed someone to get their point across."

My father hand-carried his three-hundred-page dissertation from his lab back home every night after the bombing because word circulated that the Army conducted research there as well and that the building was next on the radicals' hit list. Though they continued to protest the war, my parents wanted out of Wisconsin. My father accepted a postdoctoral fellowship at the Medical University of South Carolina in Charleston. His new job landed us in a town over a thousand miles away and twenty years behind, as my mother describes it. No antiwar slogans pierced the southern silence, just discontented grumbling about a garbage strike that roiled locals years before we arrived.

In Charleston, my pragmatic parents shed their hippie habits while maintaining socially progressive principles. They had three more intense, willful children, and drew upon all of their emotional resources to raise us. Their attention to the rights and wrongs of the outside world competed for focus with the rights and wrongs of sibling battles. But they both pursued government careers in fields that fit their idealistic-yet-practical outlook. After our family left Charleston in the early 1980s, we moved to the Maryland suburbs of Washington, D.C. Among other innovative projects, my mother founded the Brownfields program (which facilitates the redevelopment of abandoned industrial sites in order to rebuild blighted communities) at the U.S. Environmental Protection Agency. My father oversees a program office at the National Institute on Aging that explores prevention and treatment of Alzheimer's disease. I consider them public servants in the best sense of the word.

Now that my parents are grandparents in their mid-sixties living through another unpopular war, they reflect on their own youth without sentimentality. "We may have looked angry, but the truth is that we were terrified," my mother told me. "Any of our male cousins, friends, and classmates could be drafted. It's not like today. No one was off the hook then. The war affected every single family in America. We had to protest the war and take ourselves seriously because we lived in serious times."

But perspective, and her new identity as the mother-in-law of a service member, make some of the Wisconsin memories almost too distressing to recount. She feels terribly guilty about the way her peers ignored Vietnam vets upon their return, and she tries to set things right whenever she can. "I passed some soldiers in the airport yesterday," she continued. "They were arriving home from tours in Iraq. I tried to make up for the past. I walked over to them and shook each one's hand and said, 'Thank you for your service.'"

"That was nice," I said, willing myself anywhere else. Her feelings are so heartfelt and helpless. But I could barely talk about it, envisioning the scene. Since I married into the military, every soldier and sailor is my husband.

"I wanted to do so much more," she said. "I kept trying to think of something. I should have bought them dinner."

"You should have," I replied, unkindly. Her confessions pained me, too—especially because I know that in her profound remorse over the treatment of Vietnam veterans she is far from alone. I have always suspected that policymakers who orchestrated the Iraq War leveraged America's collective guilt as they whipped up support for the invasion and first phase of the conflict. No one wants to identify with the generation of protesters who taunted the troops and mocked the military. No one wants to be tagged disloyal or unpatriotic. No one, including my mom—who the year before I was born covered the University of Wisconsin's Antimilitary Ball for a journalism class assignment—wants to repeat the past.

That first fall in Anacortes, it seemed that every other Navy wife I met was mailing packages to a husband serving out an IA in Iraq. I found out later that the expertise in the specialty of electronic warfare, held by those who fly Prowlers, is in particular demand in Iraq and Afghanistan, and EOD specialists like McGowan are always high on the list of IA needs. But Martina seemed to be thriving amid the happy chaos of her four kids, and when I met a mom named Lily at my son's school, she mentioned that her husband, too, was leaving shortly for Iraq. Like McGowan, Lily's husband had just completed a three-year tour packed with deployments. The family had just begun to recover from the frequent separations with a shore tour when he was pulled away from his desk for a twelve-month IA.

"I'm so sorry," I said when she told me.

"Oh, it's no big deal," she said, waving her hand through the air as if to brush away annoying cobwebs. "They come, they go. He's never home anyway. The kids and I have our routine."

I began to see what she meant about routine. Scott left in early October for a month—his longest period away from home since the kids had been born, and my longest time alone with them—and I was running the house with the precision of a drill sergeant. I discovered early on in his absence that the only way to get the kids to bed on time (translating into a few hours of peace for me) was to make sure that everything that took place up until then was choreographed to the precise moment. We'd never been sticklers for schedules before, though we followed a basic timetable every day. Now I counted on that timetable to deliver me to the precise moment when I could sit alone on the couch, reading a book or folding laundry as night fell. I usually went to bed early, since the kids greeted each new day at five a.m.

Many of my friends had trouble sleeping at night when their

husbands were away. They were used to having a warm body next to them in bed; they were scared of intruders; they worried about bills or whether or not the car needed another oil change. The insomnia lasted a few weeks after their husbands left, and then life usually clicked back into place. Military wives are the highest-functioning people I have ever met, second only to the service members themselves.

For some reason, I never shared those worries. Only one anxiety emerged from my new Navy life: I fretted that I would die in the night and my kids would wake up alone. Of course, there was no reason I would die in the night, but once Scott left it seemed obvious this would happen, and it became imperative to plan for this eventuality.

My plans were preposterous. I placed a stepstool next to Esther's crib so that Ethan could pull her out. (This alone surely would have ended in disaster, but I blithely ignored that fact as I checked tasks off my list.) I removed the baby gate from the top of the stairs so the kids could make their way down without me. I placed all the cereal boxes in the pantry on the bottom shelf, so they could scavenge for days, if they needed to. And—intruders be damned—I left the front door unlocked overnight so that the kids could make their way into the yard on their own the morning after my demise and ask a kindly neighbor for help.

With Scott gone, who would notice if something happened to us?

This fear helped me understand the wisdom of the old Navy way, when families lived on base in houses so close to each other you could smell what a neighbor was cooking for dinner. The fishbowl atmosphere had once annoyed me. Typically, everyone in base housing knows what everyone else is doing, when they're doing it, and with what frequency. You see your friends, neighbors, and squadron members several times a day: shopping at the commissary, walking a baby, mowing the lawn. Scott and I lived in base housing in Japan, and I quickly understood that in the long run, it was not for me. But that was before we had kids. For a wandering tribe of service members and their families, knowing that someone will look after your children when you fail to pick up your morning paper may be worth the cost of a nosy neighbor.

Although Anacortes was terra incognita upon our arrival, a few scribbled phone numbers in my pocket gave me hope that firma was not far off. In the Navy, you share some of the most intense experiences of your lives with people who move away with no forwarding address, but you can usually count on running into them on a base somewhere on the other side of the country, no matter how many years pass. The Prowler community is small enough that aviators and their families are posted together many times during their careers. I finally understood why Scott never liked to say good-bye to his friends, who, like him, were constantly packing up and moving across the country or across the world.

"I'd spend all my time having good-bye lunches and good-bye dinners and promising to keep in touch, which would just be a lie," he explained once. "No one keeps in touch, but you always see each other again. You know you will, and you just pick up where you left off. It's great. You never get a chance to get tired of each other." Scott spoke to his good friends every two or three years, when their paths happened to cross in between sessions at a conference or a class, or when they were stationed together. They caught up on wives and kids and careers for fifteen minutes and digested that slice of shared intimacy for months to come.

I listened to Scott talk about his Navy friendships as if I were an anthropologist tracking the bizarre rituals of a just-discovered culture. I'm not sure if it's a gender issue or a basic personality trait, but I still chat on the phone with friends I played with at age three. I e-mail elementary, middle, and high school pals; college classmates; and my first roommate after grad school, with whom I shared the most squalid apartment either of us had ever lived in. Staying connected to people from every phase of my life is important to me because it helps me feel like I accomplished something meaningful during those periods. So Scott's theory on friendship didn't resonate with any of the truths I held near and dear.

Once we arrived in Anacortes, though, I saw how well his approach worked for our shared military lifestyle. Many of his friends from former squadrons and previous tours called to welcome us and invite us over. I'd never met them before, or even heard their names, but they greeted me with hugs and offers of help. The only acknowledgment that I hadn't been around forever came when they would politely fill me in on background to the sea stories they were recounting.

These were the people who would be a big part of our lives for the next three years—they knew it, I knew it, and we all tacitly agreed we couldn't waste any time on niceties. Any of the guys could transfer to a different base or deploy for months at a moment's notice. And since planning even a week or two in advance was hard (we never knew what the squadron schedule held or how world events would intervene), we rarely planned ahead. We all lived in the moment, calling each other for playdates that afternoon or meals that night. Military friendships are different, I came to see. After just a few months in our new home, I finally understood what Scott had been trying to tell me for years.

One element of women's friendships that is probably universal is the fast bond women build with the mothers of their kids' friends. I was lucky twice over. Martina's son Ronan and my son Ethan bonded the first day they met, so Martina and I had lots of excuses to get together. We started meeting for family dinners at Village Pizza on Sunday nights, and as the kids gobbled down their greasy slices and fed coins into pinball machines, Martina and I caught up on our week.

Despite the odds, she seemed to be doing well. I probed as delicately as I could. After all, our boys were the same age, and though I hoped Scott would never be sent away for a year, I knew that he might be tapped for an IA in the future, and I was desperate for lessons on raising kids alone. In her own way, though, Martina reminded me of every television interview with military wives I'd ever seen. The reporter typically asks, "How are you holding up?" as sympathetically as he or she can, and the military wife reflexively chirps, "We're doing fine!"

Knowing my own situation, I didn't believe Martina could be fine. With a newborn and three older kids who traded the flu like Pokémon cards, she rarely slept more than four hours at a stretch. But she looked good (if not glamorous) and sounded grounded (without going over the top), so I took her at her word.

I don't remember if Martina asked the same questions of me that I asked of her. I don't think she did. She didn't realize that I wasn't quite as immune to long absences; after all, she'd just finished up a tour in which McGowan deployed on and off for three years straight. But I wouldn't have told her the truth, anyway. The truth was that with Scott away, things were not going quite as well for us. For me it started small. I stopped folding the laundry and simply pulled clean, rumpled clothes straight out of the basket every day. I stopped unloading the dishwasher and moved clean plates straight from dishwasher to table. Then I stopped inviting people over, because the house was too messy and I didn't have the energy to clean it. I didn't have the energy to do anything anymore. Though I sat with the kids while they ate meals at the table, I ate alone either before or after they did. Their demands and antics made it impossible for me to enjoy a meal since I rose to do, get, or change something for them between every bite.

In the large, rambunctious family I grew up in, the six of us, plus any friends who happened to be hanging around the house, ate dinner together every night at six-thirty. We talked about our teachers, our friends, and my parents' colleagues, especially who was stabbing whom in the back. We debated what to watch on TV that night and where we should go that weekend. We bantered throughout the meal; my brother Charlie often laughed so hard he fell out of his chair, which inspired more raucous hilarity. We fought, but only over whose turn it was to run out to Baskin-Robbins for ice cream.

If home is where family stories are spun into art, the dinner table was our studio. My parents encouraged us to be bold and original—in life as well as at the table—and as we sat around that knotty oval slab, my siblings and I tried on new personas, pushed the limits of propriety, and learned how to time a joke. Amateur raconteurs, we tested our ability to hold each other's attention with increasingly well-wrought tales and became seasoned storytellers. Much has been written about kitchens as the soul of the home, and for me, growing up, the location was even more specific: the dinner table.

When I began looking more closely into the concept of home, to try and determine why it took me so long to transition into the peripatetic military lifestyle, I identified instantly with author Witold Rybczynski's comment about the pleasure of "installing ourselves in a place, of establishing a spot where it would be safe to dream." The popular British philosopher Alain de Botton takes the idea one step further. The house, he writes,

> *has provided not only physical but also psychological sanctuary. It has been a guardian of identity. Over the years, its owners have returned from periods away and, on looking around them, remembered who they were.*

But among my military friends, I detected a very different concept of home. Sewn onto needlepoint pillows, etched into granite plaques hanging in entryways, painted in bright watercolors and framed on bedroom walls, this simple line says it all: "Home is where the Navy sends you." *Well, actually, no,* I thought, steaming with juvenile rebelliousness the first time I saw it and every time since. (The adage echoes that of an early campfollower, Martha Summerhayes, the wife of a Civil War veteran who in 1908 penned a memoir of her experience as an Army spouse. Her devotion to the Army, which relocated her from upper-crust Massachusetts to the unsettled and sometimes violent Indian territory of Arizona, prompted her to write: "I had cast my lot with a soldier, and where he was, was home to me.")

It makes sense that some military families, lacking a beloved house or even a familiar town to return to, identify so closely with their service branch. In fact, one military-wife author urges her children to say they're "from the Navy" when others ask where they grew up. For many of our colleagues, the military itself has become their home. It shelters them, quite literally; it reinforces their sense of self, and is inseparable from who they are. "I don't know how to be a wife without being a Navy wife," one friend confided. "I got married seven days after college graduation. We've never lived in a place longer than two years. I wouldn't begin to know how to pick a place to live on my own if he retired. I don't even know what the criteria would be."

I nodded, but it meant "I hear you speaking" rather than "I understand and feel the same way." I followed the de Botton model. I longed for the sanctuary of our old dinner table, left-handed Scott on my right as we comfortingly bumped elbows throughout the meal.

My sense of adventure wasn't the issue. In high school, my friends and I boarded Amtrak for day trips up to New York City whenever the opportunity presented itself. In college, I couldn't pack my suitcase fast enough: I landed at Trinity College in Dublin for my junior year before anyone else in my family had traveled abroad. From Dublin, I explored Europe and then flew to Israel to connect with friends. I returned to Israel, the Middle East, and Europe many times after that, often on my own, and later I spent twelve months in Jerusalem as the fortunate recipient of a postgraduate fellowship. After Scott and I married and moved to Japan, we roamed Asia whenever he strung together a few days of leave.

Roaming Anacortes was not quite the same, though the town itself—peaceful and self-contained as a scene in a snow globe—was innocent of any wrongdoing. After all, this is a place where the library charges no late fees and street parking is free, a place where I once saw a uniformed police officer hop off a patrol bike to hug her neighbors.

Our problem was much closer to home. As the only grown-up in that home, I was lonely—simple as that. At dinner no one sat across from me spinning stories about the day and debating the merits of a few spoonfuls of ice cream after dinner. Ethan gobbled his meal as quickly as he could, usually fighting with me over what I served and how much he was required to eat. On a good night we sat together for five minutes, tops, before he begged to be excused, and Esther usually followed his lead.

Scott had it rough with the long, rigorous flying he engaged in during "workups," as exercises leading up to deployment are called. I tried not to complain, but he understood what was happening by the small, empty sound of my voice on the phone. I told him and others that year that my one-and-a-half-year-old and three-and-a-half-year-old—who never stopped moving, talking, or expressing their feelings—were exhausting but inspiring. I loved them more each day, but I did begin to feel that they were exhausting, period. Getting them to bed at night became the focus of my entire afternoon.

Strangely, I measured the depth of this slump only during peaks of happiness with my kids. They absolutely loved a new DVD I'd ordered for them, *Shabbat Alive*, a musically oriented, kid-friendly Sabbath service. (Since Jewish services were too far away to attend, during our time in Anacortes I relied on DVDs and CDs to help teach my kids what they would otherwise learn in synagogue.) I turned the volume up as loud as possible, and the kids and I held hands and danced around the room to "L'cha Dodi" or "V'shamru," traditional Hebrew songs punched back to life with pulsing rhythms. We learned the words quickly and sang along at the top of our lungs. By the end of the DVD, Ethan, Esther, and I whirled around in circles in the family room. They finally collapsed on top of me on the floor. *This is what being a mom is all about*, I thought, as they laughed hysterically and tried to catch their breath.

But those moments became increasingly rare that first year, as I struggled for equilibrium. I tried all kinds of things to make those transcendent moments with the kids the norm rather than the exception. Ethan loves musicals, so one day I bought the two of us tickets to the community theater production of *Fiddler on the Roof.* He sat next to me, awestruck, for the entire three hours. He wouldn't even stretch during intermission, since he feared missing something. He didn't want it to end, so as we applauded the last bow, he whispered to me, "Can we meet the cast now?"

I made sure we were first in line, and he shook the hand of every single actor in the production. We talked about it for days, weeks, months; in fact, a signed poster from the actors in the show still hangs on Ethan's wall. The performance even inspired him to request violin lessons.

But then the magical day ended. And in the manner that days do, the next one came, and then the next one. I tried to hold the happy memories close, push away the negative thoughts, let the weeks wash over me. More and more often, I found myself stopped at a red light, the kids in the backseat, wondering where I was going and how I had gotten this far. I had no memory of climbing into the car and couldn't remember if I was driving the kids to school or Safeway or the park. I couldn't even recall what I had been thinking about. My brain, sleep-deprived, soaked with worry, and distracted by the demands of our new life, was like a television screen roiling with static.

I never considered myself to be depressed, though I openly acknowledged to close friends and family that our circumstances were depressing. It seemed appropriate to be sad—I felt I had ample cause—so I allowed in "the proper sorrows of the soul," as the fourteenth-century monk Thomas à Kempis termed it. But gradually I realized I was pantomiming the motions of each day in a desperate attempt to block dark thoughts, refusing to deal directly with my situation for fear of what would greet me at the other end if I did. As a result, I lost my days entirely. My kids asked me a question, and it took me a few minutes to realize someone was speaking. Their voices, which seemed far away, brought them into focus as gradually as a Polaroid, outlines in the darkness slowly materializing into recognizable forms.

My absence from my own life became a heavy presence. *Three years of this?* I asked myself. I always hoped to be an engaged and involved mom. Now I was neither. I was Gone Mom.

Soon enough, Scott would come home—the next day or the next week or the next month. We reconnected, we told stories at the dinner table, and I returned to myself again. We spent all our free time together. Color returned to the world, food tasted delicious, and it seemed impossible he had ever left or would leave again.

4

Lost

Despite Scott's frequent absences and my struggles during his periods away, I felt more settled in as the first snow fell on Anacortes that year. But I began to notice changes in Ethan. Perhaps he was picking up on my difficulties. A sensitive soul, he detected any changes in the emotional atmospherics immediately.

During our first months in Anacortes, he seemed to adapt beautifully to his new home. Though he constantly asked when we were moving back to the old house, this seemed reasonable. He was still confused walking around our new place, heading toward the playroom when he meant to go to his room, getting lost on the way to the bathroom, or opening all the drawers in the kitchen in search of a dishtowel. Overall, though, he seemed happy during our initial transition, and I felt relieved that my gloomy predictions about how he would react to the move were proven wrong. By winter, however, it became clear that the situation was far worse than we could have feared.

The changes were gradual, and it was hard to untangle the threads. First, Ethan dropped his potty training and then stopped sleeping through the night. He woke up screaming several times between midnight and morning and panicked whenever we left his room. In fact, he refused to be alone in any room of the house. If he was watching television in the family room and we got up to walk ten feet to the bathroom, he insisted on coming with us. He wouldn't go anywhere alone, not even into the kitchen to get a snack, and soon our three-and-a-half-year-old demanded to be carried everywhere. Eventually he stopped speaking in full paragraphs, and soon after that full sentences disappeared too. He uttered single words to direct us to the object of his attention, and we didn't know how much worse it could get until he began grunting and pointing.

I woke up with a sick feeling every morning, wondering what the day held, helpless to help my own child feel better—about himself, about our family, about the world, which had shifted so mercilessly and permanently under his feet. *If only we hadn't moved, if only we hadn't moved*—it became my silent mantra. As for Scott, he convinced himself that Ethan's fragile emotional state was entirely his fault. The only thing more heartbreaking than my boy's confusion was Scott's guilt. Meanwhile, Ethan's disturbing regression, prompted by no identifiable physical condition, worsened by the day. I felt like I was watching the hands of the clock twirl crazily counterclockwise, the way old movies used to show flashbacks.

I wanted to tell someone, and since Martina and I talked several nights a week, I thought she might be able to provide a reality check. So when the phone rang one evening, I cheered to hear her voice on the other end. But she had her own reasons for calling.

"I have to tell you something," she whispered. "Can you hear me? I'm in the closet. My kids don't know I'm on the phone."

"Have you been kidnapped by midgets?" I laughed.

"I slapped Ronan," she murmured, even more softly.

My smile flatlined. Martina had adopted an antispanking policy during her teenage babysitting days, just as I had, and it strengthened after our own kids came along. We were the queens of quiet time, the regents of reasoning.

"He just said something to me—it wasn't even that bad—and I slapped him on the head," she continued. "I didn't even think about it. I just did it. It happened so fast."

"Then what?"

"He got a really confused look on his face. He's not hurt, but it scared him, and he just started bawling. I held him and told him I was sorry a zillion times." She inhaled deeply, then exhaled. "Shit. Shit. Shit."

I didn't know what to say. I could hear her gnawing on a nail.

"There's more," she continued. "I spanked Bridget yesterday."

"You need a break," I said quickly. "Is there anyone you can call to stay with you for a while?"

"Maybe. No. I don't know."

Martina's husband had just marked his fourth month in Iraq. Eight months to go. Earlier that morning, Scott had kissed me good-bye as he left for a six-week training detachment. The chilly, steel-gray Anacortes afternoons gave way to frigid, sleety evenings that descended at four p.m. The kids couldn't play outside anymore, and there was nowhere to go in Anacortes—no malls, no activity centers, no Gymboree. That first winter lasted a lifetime. I understood that there were worse fates than having to amuse kids throughout a season of snow with no husband around, but I longed for a more promising direction. I had no map, and with a dawning sense of dread I realized that Martina, my guide, was equally lost.

As I packed and prepared for our Christmas-break trip back to D.C.—our first visit since the move—Ethan woke up every morning asking if today was the day we were returning home. He clung to the notion that we would return to our old house any day now, that his lonely sojourn in the wilderness was winding down. I knew that more acute disappointment awaited him, and it broke my heart open. I reminded him that our visit would last a long time but that our new house in Anacortes would be awaiting our return. *It's going to be painful, but I'll be there for him,* I lectured myself. *You're a mom now. This is what you do.*

Ethan's pediatrician called as I was packing our last bag for the trip. When we first detected Ethan's regression, she'd responded quickly to our ongoing concerns, evaluated Ethan thoroughly, and saw him for a follow-up visit. She checked in with me frequently.

"I've been thinking more about what Ethan's been going through, and I have a few ideas," she said cautiously. Then she pronounced a judgment so unexpected that I had no ready response. "I think Ethan has post-traumatic stress disorder from your move and your husband's absences."

Like time-lapse photography, images from the past few months passed before my eyes. I had wondered more than once that autumn if toddlers are vulnerable to depression, because it seemed to me Ethan's distress was a reaction to our transition to life as a military family. I hadn't pursued the thought; I didn't know what to do with it, anyway. Who had ever heard of a depressed toddler? But now I connected the dots: the clinginess, the night wake-ups, the regression in potty training and language skills, lack of interest in food, the fear of abandonment. I had heard Ethan, during the most recent phone call with Scott, pleading with him to come home, as if the two of them had signed a contract to be together always and the contract had been broken.

Our pediatrician talked through some of the symptoms of post-traumatic stress disorder. Because of her long experience with military children, she pinpointed elements of his behavior that she'd noticed in other kids who had moved frequently and were separated from parents, especially those too young to articulate their feelings. I was not convinced that her diagnosis was correct, partly because I hesitated to compare his condition to that of soldiers scarred by the horrors of war. But the seriousness of her approach forced me to see that Ethan's issues could not be dismissed as a temporary phase.

Because of the war, more and more studies on deployment's impact on families are finding their way into print, though the focus on the behavioral health needs of military children is in its infancy. In 2008 the American Psychological Association, the American Academy of Pediatrics, and the Department of Defense Task Force on Mental Health called for increased attention to children of deployed service members. Physicians at an Army medical center in Washington state asked the Army surgeon general to fund a "Center of Excellence" on military children and adolescents to focus on the behavioral health of those left behind during a deployment. A peer-reviewed study published in the *Archives of Pediatric and Adolescent Medicine* in late 2008 was the first to examine the behavioral effect of current wartime deployments on children aged five years and younger. It concluded that children aged three years or older with a deployed parent exhibit increased behavioral symptoms compared with peers without a deployed parent.

As I read about toddlers' reactions to deployment, I started to understand the silent nature of their struggle. Older children and adolescents have different reactions and tend toward verbal aggression and rebelliousness. But younger children are physical in their grief, and so I observed Ethan closely. His behavior certainly fit the description of deployment-related distress. What I found most agonizing about this was that Ethan had become an unwitting member of the "all-volunteer force" without ever signing on the dotted line. He is a happy, sensitive soul whose greatest joys are blowing up balloons and playing with his parents. He said once that cashews are his favorite nut because "they're shaped like a smile."

But we were becoming a military family, and our son, furious and withdrawn, was an emotional casualty. After my talk with the pediatrician, I loaded up my minivan with suitcases for our flight back to D.C. Anything we pursued would have to wait several weeks. I just hoped Ethan didn't get any worse. I kept him near and tracked his every move.

5

The Provincial

Though I worried about Ethan's regression and rued the meteorological chaos of the Pacific Northwest (fall and winter rainstorms, windstorms, and snowstorms that were later determined to be among the worst in the region's history), the first months in Anacortes gradually opened my eyes to the benefits of small-town life. It wasn't just the fast, sympathetic response we got from the pediatrician or the plentiful local resources; it was as if Anacortes offered me, for the first time, an alternative way to live my own life.

What I came to appreciate about Anacortes may be true of any small town far removed from the material temptations of an affluent urban or suburban environment. Or maybe it's due to the influence of the military, whose standardized salaries tend to equalize families. Perhaps it was simple community modesty—a key value for a region stamped by the influence of its Dutch and Scandinavian immigrants and rooted in northern European Protestantism.

Modesty was not exactly a virtue I learned to appreciate in my youth. Seeing others strive for achievement, recognition, and material possessions had shaped my frame of reference far more powerfully. After growing up in Charleston, South Carolina, and Potomac, Maryland, I packed my bags for college at UMass-Amherst, followed by graduate school at the University of Virginia. Master's degree in hand, I loaded up my car again and drove to a job that beckoned me to Boston. I finally returned to Washington, D.C., where I met and married Scott. In the milieu in which I traveled during those many years, nearly everyone I knew was motivated by the same desires: a superior education, a rewarding (in every sense of the word) job, a nice house in a desirable neighborhood, children to repeat the identical cycle.

The push for more—more of everything—didn't end when those items were checked off the list. At the start of my husband's Pentagon tour, we bought a house in a Maryland suburb close to my parents, crossing off that task with great satisfaction and gratitude. But almost no time at all passed until I started eyeing the renovations and extensive home improvements undertaken by my neighbors. I also listened intently when other neighbors mentioned second homes in a nearby resort community. Our eleven-year-old car broke down, and for the first time I found myself gazing wistfully at the shiny SUVs rolling up and down our street.

Most jarring of all: Friends spoke of enrolling their kids in private school and asked about our plans, although Ethan was only six months old. We shouldered a mortgage that would wrinkle the brow of any service member, but we bought our house because of the excellent public schools less than a mile away, hopeful that we'd return to the D.C. area for a future tour or after Scott's eventual retirement.

I'd never given a thought to private school, a vacation house, or a drive-off-the-lot new SUV. Since I hadn't been raised to keep up with the Joneses—after all, both my parents were civil servants—my expectations remained fairly limited. But settling down in our affluent suburb with my young family sparked something dark and covetous that I didn't like and couldn't shake. We were blessed in every way, but suddenly I wanted what they had—whoever *they* were.

Anacortes provided a moral counterpoint to this morass of materialism. Our town is notable for many things, but during our first few months in town I paid the most attention to what was missing. No contractors' trucks parked in front of homes as workmen tore caverns in brick façades to install shiny new kitchens. No housekeepers from distant neighborhoods trudged to and from bus stops. No nannies chatted at the playground. There's no need for a vacation house in a place like this, where families live just minutes from the water and easy driving distance from the mountains. A big car or truck is useful, really useful, on nearby country roads, but it's more likely to be a Ford or Dodge pickup than an Acura or a BMW SUV.

There are no private schools in Anacortes for grades one through twelve, so all local kids attend public schools or are homeschooled. I've never known so many parents who have homeschooled their kids. I don't have the talent or patience for it, and I am amazed that mothers with the option of a full day of quiet choose instead to keep their kids close by. Some, of course, pursue a religious education, but one local mother of six told me she wanted to teach her kids at home just because she loved them and liked being near them as much as she could. In the end, the popularity of homeschooling here helped me see what motivates some people in this corner of the world. It's nothing simpler or more complicated than family. People here want to be with family, do things with family, spend time with family, and since there is little peer pressure (or opportunity) to make more money, that's exactly what they practice.

The same is true of many military families I have met. To many, a town like Anacortes fits their values perfectly. It is such a good match that military families often retire here. And these are people who have sampled the best of the world's culture during overseas

tours and have even been stationed in Washington, D.C.—one of the
most exciting places, I have always believed, in all of America.

When I was a teenager I read that the first question strangers
ask of each other at a cocktail party in D.C. is "What do you
do?" That made perfect sense to me, since people's work, where
they live, and where they were raised were the ideal trifecta of data
to help me unlock the door to their personalities. I adopted this
approach to getting to know people as an adolescent, and for years
to come silently judged those I met. As a way to understand others,
of course, my logic was deeply flawed. I saw a behavior and felt
compelled to discover the reason behind it; I hungered to ascribe
causes to everything, especially others' actions. I liked to be told
stories, so I told myself stories too—about the people I knew and
the relationships connecting them.

Trying to read people on the basis of their origins and occupa-
tions gave me insight (I thought) into anyone who'd been raised
between Miami and Maine. But after we moved to the Pacific
Northwest, that shorthand became illegible. In Anacortes, I felt as
lost as a new immigrant stymied by a simple street sign. Here, I
couldn't figure out how people from Pasco, Washington, differed
from those from Mount Vernon, Washington. I wasn't sure how to
place people who were raised in Salem, Oregon. What books did
they read? What aspirations did they hold dear? Was it assumed—or
not—they would go to college? These kinds of questions used to be
very important to me.

As for the military families who were part of my new social
circle, none of my former truths resonated, either. Few people ask
"Where are you from?" as a conversation starter at a military party.
And when I ask, no one is interested in talking about it for very
long. The military wives I meet are quite literally citizens of

America, having sampled culture, school, local traditions, and shopping in dozens of states. They're the most well-traveled people I have ever met, completing stints in every possible post across Europe, Asia, the Middle East, and South America. (A stroll through the aisles of any base commissary reveals the extent to which palates have been refined during years overseas. Our commissary, for example, imports Japanese Pocky, Filipino Sky Flakes crackers, German *Knödel* mix, and Ambrosia Devon custard from the UK, among many other items more commonly found in gourmet supermarkets or international boutiques.)

So during those first few months in Anacortes I was able to come up with no quick-and-easy first impression of those I met. I was a stranger in a strange land twice over, part of a Navy community in a region of the country for which I possessed no guide. As a result, something unexpected happened. Since I couldn't judge people at a glance anymore, I stopped trying to. Like a first-year language student, I finally understood the slippery and undependable nature of words. I grew to rely on my new friends' actions, rather than their statements, as I sought insights into who they were. For someone as logocentric as I, it's surprisingly liberating to be able to disregard someone's comments entirely, depending solely on their behavior to see into their heart and mind.

It was at that point during our first fall that I recalled the writings of Alexis de Tocqueville. Since I now felt like an outsider in my own country, I wanted to reread the impressions of a true foreigner interpreting our fledgling democracy. Tocqueville never journeyed to the West Coast, of course, but when he wrote that "to try to present a complete picture of the Union would be an enterprise absolutely impracticable," I could relate.

My lifelong experience on the East Coast convinced me I knew America. Pollsters and pundits proclaimed otherwise, voting patterns exposed the reality, but still I believed. I surrounded myself with people who felt just as I did. It was comfortable, it was easy, and on my own I never would have thought to change in any way. Then I married into the military. The Navy moved me into the heart of the country, and it turned out to be a small town as far northwest as one could possibly travel without swimming into Canada. So at age thirty-seven, and with the stunning realization that it was I who all along had been the provincial, I finally became an American.

6

Pippi

Away for six weeks, home for four. Away for four weeks, home for one. Away for five weeks, home for two. Once the squadron entered the most intense phase of its pre-deployment workup period, Scott drifted in and out of our family's life. Mostly out.

The afternoon we met the jets on the flight line when the squadron returned that spring from a month away was like every other time we'd greeted Scott's plane—lots of waiting, multiple delays—but we didn't care. The kids and I crept step by step from the hangar onto the tarmac to watch the four planes land. We didn't run to greet him immediately because we never knew if the helmeted, goggled figure who climbed out of the cockpit was Scott or one of his crew members. In their identical flight suits and gear they all looked alike, creatures from a bad science fiction movie.

But Scott knew it was us squinting into the sun. He stopped, pulled off his helmet, and started waving crazily. He knelt down and held his arms out for the kids, who finally ran to him. He scooped them close, and the three of them hugged tightly. I gave

them a few moments together as the wind whipped my hair into
my eyes and tears of relief and happiness clouded my vision.

It took us a while to gather Scott's bags. After his debrief in the
squadron ready room, the four of us headed toward the air terminal
on base, one building away, to greet the airlift. Two cargo planes full
of the squadron's nonflying officers and enlisted sailors were also
scheduled to arrive home from the boat detachment, and the aviators usually tried to greet them and thank them for their hard work
as they stepped off the plane. The air terminal teems with family
members at these events, so it is a good opportunity to shake hands
and tell the wives or parents of the sailors what an excellent job
they performed while away.

I love greeting the airlift, just as I love sitting in the arrivals
terminal at any airport. There is nothing like the exhilaration of a
hug that really means something. It's a clean slate, a fresh start, a
whole heart.

At first, I had no clear notion of the perceived differences between enlisted sailors and officers and, since no military wife exists
exclusively on her own terms, those between sailors' wives and officers' wives. I hadn't had much of a chance to get to know the
spouses on the "other side," though I had met a few as I brought
meals and gifts to new moms and babies. Because their husbands
were often so young and worked in junior ranks, many of the enlisted wives I met lived in Navy housing or in small houses or trail-
ers off base. And while it was obvious in some cases that our
backgrounds, lifestyles, and choices were different, some of us had
enough in common that I walked away from their doors wondering
why the two groups didn't combine their efforts, especially when
our spouses were deployed.

The quiet class warfare at the heart of many of the unspoken
feelings between officer and enlisted families has a long historical
reach, stretching back to the Old Country. America's fledgling Con-

tinental Army built itself to compete with its forebears and ultimate adversaries, the army and navy of Great Britain. Merry Olde
England was not exactly known for its democratizing impulse; aris-
tocratic officers typically purchased their commissions or were
appointed by royalty. The "serving class" of enlisted men were less
fortunate souls with few options in life, and the merit-based system
associated with today's military simply did not exist.

America's anxiety of influence played to this weakness. Perhaps
it was lack of imagination or the most likely culprit, lack of funds.
The destitute Continental Army could barely support those who
fought in its name. Continental Army officers were often elected by
their men, but many officers were well-to-do businessmen or land-
owners who bought their own uniforms, housing, food, and even
ammunition, and paid for more comfortable transportation for
themselves and their families between encampments. The contrast
in lifestyles was obvious, and enlisted soldiers expressed consider-
able resentment. A caste system developed in the American military
even before there was an American military.

Now, however, service members can bridge professional gaps or
transition to a higher socioeconomic class in a military that prides
itself on merit-based progress. Many programs exist to help high-
achieving enlisted troops climb the ladder; pay and benefits for
senior enlisted service members are respectable and often cited
as motivators among junior sailors seeking reenlistment. High-
achieving sailors can make the transition into the commissioned-
officer corps, and the sheer numbers of these "mustang," or former
enlisted, officers make it clear that many opportunities exist to
crash through the glass ceiling of the past. (This is a dramatic im-
provement on previous practices: Though apprentices aged thirteen
to eighteen served on board American naval vessels beginning in
1837, as a rule very few enlisted sailors ever received an acting appointment, regardless of the length of their service or the quality
of their performance.)

Then, as now, wives of service members operated within a parallel social structure in their own ranks. In the early days of the
American military, enlisted wives sometimes worked as servants for
the officers' wives or as maids in their homes. Linguistic barriers
existed as well: Officers' wives were known as "ladies," while the
spouses of enlisted troops were referred to as "wives" or simply
"the women," a practice that continued in some circles through the
late 1960s. Everyone knew her place in the hierarchy, even those
women who never signed on to serve. As one mid-nineteenth-
century frontier soldier wrote to his hometown newspaper:

> *It is really curious to observe how well and how strictly the three*
> *classes of women in camp keep aloof from each other. The wives*
> *and daughters of colonels, captains and other officers constitute*
> *the first class. The rough cooks and washers who have their hus-*
> *bands along . . . form the second class. The third and last class is*
> *happily the smallest; here and there a female . . . truly wife-like*
> *in their tented seclusion, but lacking that great and only voucher*
> *of respectability for females in camp—the marriage tie.*

Some of the barriers that separate officers' wives and enlisted wives
still exist. For example, there are distinct on-base housing areas for
each group. But many people work hard to find common ground
among the spouses and to eliminate old-fashioned divisions. The
Army has made great strides recently in combining enlisted and
officer families of the same unit for social events and for purposes
of general "readiness" (which typically means preparation for deployment, disaster, or casualties). The Navy also encourages cre-
ation of all-squadron Family Readiness Groups in a move away
from the bifurcated officer-spouse-group/enlisted-spouse-group
model. But change is slow, and there are pockets of resistance
among both camps. When I mentioned to another officer's wife that
I hoped to transition our squadron to a Family Readiness Group

model, she cautioned me that the enlisted wives wanted nothing to do with us. This presented itself as: "Would *you* want to hang out with your husband's boss's wife?"

Maybe not. I didn't want to be willfully blind to class issues in the military, since they are real, and I wasn't going to be able to change them on my own. I certainly didn't want to make anyone uncomfortable. But greeting an airlift wasn't the same as asking someone over for dinner, and I was eager to meet anyone who wanted to meet me. Scott and I arrived early for my first airlift, so I walked around introducing myself to the families of the enlisted sailors and getting to know their kids. I took my cue from Scott and his then CO, who were doing the same thing. It felt awkward and forced at first, but it became easier. The wives were friendly and kind; they knew what I had to do, and they made it easy for me. Unlike with some officers' wives, whose husbands worked directly with Scott, I didn't sense any ulterior motives on their part. There were too many layers of command between their husband and mine, and they weren't preoccupied with making a good impression.

That was the biggest difference I saw between them and the officers' wives I knew. In a military that prides itself on social performance, these women waiting to welcome their sailors weren't acting a role. Freshly showered and made-up as they were, their exhaustion still seeped through. I walked up to a woman who appeared to be in her early twenties. She had long red hair and freckles, and held a toddler on one hip as she cradled an infant in the other arm. In her snug T-shirt and low-slung jeans, she looked like a hipster Pippi Longstocking.

"How did you survive the month?" I asked.

Pippi rolled her eyes. "You know how it is," she sighed.

Did I ever. But I'd never heard anyone express the thought with such bluntness and resignation. It was—horror of horrors—negative.

"How old are the boys?" I asked.

"Twenty-two months and nine months."

"Wow," I said, imagining how badly I'd deal with two kids so close in age.

"It's those damn boat dets," she said, grinning as she read my mind.

I smiled back. It could mean only one thing: that the joy of greeting her husband after a month away following some prior detachment had led to an unexpected surprise nine months later. I hoped Pippi and her husband were more careful this time. She looked like she'd had about as much as she could take.

"See this bruise?" she said, pointing to her infant's eye. "I found him crawling around the bathroom, crying, when I was dealing with this one." She nodded to her toddler. "There's no way to watch them both at the same time. So I took him to the emergency room on base."

"What did they say it was?"

"They wrote me up for frickin' child abuse!"

I was shocked this poor woman was spilling her heart out to me. Most of all, though, I couldn't believe all this had happened while her husband was away. She stood her toddler on the ground and hooked a baby leash to the backpack strapped across his shoulders.

"By the time I got home from the ER someone from Child Protective Services was at my door," she continued. "The only good thing is they're going to send over someone to help me during the day."

"So has the case been resolved?" I asked. For the first time, I thought that maybe I could help. I hadn't asked for any authority in the squadron or done anything to deserve it, but I had it and figured I may as well put it to good use. At the very least, I could ask Scott to help.

"Not yet. The hospital called my husband's chief. Now he has to file a report."

Very few family issues remain secret in the service. For enlisted sailors and officers alike, squadron leaders are contacted anytime a service member or an immediate family member breaks the law, needs financial or legal assistance, or seeks significant medical care. The personal and the professional are tightly intertwined. (In fact, an officer's approval used to be required before soldiers got married, and in some cases today approval is compulsory if a service member at an overseas post wants to marry a citizen of the host country.)

Often, the service member's boss acts as an advocate on the sailor's behalf, especially because a junior sailor usually has relatively little power or resources. That seemed to be the case here. Pippi's husband's immediate boss planned to accompany the family to the meeting with Child Protective Services and to work with local child welfare agencies to coordinate aid and other assistance.

I gave Pippi my number and asked if I could call her after the weekend. I walked around the terminal and greeted other enlisted wives. Finally, we all heard the longed-for shouts, staccato explosions like fireworks on the Fourth of July: "It's here! It's here!"

The airlift landed. I found a seat in the back of the room, where I watched the scene through large picture windows. As the door to the plane opened, uniformed men and women carrying enormous green duffel bags carefully stepped down, blinking against the sunlight like baby birds.

The children standing at the picture window jumped, screamed, and pointed as they spotted their parents. The male sailors crossing the tarmac walked slowly—or perhaps everything about the reunion took place in slow motion. With their parents in view, the children waiting at the window grew more hysterical by the second. I spotted one little boy about Ethan's age sob as the tension of the moment became intolerable, then slap the tears off his cheeks as if they were annoying mosquitoes.

"Run, you dogs," one of the wives near me mumbled angrily under her breath, directing her quiet wrath at all of the sailors. "Run to your kids."

The slow procession of shy fathers finally arrived at the door of the terminal. That's when I spotted Camille stepping off the plane. Camille, a twenty-five-year-old sailor in the squadron's administrative department, had just distinguished herself with a promotion, scoring exceptionally well on the required advancement exam. I'd met her early on in our tour as we worked together to plan the squadron's social events. She was personable, highly capable, and able to come up with creative twists for even the most formulaic military ceremonies. Her seven-year-old daughter lived with grandparents during the squadron's away periods. Camille scanned the scene as soon as her feet touched the asphalt, and I knew she was searching for her girl. I saw the girl at the window wave excitedly, and the two locked eyes through the glass that separated them.

Camille walked quickly, her giant duffel bag banging against her leg with each long stride. She never took her eyes off her daughter, except to assess whether or not to pass the infernally slow sailors trudging along in front of her. She had no choice, of course. With her daughter's gaze upon her, Camille moved faster and faster until suddenly she was running, pressing her duffel bag close by her side to stop it from hitting her leg. She passed all the dads. At the door to the terminal she grabbed her daughter, and the two wrapped themselves around each other with a ferocity I'd never witnessed before. They sank to the ground together. There they sat for the next ten minutes, Camille cross-legged on the tiles of the terminal with her daughter in her arms. The rest of the sailors simply stepped around them, eyes scanning the room like searchlights as they crossed the threshold.

———

The terminal was finally empty. Scott and I picked up leftover goodie bags donated by the USO. He made sure the last of the single sailors waiting in front of the air terminal had a ride to the barracks. We reached our own car. Scott strapped the kids into their booster seats and climbed into the driver's side of my minivan. He slid the seat back, adjusted the mirrors, and put the car in reverse. He backed out of the parking spot. As we drove off base, he held out his right hand, pulled my left hand toward him, and kissed it.

7

O'Dark-thirty

During Scott's first few days home from a boat det I always smiled to see his olive-green flight suits littering our laundry again, the Velcro soft and fuzzy where he peeled off his patches before throwing them in the wash. Just when it seemed like we finally had hung the last of his clean uniforms in the closet again, it was time to fold them and pack them, and he was gone.

During his two weeks at home from that particular det, an avalanche of advice from the other wives rolled down on me. Lily, the Montessori mom with a husband in Iraq, said it best: "Workups are much harder than deployment. During workups, they're in and out. It's so disruptive, especially for kids. With deployment, they're just gone, and you can get on with your life."

It made a certain sense, especially because I knew that she and the others who'd said the same thing really wished the deployment to hurry up and start so they could begin counting down the time until it was completed. For all of us on sea tours, prospective deployments hover over our lives like bumblebees, circling closer and closer overhead and finally making it impossible to eat, or move, or think about anything else except the incessant buzzing and the inevitable pain. During workups, the bee buzzes around our brains for months on end. There's no avoiding the sting of deployment.

"I just want him *out* of here," said Martina, to the point as always, referring to her memory of McGowan's past extended training periods. "The sooner he's gone the sooner he's back."

Martina felt especially bitter. McGowan had just arrived home from Iraq for a two-week leave period, granted at the midpoint of his yearlong IA tour. She and the kids had counted down the days until his arrival and festooned every inch of the house for Christmas, right down to the white spray-painted pine needles twisting around the lamppost. The day of his return, they arrived at the airport to meet his flight three hours early.

Though I looked forward to meeting McGowan, I wanted Martina and the kids to enjoy their time with him without any interruptions. I met him only briefly during his visit home, during a kids' birthday party at the bowling alley. On that afternoon, in the dim nooks of San Juan Lanes, his face appeared lined and weary. It was surprising in a man approaching his late thirties, but I became used to that weathered look in the months to come, as more of my friends' husbands returned from Iraq. Despite McGowan's obvious exhaustion, I saw a deep soulfulness in his dark blue eyes, and in his good-natured smile it was clear he was thrilled to be with his children. That feeling, I discovered, was not necessarily mutual.

"It's not going well," Martina admitted, when I called her.

"What happened?" I asked, stunned.

"Ronan's just mad at McGowan. He's mad all the time. Bridget's worse; she's scared of him. She has no idea who this intruder is, so I have to hold her all the time. She won't even sleep in her own bed. It's worse than when McGowan was away. Then at least I had a few minutes of peace. Now I don't have any peace at all."

"What about number one and number four?"

"Maeve is happy as long as she has a book in her hand," Martina said of her seven-year-old. "As for the baby, she's sick. Up all night."

"Oh my God."

My heart broke for Martina, who hadn't slept in months. And for McGowan, too, the mysterious ghost who had floated through my consciousness since I met her. I could picture him in his Baghdad quarters, surrounded by photos of his family, dreamily imagining his trip back home, the kids running into his arms. All he wanted, I was certain, was a happy family.

The children weren't exactly winners in this scenario, either. Ronan's rages continued after McGowan returned to Iraq. He started fighting at school, and his mood at home became sullen and rebellious—a far cry from the sweet, easygoing kid I knew. Martina called me to talk through counseling options, since I had learned my way around the local child-therapy system during Ethan's December distress. For insurance reasons, many doors were closed to her, and she fumed against the system that sent her husband away but provided few mental health resources for families to cope with the loss. After several weeks, she finally connected with a social worker on base.

"What did she suggest?" I asked.

"She thought Ronan might feel better if he talked about McGowan at school more and showed off some of the things his dad sent him. That if he sensed the other kids' interest, and they counted down the deployment with him, it would help."

"Sounds reasonable," I said, mentally filing that one away. "What else?"

"She suggested I tell Ronan that his dad is fighting for freedom, so he'd develop a sense of pride and understand why it was important for him to deploy."

I put my pen down. I always felt uneasy listening to jingoistic bromides, and I couldn't imagine repeating one to my young kids.

It reminded me of the platitudes I hear when some strangers, in an effort to make me feel better about spending so much time without my husband, advise me to stay strong by looking at "the big picture." I heard a lot about "the big picture." Though I am tremendously proud of Scott's naval career and his dedication to the squadron, it was all I could do to focus on the small picture: emotional survival. In our case, pride was a good breakfast but a poor lunch, and by suppertime we were often starving.

As for what to tell kids, any mention of fighting for freedom struck me as unnecessarily political and not very age-appropriate in its level of abstraction. (I would face exactly the same question in the coming months, when Ethan and I visited a different social worker on base, our first and last appointment there, and received the same suggestion.) But I didn't know where Martina stood on the war. We never talked politics; she told me once she didn't watch the news or read the paper because it made McGowan's deployments to combat zones easier for her.

"What do you think about that?" I asked, as neutrally as I could.

"Well, the other night I told Ronan that his dad was going away to play with Iraqi kids. I read about that one in a magazine. But he just looked up at me with his giant eyes and asked, 'Why does Daddy want to play with other kids and not me?' I wanted to *kill* myself. I wanted to *burn* the rag that gave me such bad advice. So I don't know what to do. I want the kids to be proud of their dad, but I don't want to tell them too much about why to be proud."

I was intimately familiar with that dilemma. For months I had said nothing at all to Ethan and Esther about Scott's job. As Ethan began asking questions, I told them Daddy had to go away to fly his plane. Later, I mentioned he was really good at his job and that was why he had to fly so much and stay away for so long. They appeared satisfied with that explanation for the moment. But the thought of transmitting any more information to my four-year-old and two-year-old paralyzed me with fear. The word "Iraq," uttered in their presence, made my blood run cold. I just prayed they didn't hear about the war from anyone else. It was a stunningly naïve approach, and eventually it backfired with tremendous psychic violence.

Martina never told Ronan about the war, and she never did mention to her kids the idea that McGowan was fighting for freedom. But she continued to wonder if it would have been better if he hadn't come home on leave after all. After several workup cycles, and my kids' fragility before and after Scott's many departures that year, I also began to wonder if it would be better to take the pain of a protracted absence up front.

Often, Scott left during one season and returned in another. When he pulled into our driveway that spring, for example, he saw flowers blooming in a yard formerly covered in frozen brown grass. More significantly, he returned to find Ethan and Esther embracing new concepts and flaunting new skills. Esther had turned two during Scott's most recent workup cycle, and he said that she seemed like a different child entirely.

"What happened to our little baby?" he asked me as we sat on the couch, watching Ethan and Esther playing with a dollhouse. Esther tucked one of her dolls into bed.

"You bootiful," she crooned to the doll. "Evybody loves you. You so special. You a good girl. Night-night, little boo." It was a word-for-word repetition of her own bedtime routine, when I rocked her and whispered softly into her ear.

"Oh, I forgot to tell you," Scott said excitedly. "Esther put her shoes on all by herself when we left the house earlier." I never knew what to do when he told me things like that. Esther had been sliding her shoes on by herself for a month; he just hadn't been around to see it.

"That's great," I said quietly. I hesitated to dampen his enthusiasm or make him feel even worse about missing the kids' milestones.

"And Ethan showed me the pillow he sewed at school today. I couldn't believe he had such good manual dexterity."

That was actually the fifth or sixth pillow Ethan had sewn at school during the last week; he was in a frenzied pillow-making period, delighting in his newfound talent and the praise his Montessori teacher and I heaped upon him.

"He loves those pillows," I said carefully.

I tried hard to catch up Scott on everything that had happened while he was away. Though we e-mailed daily when he was on the boat, it's hard to capture all the little things that kids experience for the first time, all the dazzling things they say. It's like explaining a joke: It stops being funny or clever when you repeat it. But one of the ways we stayed connected was to make a concerted effort to talk about the little things, so we didn't drift apart. Scott didn't want to feel like a stranger to his kids, and I didn't want him to feel like a tenant in our home.

Sometimes, though, it was hard to catch up with him, and it wasn't because he was at the squadron all the time. In the first twenty-four hours home after the boat det that spring, he washed, folded, and put away four loads of laundry; emptied and then repaired the dishwasher; bathed the kids; replaced all of the burned-out light bulbs; screwed in a handle that had fallen off a dresser; threw out all the old food in the refrigerator; and reorganized the pantry.

"I'm just trying to help, honey," he said, when I pleaded with him to relax. He smiled at me, but his eyes flashed sad. I knew him well enough to understand that he aimed to make up for the time he'd been away. But he had no reason to feel guilty. After all, he was helping to prepare and lead a squadron into war, and as the months ahead would prove, it required every ounce of his energy, intelligence, and skill.

Mommy?" Ethan woke up asking for Daddy and grew more frantic by the second after I told him Scott had already left for the office.

"Yes, my love?

"I don't want Daddy to leave again!"

"He's just gone to work," I comforted.

"But he's going to be gone forever and ever and ever," he cried.

"No, tonight he'll be back for dinner," I reminded him.

"He's on his big aircraft carrier, far far far away," he continued.

"Not now. He's home for a little while."

"Is the boat back?" Ethan asked, suddenly cheerful.

"Daddy's back for a little while."

"Oh."

Silence. I could see the wheels in his head turning.

"Is Daddy going to bring me another treat?" (I always readied presents for Scott to give to the kids when he returned from a det.)

"Not tonight, because he's back for a little while."

"Oh. That's okay. I still love Daddy, even if he doesn't bring me a treat."

We spent every evening together during the two-week period Scott lived with our family that spring. Our routine was as automatic and sacred as a genuflection. After we tucked in the kids, Scott blended a fruit smoothie for me, we watched *The Daily Show*, and we chatted quietly about our day. Our bare feet overlapped each other on the rug.

I was lulled, again, into normalcy. The shelter of Scott's presence was all the home I needed. I tried to remind myself that we were not like regular couples, that this was not what our life was really like, and that I should not get too used to it. That soon I'd be watching Jon Stewart by myself again. Soon I'd be marching upstairs to tuck in Ethan for the fifth, sixth, seventh, or eleventh time, listening to him cry, "But I miss Daddy!" As if that feeling was so monumental, so overpowering, that it was absurd to think that something as mundane as sleep was even possible.

But those sweet, slow evenings with Scott at home overpowered logic. I let myself forget; I lost myself in the time we had. So when the two weeks neared an end and Scott again surrounded himself with mountains of laundry, sorting and washing and folding clothes, I simply watched, shocked into silence. *Not already*, I thought. *You just got here.*

I knew he was mentally preparing to go away again. His flight back to the boat briefed at seven the next morning, which meant he'd have to leave the house at six a.m. Or, as he and his colleagues called any early-morning report time, "O'dark-thirty."

"I'm just trying to help, honey," he said when I asked him to return to the couch. He was missing Jon Stewart, which felt like a catastrophe. But it was as simple as me missing Scott already, though he sat cross-legged just a few feet away. That sad look flashed across his eyes. "I don't want you to feel overwhelmed with housework when I leave." He folded another shirt, laying it atop a tower of clean clothes.

The next morning, he woke up Ethan to say good-bye and carried him downstairs. Our boy wrapped himself around his dad like a koala bear hugs a tree, hands and feet meeting at the other side and clinging for dear life. Scott gently lowered him into his favorite comfy chair.

"I love you, Daddy," Ethan said.

"I love you too," Scott said. "Be good for Mommy."

"I don't like it when you go away, Daddy."

"I know. I don't like it either."

Ethan covered his eyes with his hands, bowed his head to his chest, and curled himself into a ball on the chair. I picked him up, and we walked Scott down the hall. It was an hour before sunrise. Ethan and I stood at the door, waving good-bye in the dark.

I discovered over and over throughout the squadron's workup cycle that the ability to be on one's own is a muscle that atrophies if unused. When exercised again, it's just as resistant as the first time, and achingly, intolerably sore in the days that follow. With training, the muscle strengthens. It becomes impervious to the weight of the pain imposed upon it. But few undertake this practice voluntarily.

8

Flat Daddy

Regardless of the turmoil I experienced throughout the first year of our tour, out in public I kept smiling. We were doing it: living as other military families have since the days Penelope waited loyally for Odysseus. My nonmilitary friends marveled at our situation. I understood their mystification; after all, I would have felt the same way, had I not been granted my own set of keys to the fortress. In the past I had always been indifferent to and ignorant of the military, qualities that many others share and that continue to separate an all-volunteer military from the public it defends. Regardless of my new status as an insider, I never knew how to respond when others asked, "How do you do it?"

What choice do I have? I wanted to say. *Scott entered into this life long before he met me.*

Instead, from our earliest days in Anacortes, I tried to emulate other Navy wives' handling of their husbands' long absences. Often they put on a brave face and brushed it off as insignificant, almost a nonissue. One night when I celebrated a birthday with two other military wives, for example, we saw a woman we knew and called her over to our table. Her husband had left for a six-month deployment a few weeks earlier, but he'd suffered a burst appendix and returned home to heal.

"You have to tell us," one of my friends whispered, leaning in close to the woman whose husband had just flown home. A spouse returning early from deployment was a dream none of us could afford to indulge in. "How does it feel to have him back?"

She considered us for a moment. "Actually, I was really looking forward to having some girl time with my friends," she answered coolly. "It's been a few years since he deployed, and I was just going to kick back and relax for a while."

I took my cue from her, and from others who convinced me that they looked forward to their husband's deployments to pursue their own hobbies or interests. Women with kids often told me they try to maintain the same routine when their husband is home as when he's away, so he can slide neatly in and out of their lives without the kids even noticing. "He fits into our schedule," a mother of two boys told me. "So it doesn't matter if he's away or not, we do the same things regardless."

"He's gone so much the kids don't even know the difference," I heard over and over. "Even when he's home, he works so late the kids can go a week without seeing him."

Early on, I followed the advice I received from every quarter, since these women had been through it all before. After all, they had survived careers packed with deployments that may otherwise have been devastating losses. So throughout the squadron workup period leading up to deployment, when Scott went away for four to six weeks, then returned for a few days or weeks, then went away again for a month, I didn't vary Ethan and Esther's schedule. I didn't make a big deal about Scott's departures or arrivals.

As for me, I buried myself in work. I started looking forward to Scott's absences because it meant I could type late into the night. And I was so productive! When Scott called from an airport or a hotel to tell me he missed me, I could hear longing and love in his voice. I told him I missed him too, but I was secretly eager to start tapping the computer keys again. In those days, my personal trinity—denial, avoidance, and evasion of the truth—worked wonders. When friends said, "Your husband must be coming home soon," I was always surprised, since I hadn't even been keeping track of the remaining days.

My heart wasn't hardening. I didn't love my husband any less. I loved him so much that when he went away, I had to turn off that part of myself so our family could continue to thrive. Over time, I spun a web of distractions that cradled the four of us gently in its net. It was a sort of refuge, I suppose, and I lived in it comfortably for many months, unaware that it would unravel in an instant.

One night during dinner with a neighbor at Village Pizza, Ethan ate two slices of pizza, and as he took a bite of a third slice, he threw up all over the table. Esther, not to be outdone, followed by dumping an entire cup of ice over her head. Ethan then laughed so hard he fell out of his chair. He immediately began crying as hysterically as he had just been laughing, as if his heart rather than his elbow had been scraped raw. Esther unbuttoned her soaking-wet shirt, threw it on the floor, and ran crazily around the room.

Because the restaurant was empty, I decided to let the kids run wild for a few moments to get a short break from the chaos. I was confident that Esther had sequestered herself in the back room, where a pinball game and novelty machines usually enticed her. But when I got up to retrieve her, but she wasn't in the back room. I checked the front room again. No Esther.

I circled back to the games, calling her name, and then heard her kittenish voice answering, as if from very far away: "Hi, Mommy! I'm in here!" I followed the faint sound to the bathroom, where I tried to open the door. It was locked. My toddler had locked herself in. Luckily, one of the teenage cashiers heard my panicked pleas and came running. He stuck his fingernail in the lock and jiggled it open. Esther sauntered out of the grimy, pitch-black bathroom with a big grin on her face. I scooped up her half-naked self and returned to the table.

"I don't know how you do it," my neighbor said, shaking her head.

"I'm dying inside," I answered, smiling. (At that time, I said everything with a smile.)

My words hung in the air like a scribbled phrase in a cartoon bubble. I almost looked around to see where they came from. I was shocked that they emerged from my own mouth. But it felt right, and it felt good to say it, even though the confused look on my neighbor's face made it obvious I had just breached some boundary.

So I decided to try it again. A few nights later when a college friend repeated to me on the phone the words I now heard in my sleep—"I don't know how you do it"—my most honest response kicked in. "I'm numb inside," I said, this time without a laugh. "I don't feel anything at all."

That felt right too. Such a long time on my own with the kids—without Scott to lean on, without his sweetness to remind me what our family enterprise was all about—had drained my energy. The thought of our future deployment now crushed me, as the situation was only going to get worse. During workups, at least Scott returned home every once in a while. Squadrons on deployment never come home, and there's typically no way of seeing anyone on the boat unless there's a port call in a convenient location overseas. With little kids, however, port call visits, which last only a few days and are often relocated at the last minute, are all but impossible to co-ordinate. *Six months away,* I kept thinking. *Six months.*

Then late one night Scott explained that the Navy's senior leaders had just extended his cruise to seven months and could possibly lengthen it to nine. A colleague in another squadron had been given exactly the same news. Later that week, I lunched with a Navy wife whose husband had recently walked off the boat following a ten-month deployment.

I understood then that I couldn't do what I admire and respect most about the Navy wives I know: I couldn't pretend I didn't mind that my husband was rarely around or that my kids weren't suffering. But complaining never felt right, either, since many service members' families experience challenges far more difficult than ours. Whenever I started to feel sorry for myself I remembered those military spouses whose partners deploy for twelve to fifteen months, and even nineteen months in some cases, serving repeated tours of duty with ground forces that place them directly in harm's way. America's war on terrorism created a completely new and unwelcome reality for families who had never experienced such long deployments, and it became impossible to wallow in self-pity with those numbers wailing like sirens across my consciousness.

The Navy has always sent its people on cycles of deployments. Even in peacetime, sailors never stayed home for long. If you're in the Navy, you go to sea. Period. That's why the Navy exists. And that's why Scott gave me the Big Talk in my apartment the night he broke up with me for the third time: He knew I'd be on my own more than I wanted to be. Wars in Iraq and Afghanistan set in motion for the Navy a more aggressive deployment schedule, with longer, more frequent, and unpredictable cruises for each squadron. That reality makes life different and challenging for Navy families now.

But in my darkest moments, I tried to remember the spouses left on their own who have more kids than I do or whose kids have health problems, who have financial worries, who don't have extended family to depend on, who don't have time for outside interests or move so often there's no hope of a fulfilling career. As it happens, many other people are also thinking about military families and the children of deployed service members. Through Internet searches and word of mouth, I began to discover the numerous resources created by generous, entrepreneurial individuals, agencies, and nonprofit organizations. Some of these initiatives help service members' spouses land jobs, repair their roofs, get a new computer, or support a sick child. Others provide emotional boosts, like mailing a stuffed animal signed by the deployed parent on a child's birthday.

And then, of course, there's Flat Daddy.

I had read about the Flat Daddy program in local newspapers, where writers told of young children toting around three-foot-tall photos of their smiling fathers in uniform. The tone of the articles was sympathetic and patriotic. The accompanying pictures showed children pushing Flat Daddy on the swing, sitting next to him in a restaurant, riding beside him in the car. Though the real father was stationed overseas, presumably in difficult if not outright hellish conditions, Flat Daddy was always happy, immortalized on photo paper and smoothed onto a stiff foam core.

Though I now promised myself to face Scott's absence head-on, the idea behind Flat Daddy seemed vaguely Orwellian to me. The idea of pretending a proxy dad was home doing all the things a real dad did—when the real father was fighting a war with no end in sight—sparked a sense of dread that I couldn't shake. And the Flat Daddy poster (I admit I have a morbid turn of mind) reminded me of something propped up next to a casket at a funeral home.

I doubted that Ethan and Esther would fall for the Flat Daddy concept. But with Scott gone again, both kids were acting strangely. Ethan woke up crying several times per night, sparking my memories of the upheaval we endured the previous winter. Esther spent the first two days of his absence walking around the house aimlessly, alternately whining and sobbing. It was totally unlike her; she was such a happy kid that she'd tickle her own tummy to make herself laugh if nothing more interesting was going on.

Looking for advice, I talked to a friend with twins in kindergarten. I was really confused: Was it better for my kids to forget about their dad and not mind he was gone? Or should I allow them to go through the grieving process every time he left, though it was so painful? I still felt so new at this Navy mom business. I wanted to help my kids experience what they needed to, but how heartbroken did they need to be before I stepped in?

"It makes me sad that my girls adjust to Del's absence so easily and don't seem to care that he is gone," my friend admitted. Her husband was in Afghanistan indefinitely; their squadron didn't even have a return date. "But if we are going to live like this, it makes it easier for all of us."

Our conversation left me unsettled. I didn't think I could ever be happy with the kids not caring that their dad was gone, even if it meant they were well-adjusted Navy children. So I flashed back to those upbeat articles about Flat Daddy, and I reconsidered. The families featured in those stories seemed to be having so much fun. Maybe they knew something I didn't.

The moment Flat Daddy arrived, he confirmed my hopes. Esther held him and kissed him as if he were the real thing and even dragged him into her crib at night. In the days that followed, she and Ethan took him everywhere: out for dessert, where they fed him ice cream; to the library, where my son balanced Flat Daddy on his shoulders and raced through the aisles; into the backyard, where he accompanied them down the slide.

"Daddy's home!"

Every time they shouted those words, my heart leaped. For one joyful moment I thought my husband had somehow found his way back to us. Of course, the children were just enthusiastically greeting Flat Daddy, who was leaning against the wall in the foyer. We brought to life countless newspaper photos. For the first time since marrying Scott and having kids, I saw myself as if from afar: I was keeping it together, the cheerful, agreeable woman "who took life in her stride," finally following the exhortations of *The Navy Wife*. Except that Flat Daddy made keeping it together that much trickier. With his smile literally hovering over us, Ethan and Esther now queried me nonstop: Why did Daddy have to go away? When was he coming back? Tomorrow?

"Not tomorrow," I'd explain. "He's going to be away for a long time, but he still loves you and thinks about you every minute." Or I'd say: "It's his job. He loves you very much and doesn't want to be away from you, but it's his job, just like your job is to put away your boots in the laundry room."

Flat Daddy did help them remember Scott, but the problem now was that we talked about him incessantly. Every picture they drew, every song they sang was for Flat Daddy. I found Esther sneaking him sips of her apple juice, holding up the straw to his lips. I discovered Ethan caressing his cheek. All of that was beneficial for them, I believed. But even though I had vowed to face the music, living with Flat Daddy struck a sour note as spring slid into summer—and not just because of the children's jackhammer-speed questions about Real Daddy's eventual return. Flat Daddy was a fake husband whose frozen cheerful expression gave me no comfort. He reminded me only of the Scott I was missing. I would walk by and remember our first kiss, the crush of the glass under his black patent-leather shoe at our wedding, the gentle way he cradled our babies, and I'd think, *Why have you left us?*

But Ethan and Esther loved hanging out with Flat Daddy, so I couldn't remove him (it?) from their lives. Instead, whenever I needed a reprieve I'd sneak him into the upstairs office, where they rarely ventured, and then I'd feel guilty and immediately return him to the family room. Once I accidentally banged him against the wall, then patted the cutout, catching myself before I apologized.

I almost let my son draw on Flat Daddy, thinking that if he were defaced I'd have an excuse to move him to Flat Daddy heaven. This supposedly clear-eyed preparation for deployment was preparing me for a total breakdown.

As it turned out, I wasn't the only one. One morning we said good-bye to Flat Daddy as usual and headed off to Ethan's Montessori preschool, where that day Lily's son, who was also four years old, was giving a presentation about his dad. Together, Lily and her son had pasted pictures on a poster, brought in items his dad had sent from Iraq, such as a carved camel, and planned to share a book about how to deal with sad and angry feelings. But Ethan refused to enter the classroom, crying hysterically and clinging to me as I tried to leave. When the teacher explained to him that the little boy was going to talk about his daddy because he missed him, Ethan started screaming, "But I miss *my* daddy!" I tried to comfort him, but he was inconsolable. Finally, I offered to go home to get Flat Daddy. My son looked at me as if I had lost my mind, then burst into a fresh round of crying. "Flat Daddy's not real," was all he could say, each word pushed out on a sob.

My brave boy was ready to call it as he saw it: The emperor had no clothes. Watching my children feed ice cream to Flat Daddy and swing with him in the backyard may have been hard for me, but it turned out that it was even harder for Ethan. I had to ask myself: Had this been a show he was putting on for me all along, being strong to make Mommy feel better?

Despite my original reservations, I'd allowed this doppelgänger to lull me into a hazy daydream of us as a family again and make me believe my children were fine. But Flat Daddy was no substitute for an ongoing conversation about how Real Daddy's absences were affecting us. Watching my son come unglued forced me to see that Flat Daddy wasn't fooling anyone and neither was I. Because when Ethan said that he missed his daddy, I finally started crying too—for the husband I longed to be with; for my son's pain; for Lily's son, petting the carved camel as he waited for his dad to return; for the ones whose parents would never return. And for the fear my son would be one of them.

I understood that we couldn't continue like this. After I reflected on the avalanche of emotion that had accompanied both denial and acknowledgment of our situation, I realized that I was, very simply, afraid—afraid to experience what was quickly proving itself to be the most significant event in my adult life. Bigger than marrying Scott, bigger than giving birth to Ethan and Esther, was sending my husband off to war again. This time the stakes were even higher for us than they had been when I was pregnant with my first child. This time we had a family, including two complicated creatures whose psychological well-being lay in our hands.

I stood at a crossroads, unsure of which direction to take. Denial, as I discovered, didn't make our life as a military family any easier; our days were more chaotic than ever before, prone to meltdown at a moment's notice. And if acknowledgment of our status meant facing down Flat Daddy every day, I would just have to throw in the camouflage towel.

Before I left to pick up Ethan that afternoon, I walked over to my jewelry box. Scott's training cycle was going to keep him away from home during Mother's Day, still a few weeks away. Before he left he'd sneaked away with my gold charm bracelet, arranged for two new charms to be attached, and presented me with my gift before he flew out. The new charms, a Prowler and a pen, were hooked together on a single O-ring.

"Our twin passions," he had said in his deep, quiet voice, placing the bracelet in my palm. "Flying and writing."

Flying and writing. I took it to heart, maybe more literally than he meant it. I'd write about his flying—about this tour, about the kids, about becoming a military family. "Tell all the Truth but tell it slant," as Emily Dickinson exhorted. Indeed, despite the profound challenges, there was a brilliance that dazzled gradually, just as Miss Dickinson predicted. I wasn't sure how to start, but I had a feeling that, when the moment came, it would come fast and there would be no turning back.

9

A Day of Mother

We'd lived in Anacortes almost a whole year when I finally began inching closer and closer to the me I used to be—before I'd convinced myself that becoming a military wife meant I had to change fundamentally. Mother's Day was a real test. It's perfectly fine to believe that Mother's Day is just another Sunday or that it's a Hallmark holiday. That's what I told myself, anyway. Scott was still gone, and though I'd tried to make plans with many people that weekend, no one was available. Even my friends whose husbands were deployed had mothers and sisters in town. The squadron wives' club members hadn't planned ahead, so we didn't have an event on the books, either.

I knew my parents would be celebrating Mother's Day with a big family brunch, just as they did every year. The guests and the menu were all so familiar to me that I could smell the soufflé, hear the laughter all the way across the country. So when I woke up on Mother's Day that May morning, the sky wasn't the only thing that was overcast. But this was the old me—me, redux. I gave myself a talking-to, just as I used to do. I asked myself how to turn things around, make Mother's Day memorable. I'd spent so much time since our move to Anacortes feeling guilty about my emotional absence from Ethan and Esther that I lay awake every night lamenting my actions. The fact that friends and family who witnessed my interactions with the kids felt that I was fully engaged gave me scant comfort, as only I understood what my children needed, I believed, and therefore only I knew how far short I had fallen.

So my gift to myself on Mother's Day, I decided, would be a peaceful night's sleep. I'd give the kids a day to remember, a day of Mother rather than Mother's Day. I vowed that when I went to bed that night, I would have no regrets. It didn't matter that Scott wasn't with us, I told myself, because this is my time with the kids. Today, the three of us are all we've got.

I closed my laptop, packed our lunches, and dressed Ethan and Esther in their warmest layers, with windbreakers on top.

"Where we going?" Esther asked, as I strapped her into the car seat.

"We're having a picnic on the beach," I replied.

"Yay, yay, picnic on the beach," both kids sang, overlapping each other like the peals of cheerful, chiming church bells.

Washington Park, a 220-acre state park, is only ten minutes from our house, and its rocky beaches and heavily wooded trails are glorious when the weather cooperates. That morning was cloudy and gray, but I didn't care. All the picnic tables were empty, so I set up our lunch at the one with the best view, facing the pier. We watched boats launch, one by one as if on an assembly line, splashing softly into the water and gaining speed in the deep. We searched for Blinky, the one-eyed seal we'd spotted many times before, but he was too shy to show himself.

After lunch, Ethan and Esther ran up and down the beach, stopping occasionally to balance single-file on beams of driftwood bleached bone-white by the sun. I even let them take their boots and socks off and wade into the frigid water. Esther lay down to make a sand angel, and when she stood up again, the grains glittered in her pores, catching the sun's rays as she literally sparkled from the inside out. Ethan clambered up a boulder before I had a chance to spot him, and balanced precariously as a tightrope walker. I was breathless, from both my own fear and my awe of the fearless boy he had become.

Together, we poked dead jellyfish, collected shells, waved at kayakers. After a few hours I realized we had wandered to the end of the beach, in full view of the newly constructed condos encroaching on the park. I gazed down at the picnic tables we'd meandered from, which were now full of families. Smoke billowed from grills sheltered in gazebos. Other families were spreading blankets on the sand and unpacking picnic baskets. Parents—moms and dads who instantly reminded me of what my kids were missing—chased their toddlers around in circles.

Other military wives tell me that their loneliest days are Sundays, when they feel most acutely the absence in their own family. Watching other families enjoy a simple day on the beach, I understood that, and I felt with an empathetic stab the pain that single moms—whether they are divorced, widowed, or never married—must live with all the time. Though I remained grateful for Scott's full emotional and financial support, I began in those months alone to understand the isolation, pressure, and fear single moms experience every day of their lives. And as I shared stories of our family's long separations with my married civilian friends and listened to them relate their own suburban struggles, I grew to believe that all marriages experience some sort of deployment. It could be a drawn-out business trip, an illness, or the death of a parent that separates two loving partners for some period of time. Depression, a deployment of the heart, can banish lovers to opposite ends of the earth, farther away than any aircraft carrier can steam. Solo immigration of the family breadwinner sunders solid families for years on end. Even a happy event like the birth of a baby, which shuffles each family member's ranking and status, can create an emotional rift between a husband and a wife more agonizing than any physical separation.

Our family's separations may not have been easy, but each detachment and deployment came with an end date, I reminded myself that day at the beach. So when sadness seeped through my resolve, I faced it down. I forced myself to stay in the present. But that didn't mean we had to stick around.

"Time to go, guys," I ordered. "More fun stuff ahead, but only if we leave now."

Back home, the kids and I baked brownies together, and we all played with Esther's dollhouse. After I tucked in Esther for her nap, I told Ethan I was going to close my eyes on the couch while he watched a video.

"Can I lie on you, Mommy?" he asked.

"Sure," I said, holding out my arms.

We lay like that for a few moments. I remembered sleeping with him in the exact same position when he was a newborn. I dreamed of Scott's return then too. Suddenly, Ethan sat up. He pulled the hem of my shirt to one side, then bent over and kissed my stomach.

"I love your big, squishy tummy, Mommy," he said, serious as a marriage proposal.

I had gained ten pounds since our move to Anacortes. That big, squishy tummy, streaked with silver stretch marks, was a touchy subject, indeed. But when Ethan kissed my belly, nothing else mattered. That Mother's Day, my first alone, was the best day I'd had in a long time, and I slept peacefully all night.

10

Cryptology

It's been almost eight years since I watched the documentary on NASA wives at Scott's former house in Pax River. The truth is, since our relationship was only weeks old then, I felt that Scott's proximity to me was much more worthy of my attention than what those women with the beehive hairdos were discussing onscreen. But one moment haunts me. After astronaut Elliot See dies in a plane crash, fellow astronaut John Young calls NASA wife Marilyn Lovell and asks her to visit See's wife. "You want me to tell her that Elliot was killed?" she responds, in the documentary dramatization. "No," Young replies, "I want you to do something much harder—not tell her. Somebody should be there with her right now, but she can't be told anything until I can come over and notify her officially."

Notification of deaths wouldn't happen like that anymore. But I was forced to think through that contingency when I answered the phone at midnight during the squadron's workups. Scott rarely calls that late unless he needs an extraordinary measure of comfort; if I hadn't been so tired, I would have picked up on it right away.

"Are you sleeping, sweetie?" he asked.

"That's okay," I said. "Is everything all right?"

"I just want to let you know I'm fine," he answered. Usually that response would have been enough. There was a hidden message in that statement, a code. But I was still waking up, and my cryptological abilities weren't operational yet, so I told him I loved him, and we said good-bye.

A minute later, lying in bed with my eyes wide open, I called him back. It always took him a while to give me bad news, so I let him get to it on his own.

"How was your day?" I started.

"It went fine for me," he answered. There it was: the emphasis on the "me."

"Everything okay in the squadron?"

"The squadron's fine."

I didn't respond. After a few silent moments, he took a deep breath. "There was a mishap tonight," he said. "The air wing lost an aircraft."

The word *mishap* sounds so innocuous, like someone has spilled milk or bumped into a table. The word *lost* hints at a temporary, fixable condition. What's lost, after all, can usually be found. Being lost isn't a permanent situation. But the Navy has its own Talmudically precise lexicon. I picked up on that years ago, when I first started answering similar midnight phone calls about Scott's colleagues at test-pilot school.

Now I understood. Scott was telling me that a jet or helicopter taking part in his air wing's training mission crashed, and people had died. He was required to be evasive, since the Navy would not release details or names until family members of the dead had been notified. But when CNN reported the news, hours from now, at least I would know that our squadron wasn't involved.

"Can you tell me what happened?" I asked.

"Not really," he said. "We don't know much."

"That's awful," I said. "How'd you find out about it?"

"I was flying." That meant close proximity.

"So what did they say about it on your radio?" I don't know why that mattered. I could have asked him trivial, irrelevant questions for a solid hour. I guess I was trying to help him, simply by keeping him talking, because I could hear the pain in his flat, low voice. He was slipping away into his own world of sadness. I wanted to do anything to keep him on the line, since I knew he'd soon be inaccessible to me.

"I can't really talk about it, okay, honey?"

He was gone.

During the next few days, details emerged about the five officers and aircrew who died in that training flight over the Nevada desert. (A base spokesperson told the news media that that collision stood out as the worst in recent memory.) As with the mishap during test-pilot school, Scott witnessed the crash, a fireball that flared up below his aircraft. Learning these particulars, words from the Rosh Hashanah prayer rushed through my head: *Who by water and who by fire.*

My monthly spouse club meeting convened later that same week, so we talked, haltingly, about what we had learned from our husbands about the mishap. There were six of us at the meeting, all wives of officers in the squadron. Agendas for the meeting lay in front of us on the table, but we looked away from the paper and at each other. We contributed what little we had heard while trying hard not to whip up fresh rumors, since scant official information circulated at that point. We knew that the CO of the sister squadron had been killed on that flight and that he had been a friend and close colleague of our husbands. The CO who died had a six-month-old baby, and one of the lost airmen left a pregnant wife. That was especially tough to hear. We all averted our eyes from the two pregnant women at our table.

It was as if some unseen hand had written the words in black marker on our foreheads: *It could have been me.* In our solitary moments, most of us had secretly imagined the worst, but we never talked about it. As a group, aviators and their spouses are usually too superstitious to discuss morbid scenarios.

"Trey was talking to the pilot in the ready room a few minutes before takeoff," the woman next to me said. "It's surreal."

"I just felt so guilty, getting the call," another woman admitted. "When I heard what squadron it was, and I knew it wasn't ours, I felt relieved. Glad, even. But those families are totally destroyed now."

I knew what she meant. In the spring of 2003, during six weeks of mandatory bed rest in an attempt to stave off preterm labor during my pregnancy with Ethan, I watched news of the just-proclaimed Iraq War every waking moment. I tracked the progress of Scott's squadron, which was then based in the Persian Gulf on the USS *Kitty Hawk*, via the laptop next to me in bed and the television across the room. I was enormous—nearly eight months along and so uncomfortable I slept only an hour or two at a time. I'd moved into my childhood bed at my parents' house once the doctors told me to lie on my side twenty-three out of twenty-four hours per day.

One early morning, I rubbed my eyes, clicked the remote on, and propped myself up on my elbows. As I peeked over my belly, I read the text that crawled across the bottom of the screen. An airplane flying off the USS *Kitty Hawk* had crashed in Iraq. That was it. Nothing else. I searched every Internet site I could, trying to track the downed plane or uncover any other piece of information that I could factor into my decision to panic—or not. I didn't assume Scott's plane had crashed; in fact, I assumed it couldn't have been Scott. I naïvely decided that he couldn't die when I was pregnant with our first child. He couldn't die in a war he shouldn't even have been in to begin with. After all, he had been slated to return to D.C. from our last assignment in Japan months earlier but had been kept on—and on, and on, and on—because the squadron desperately needed an extra pilot for that phase of the air war. Orders are not options, as they say in the military. Anyway, not even I was petty or selfish enough to begrudge our friends in the squadron the manpower they required as they literally fought for their lives and for the safety of troops on the ground.

My phone started ringing as friends and colleagues woke up and saw the news. I didn't answer any of the calls because I didn't trust myself to talk to anyone. Although I continually assured myself Scott couldn't possibly be dead, I couldn't stop crying, either. My parents checked in on me every hour, but they stayed downstairs. They were crying privately and didn't want to make it worse for me. We couldn't face each other. There was just nothing to say.

Finally, the call came. The head of my former wives' club reached me from base in Japan. She told me the name of the downed pilot, Lieutenant Nathan White, and mentioned the squadron to which he was attached. Back on base, she was helping his wife and their three young children the best she could. They lived just a few doors away. Everyone in the neighborhood grieved, and the streets resembled a ghost town, she told me. It was a bleak day. (Years later, reports reached the news that White's F/A-18C Hornet was shot down by a U.S. Patriot missile, one of the first incidents of "friendly fire" during the war, and the story of his life and death was featured on *60 Minutes*.)

I remained upset, even after I found out that Scott was safe on deck. After all, he knew Nathan White, and we both knew many aviators and families in that squadron. I imagined his wife's grief, and that of White's parents and friends. But my sadness was paired with overwhelming, shameful relief that our squadron had escaped injury. When the next call came, I answered it right away and started spreading the news.

11

Starfish

S ummer sped in as we rounded the circle of our first year in Anacortes. Without the stifling humidity I'd grown accustomed to during a lifetime of sweaty East Coast summers, the mild warm weather of the Pacific Northwest was sheer pleasure. Suddenly, it didn't matter that there were no Gymborees, no malls, no schools in session. The entire town became our playground. There was always a new beach to explore, a park to run around in, or a trail that harbored undiscovered treasures, like a nest of herons we spotted in the V of a tree in Washington Park. When it rained, we drove a mile down to the end of Commercial Avenue and sat in the car watching trawlers being repaired at the Dakota Creek shipyard. Welders' yellow and orange sparks flew with the grandeur of Fourth of July fireworks, enthralling the kids longer than I ever thought possible. Just one street up, if we timed it right, we could glimpse the U.S.A.'s America's Cup racing yacht under construction in a high-security, three-story shed converted into a purpose-built boat construction facility.

We didn't venture out every day. Sometimes, the kids were satisfied with swinging in the backyard or playing with the other children in the cul-de-sac, where we could almost always join a game of kickball or a gentle sword fight.

For the first time since we moved, both kids seemed grounded, happy, and healthy—healthy in every way. Our winter-break visit with grandparents, aunts, uncles, and cousins had reassured Ethan that his old life still existed, and he found comfort in the knowledge that the people he loved welcomed him back with open arms. He cried when we left but settled back into our routine in Anacortes with an ease I hadn't anticipated. And in his summer wardrobe of shorts and T-shirts I saw how much my four-year-old had grown physically in the last several months. Each day we spent at Bowman Bay, Little Cranberry Lake, or Washington Park deepened his nut-brown tan. His dark eyes sparkled as he hunted for hawk feathers or rolled rocks over to watch baby crabs scuttling across the sand.

Esther shot up like the tall, strong stalks of daisies that bloomed across our front yard. Like a flower, she sought the sun and became even fresher, more and more herself, under its warm embrace. Her porcelain skin was too fair to tan, but a sprinkling of new freckles dotted her tiny nose and both cheeks. She entered her second year with a vengeance, challenging me and negotiating the terms of her meals, bedtime, and outfits in a high-pitched, forceful voice. But her sweetness never left her. She awoke with a smile each morning, she was the first to hug someone who looked upset, and she still snuggled up close when we read books together.

Scott was missing it all, but I tried not to think about that. Especially when I realized how much time was passing. One day at Guemes Island, as the kids and I searched for hermit crabs, Esther spotted a live starfish in the shallow water. As she pointed it out, I saw that her hand was nearly as big as the starfish, her fingers as long and elegant as its softly waving arms. I suddenly realized that she wasn't a baby anymore. Years before, when that same thought flashed through my head about Ethan, Scott and I decided it was time for another child. But getting pregnant during the tour at

Whidbey looked less and less like a brilliant idea, since Scott's schedule promised nothing but long absences. We had no idea what the tour after this one would hold, or where in the country—or the world—we would move. And there was always the chance of a future IA. I couldn't count on Scott to be around, and I didn't think I could handle three small children on my own.

The Navy intruded on our most personal decisions at every turn. But I set those thoughts aside because Scott returned home for several weeks in June. We were a family again, and after a transitional year of upheaval and unhappiness, our life seemed gloriously normal.

Normal, with one exception: I'd never had both kids totally on my own, without school or day care, for such a long period of time, and I didn't see how I could continue working through the summer if I was with them all day. Not working didn't ever occur to me; it helped me stay sane in the midst of domestic chaos, and it was just what I had always done. From the time I hit thirteen, I had worked part-time jobs, whether as a camp counselor or drugstore cashier, office receptionist or temporary secretary. Continually writing and editing the script of my life, my career-minded mother helped me snag competitive summer internships at D.C.-area agencies as soon as I started high school. She believed, rightly, that the exposure would give me a sense of what I wanted to do with my life. It started early, but I didn't mind; I never had any desire to hang out at the pool or play video games during school breaks. All I ever wanted to do was read novels, and I could finish off a book every two days on my Metro commute in and out of the city.

There was more to it than that, of course. If first-child syndrome is a disease, I had it bad. I tended to envision myself as a little adult, so it never felt strange to put on a skirt and blouse every morning of my high school and college summers and wait for a county Ride-On bus to deliver me to the Metro subway station. My mother went back to work soon after I started first grade, and as a child I studied her carefully every morning as she curled her hair in the mirror, pulled on panty hose, and picked out a dress while nibbling the English muffin on her vanity. She was my world, my entire and exclusive frame of reference for how to be, and so I figured that was what all women did.

By the time I was a senior in college I juggled three part-time jobs, and I continued to work extra gigs and hold down internships through graduate school. Like many English majors lacking a trust fund, I worked hard because I needed the money. But twelve years later—when I married Scott and had the option to quit my job—I realized I loved working too much to stop. I enjoyed everything about it: strategizing over challenges, untangling office politics, speaking at conferences, finishing projects, meeting goals, solving problems. My biweekly paychecks oiled the gears of my young adult life, and as I paid bills at night, I felt a responsibility and in-dependence that made writing the checks almost pleasurable. My money was my own, and I could make my own decisions about how to spend it.

That's why I feel acute sympathy for military wives who have never landed in one place long enough to establish a career. Often, the unpredictability of their husbands' schedules makes it difficult for employers to depend on them, a vicious cycle that renders mili-tary wives, and especially mothers, less attractive job candidates. In addition, because military spouses move frequently, they often fail to meet residency requirements for benefits such as unemployment compensation and in-state tuition, as a Department of Defense re-port has found. However, these same spouses must usually file and pay in-state income taxes, forgoing a benefit afforded to active-duty members that allows long-term maintenance of residency in a single "home" state.

Overall, state-by-state statistics on military-spouse employment are scarce because military bases are excluded from calculations of the national unemployment rate, but the U.S. Department of Labor has released figures showing that the unemployment rate among military spouses is three times that of their private-sector counterparts. Regardless, military spouses are a motivated workforce. Studies show that most military spouses are in the labor market, either holding down a job or looking for employment, though on average they earn three dollars less per hour than their civilian counterparts, and their unemployment rate is three times as high as that of civilian spouses.

Military spouses who do work often settle for stopgap jobs that pay less and have limited career growth. Most of these women are resigned to the reality of limited career options. One young wife I know, a college graduate, worked a series of jobs in jewelry stores around the country during her first few years of marriage, but even those minimum-wage calls dried up when potential employers tracked her frequent moves. With no one to hire them, some military wives get creative, especially spouses of enlisted sailors, whose paychecks don't stretch far enough. To supplement their husband's paycheck, some host foreign exchange students, hire themselves out as surrogate mothers for couples who are unable to get pregnant, or set up day-care centers in their family rooms.

If they established a career before marrying into the military, extreme mobility forces the loss of seniority and also makes it difficult to stay current with licensing and certification regulations. (One study found that the relocation rate of the military is four times that of the civilian population.) State-by-state requirements create delays and add layers of additional added expense in the form of exams and fees. Wives with specialized skills, including graduate and professional degrees, face other challenges. I've seen this firsthand: My friend Isabelle was a programmer at Microsoft when she and her husband married, but after just one move, she fell behind in the critically important technical training that keeps programmers competitive. A few years and several more relocations rendered her degrees and employment history irrelevant.

Many ambitious professional military wives have made heart-wrenching choices to maintain or finally abandon a successful career. One friend started teaching in the local school system when her husband was a junior officer and gradually worked her way up to vice principal while pursuing her Ph.D. To reach those goals, she'd stayed in one place for the fifteen-year period her husband took assignments that relocated him all over the country. At one point, they spent nearly six years apart, three tours in a row, during which time they saw each other one weekend every other month if they were lucky.

"It was horrible," she told me, shuddering at the memory. "I'm never doing that again."

So as her husband pondered opportunities for his next tour, she readied herself to accompany him and gave up the chance to be principal in the school system that nurtured her career.

Recently proposed initiatives may address some of these problems. The Department of Defense is collaborating with the Department of Labor to help spouses find meaningful work, claiming that "military spouse employment is a critical component of the Department's Social Compact with military families." The DoD's Military Spouse Preference Program also aims to help spouses reenter the labor market. In late 2008, an executive order was signed to make it easier for spouses of service members to get federal jobs; it authorized noncompetitive hiring of spouses of active-duty and Reserve service members to streamline bureaucratic requirements. And in another example of growing attention to the cause of military spouses, one congressman has proposed legislation that would allow them to claim one state of domicile regardless of where they are stationed, just as the service member is permitted to do. These initiatives are all due in part to studies showing that personnel are leaving the service because of their spouses' limited career opportunities.

It's only relatively recently that an officer's spouse was assured of the right to work in the first place. A "two-for-one" mentality long reigned in some military services, and the assumption was that a spouse would forgo career aspirations of her own to support her husband's career and his unit's well-being. In 1988, following an Air Force inquiry that found that two wives of senior Air Force officers had been warned that their husbands' careers would suffer if they did not quit working, the Air Force adopted a formal policy stating that spouse employment was a private matter forbidden from consideration in the service member's evaluation for promotion. Then Secretary of Defense Caspar Weinberger ordered each service branch to issue a policy holding that military spouses have the right to work at jobs outside the home. Furthermore, Weinberger's order stressed that "No military member will be adversely rated or suffer any adverse consequences from the decision of the member's spouse. . . . Nor shall a spouse's employment be a consideration in either assignments or promotions." This was a breakthrough for military spouses, whose institutionalized roles (as volunteer and fund-raiser for military causes) had never been challenged formally and certainly never at such a high level.

Memory of this is misty at best in my postfeminist generation. In any case, the right to do something in theory doesn't necessarily make it easier to do in practice. The officer wives in my orbit, most of whom are college graduates, focus on their children and volunteer their time to organizations on base. In their premilitary lives, their careers ran the gamut: they were attorneys, stockbrokers, flight attendants, teachers, defense industry analysts, entrepreneurs, IT specialists, human resource managers, nurses, and physical therapists. Those in professions that travel well, like health care, real estate, or education, usually find a way to work (at least part-time) wherever their spouse's new assignment lands them. But the complexity of being a military wife—following a spouse who rarely stays put, and parenting alone—sometimes forces the choice to stay home, even when it places the family at a severe financial disadvantage.

Before I married into the military, I would have viewed these unemployed spouses far less sympathetically, as women who required someone else to take care of them. Little did I realize that military wives know better than most how to take care of themselves, their families, and anyone in need.

A fter I finished graduate school and launched my career in the publicity department of a publishing house in the Boston suburbs, I'd been juggling multiple gigs for so long that I didn't know what to do with myself at night or on weekends. One full-time job seemed like ridiculously little work for a single girl. I read voraciously in my free hours, but I could finish a book in a day, and after a few months those towers of novels next to my bed seemed reproachfully self-indulgent. I started to believe I was reading my life away, substituting the excitement of other people's adventures for my own. For the first time, my self-image as a reader fought with my self-image as a hard worker. Neither could afford to lose. That's when I started writing again, though my first essay wasn't published until several years later. Until my kids were born, I balanced two jobs: a full-time position and my freelance writing on the side. Once Ethan and Esther arrived, I scaled back dramatically. But scaling back was a far cry from giving up work altogether, and that's the decision I faced our first summer in Anacortes, when I became my children's full-time mother, companion, and educator.

I hadn't taken a summer off since fifth grade. It was a tough

idea to come to terms with, since *not* being a typical Navy wife
was important to me then, and staying at home with kids is a very
Navy wife thing to do. But we were now Anacortesians. Since the
sun shines brightly only three or four months out of the year, I
gradually eased my way into the town's live-it-up mentality. I
stopped looking at my watch, fractioning my time into the next
conference call, the next e-mail, the next project deadline. Few of
my mom-friends in Anacortes worked, and many of those who did
also took the summer off, so setting myself free was a little less
strange than it might have been back in D.C., surrounded by neighbors rushing to and from the office.

Since Anacortes is a tourist haven, and many people wandering
around town are fresh off the ferry, I fit right in, at least as I justi-
fied it to myself. I still believed that Anacortes was just an interruption in our life, a temporary hiatus in the flow we had established
as a family.

12

Beautiful World

By the time Scott left us again, for the month of July and another set of workups, the kids and I were conquering a new corner of town each new day. Ethan and Esther played together better and better as they grew older, and Ethan, who had never been comfortable on his own, now entertained himself with drawing or crafts during Esther's naps. He and I spent quiet time together we hadn't enjoyed since Esther was born. His feelings toward me turned almost romantic.

"Mommy, I fell in love with you when I was a little baby," he confessed one sunny afternoon, as we built a Lego tower. His root-beer–brown eyes softened with affection.

I thanked him and smiled before I asked, "And how do you feel about me now?"

"I just love you more every day," he confirmed.

The feeling was mutual. By dinnertime I shook with exhaustion, and by the kids' bedtime I was crankier than a toddler. But I saw Ethan and Esther in an exciting new way. The three of us grew closer as we picked wildflowers, pointed out newborn ducklings to one another, examined crabs' abdomens to determine gender, or stood aside while baby snakes slithered slowly across our path. Ethan loved the sensation of ladybugs crawling on his hands, and he laughed as their tiny feet tickled his palms. I discovered that Esther was terrified of spiders, but she didn't hesitate to pick up a dead mole and carry it across the yard to present it to me. Together, the three of us banded together, a team of explorers conquering fresh territory. I'd never enjoyed such uninhibited access to nature or the time to make my own way through it, pursuing my own paths and exploiting the freedom to return to the nooks and crannies that haunted my inner landscape long after I returned home.

Beautiful World, more than any other new discovery, enchanted me. It is a trail around the corner from our house that winds through a vast, self-contained forestland. Ethan christened it Beautiful World after one of our first visits, and the name stuck, out of sheer appropriateness. Usually the kids rode there from the house in their red wagon, which I pulled down our street, up a hill, and around a sharp bend. As we hit the lip of the path, they clambered out, all hands and feet, and ran as fast as they could. They climbed a giant dirt pile first. After that, we picked left or right, then left or right again, and a few steps later, the gifts lay before us in near-unimaginable abundance. We emerged into what seemed to me prehistory itself.

I felt like a Lilliputian amid the giant ferns, the elephant-ear–sized leaves, the toppled trees longer than train tracks and wider than any railroad car. Even on the sunniest days Beautiful World remained shady and cool, and so breezy that branches creaked continually in the wind, back and forth, back and forth, like doors in an eerie old mansion. The quiet pressed upon us almost seductively. Both kids grew calm as we hiked deeper into the antediluvian forest, shadowed by owls, butterflies, and slugs.

Though I often took the kids to Beautiful World on my own, we always returned when Scott flew back to town. The moment Esther's legs gave out, he lifted her to his shoulders. She giggled as berries hanging from the higher branches tickled her neck. Whether or not Scott walked with us, the kids and I never hurried through our hikes, and we always discovered something new, like the time we stumbled upon an enormous pond covered with a carpet of lily pads.

I like to think that Ethan named the path Beautiful World for its natural glory, but I suspect he really craved our hikes for the tiny treasures he found: shards of colorful glass; giant rusty nails; an ancient padlock, poetic in its possibilities; a matchbox car encrusted with mud. I started a Tupperware curiosity cabinet for him, a poor man's *Wunderkammer*, and he became an amateur curator—of trash—as he sorted through his finds every day to decide which to retain and which to discard.

One late afternoon that summer, when Scott had been away a few weeks and would not return for many more, both kids grasped their objects for the curiosity cabinet as I pulled the red wagon behind me on the way home. My head hung low. The wagon, heavy with their combined weight, seemed harder and harder to pull with each step. Suddenly, something in the air lifted my attention straight up. Two birds circled above me, close enough that I could clearly distinguish their white heads and long, sleek black bodies. I'd never seen a bald eagle before, except in an encyclopedia, and I doubted my own eyes. The pair arced in a wide, soaring circle, gliding the same simple path, like ice skaters. They tilted into the breeze, slowing as they reached a certain invisible spot, until the wind compelled them forward again. They carved the air into perfection, a precise O, over and over.

Time stopped. I held my breath. I couldn't take my eyes off these eagles, which barely fluttered a wing as they circled round and round. It was as if they'd been sent to hypnotize me. The air they flew must have been cool and crisp and, best of all, silent. I envied the silence, since the kids' demands to keep moving blurred the edges of my reverie. I straightened up and began walking again, facing the peaks of Mount Baker. In the glittering, four-o'clock sun, the melting snow on its side glowed like gilded silver, and the reflected rays reached out directly to me.

That's when the *I* that I had so carefully constructed during the past decade melted away too. In creating the image of myself as the semi-urban professional-turned-mom, I had ignored the possibility of any of this. Long ago, I decoded myself as I had always tried to decode others, but I was as wrong about myself as I had been about the Navy, Navy wives, and the life that awaited us in the Pacific Northwest. The emptiness was suddenly attractive, not because of the isolation, and certainly not because of the loneliness, but because of the possibilities.

It was the most internal of transformations. I suddenly saw this tour as much more than an interruption, a temporary hiatus from my mostly scripted life, which I would at some point in the future return to unchanged. After all, I was watching my kids grow into people, spending more time with them than ever before, and even though it was rough going, I was feeling for the first time like a real mom. I finally realized that I could be dependent on Scott emotionally and grieve his absences while continuing to thrive. My outreach to squadron wives gave me hope that I had made a difference in at least one or two lives. Most surprising of all, I was connecting in a deeply personal, authentic, and sustained way with the natural world. There was no text for that. All it required of me was to pay close attention, which I'd been practicing since I could remember.

The losses following our cross-country move echoed profoundly throughout that first year. But when those eagles soared above and Mount Baker shone ahead, I understood that Anacortes wasn't going to be the end of me. It was, instead, the beginning of who I am.

M ommy?"
     "Yes, my love?"

I pushed Ethan on the backyard swing as a moody orange sun hovered above the horizon, as resistant as my boy to going to bed that night.

"I can close my eyes, open them, and see Daddy on the deck."

"Really?"

"Yeah. He comes out of my imagination, and I can see him walking there"—Ethan pointed toward the outdoor dining set—"and then I close my eyes, and he goes back into my head." He wore his secret smile, as if he had solved a difficult puzzle completely on his own.

"You're lucky you can do that," I said. "That means you can see Daddy anytime you want. He's never far from you."

"I have magic powers," he said excitedly. "I'm a magical person."

"Yes, you are," I answered.

13

The Loved Dog

O f all the American narratives now accessible to me—small-town life, military culture, stay-at-home motherhood, nascent naturalist—one combination held particular surprises. In Anacortes, I recognized faces at the library that I'd seen moments before at the grocery store. I smiled at strangers dining at an outdoor café because I'd just crossed their path at the park. And the few times I started to honk my horn in frustration at a car making a stupid move, I stopped because the shadowy profile in the vehicle ahead looked a little too familiar.

I had lived that sort of fishbowl existence once before, around the time Scott and I married. At that time he was stationed at Naval Air Facility Atsugi, forty miles outside of metropolitan Tokyo. On a military base, of course, life is even more claustrophobic and circumscribed than it is in a town—even a small town like ours. At Atsugi base, I stumbled upon many impromptu spouse club meetings convened in the aisles of the commissary, where by chance everyone had gathered to shop at the same time.

People left base all the time, of course. Many local restaurants and shops beckoned; convenient trains, just a short walk away, sped us into blindingly glamorous Tokyo in under an hour. But life was simpler inside the gates, and people often stayed close. We bought the same issues of *Vogue* and *People* that our friends were paging through back home, paying for them with American dollars at the base bookstore. The food court offered Taco Bell, Subway, Baskin-Robbins, and other familiar comforts. And though cars on base drove on the left side, per Japanese road rules, English-language street signs eased navigation and calmed the nervous newcomer.

But I soon discovered that on-base living is not always easy. No boundaries separate those in such close quarters: Antagonistic bosses dine alongside sheepish subordinates at the Officers' Club at night, colleagues competing fiercely for upcoming promotions attend the same barbecues and baseball games, and babysitters are often children of shipmates. In Navy housing, comings and goings are community business, as are new purchases (since empty boxes appear curbside on trash day), visitors, and children's behavior.

Living small had a certain charm, though. I liked all my neighbors, which helped. We left bikes outside, cars unlocked, front doors wide open. If I got lost amid the identical rows of semi-detached homes, I simply knocked on a stranger's door and asked for directions. I was pregnant and alone most of our year in Atsugi's Navy housing, and many friends dropped in to check on me. I took myself on walks around base at ten or eleven p.m., when I was too anxious and lonely to sleep, and I never worried about my safety; drivers often pulled up to ask if I was all right or to offer me a ride back home.

Proximity made it easy for me to be altruistic too. If a friend caught the flu, I crossed through the backyard in my bare feet and delivered a pot of chili to the family. If a squadron mom needed a few hours on her own, her children ran over to my place, and I entertained them for a while before watching them scurry back across the grass.

I quickly saw the advantages to living within butter-borrowing distance—advantages to the Navy, too, of course. Everyone looking out for one another meant that anything untoward was spotted immediately. People worked extra hard to maintain community values (like mowing the lawn once a week) and uphold standards of behavior (like never driving drunk). You learned fast to be nice to strangers, to smile at everyone, to avoid overreacting in a tense social situation. On such a small base, you were bound to claim some connection to everyone whose path you crossed. The cashier at the Exchange who refused my return, for example, could very well be the wife of a sailor in our squadron, practiced in circulating gossip faster than a "Reply All" e-mail.

Living on base was a crash course in civility. These simple courtesies had seemed unnecessary in the anonymous suburbs of my past, but partaking in them opened my mind to the possibilities of what a community could be. That realization has served me well ever since, both in the military and the civilian worlds, and now in Anacortes, where our Navy experience pairs itself with the requirements of life in a small town. It is as if the Navy and Anacortes overlap like ovals in a Venn diagram, interlocking in the middle to form an island where everything converges.

That awareness was especially helpful to me during one of the strangest dramas I've ever played a role in. It happened midway through another one of Scott's absences that first summer, during my brother Joshua's mercy visit. A Ph.D. candidate in neuroscience at Vanderbilt University, Joshua typically spends his days scanning brains with an MRI machine. Despite his expertise in the workings of the human mind, nothing had prepared him for the havoc two intense, talkative little kids wreak on one's mental health.

Sometime that week, Ethan had started to realize that Daddy was really gone. Gone a long time. Gone forever, probably, in his mind, since a month seemed like forever to me at that point too. Though Ethan's outlook had improved tremendously since signs of his initial distress, each of Scott's absences that first year ushered in a new and surprising (though usually temporary) setback. That summer, Ethan started calling my brother "Daddy," in an absentminded, reflexive way, and Joshua kept correcting him. We always reminded Ethan that Scott was coming back and that he loved him very much. But Ethan was sad and mad. Ridiculous requests were followed by vicious tantrums, topped by howling sadness. He pinched and bit his little sister and lashed out with rude comments to all.

I understood that poor little kid better than he understood himself, and I worked hard to stay calm and patient. I would have never guessed that the unexpected intervention of a stranger would do more to refocus my efforts than any parenting manual, but that's exactly what happened one evening as Joshua, Ethan, Esther, and I sat at our usual spot in the back room of Village Pizza. Ethan's discontent had been building all day, and our nerves were frayed. Once seated, he erupted with the angry force that his earlier rumblings had portended. I walked him out to the car as he hollered. I opened the door and sat him inside. Then, with the door still open as I stood on the sidewalk beside him, I talked and he screamed. After fifteen minutes of ear-splitting drama, he finally calmed down, and we walked back inside, hand in hand, and sat down for our pizza.

As I took my first bite, I looked up to see a woman standing at the head of our table. She held a book in front of her. "I just wanted to tell you that I was listening to everything you said to your son outside," she quickly explained. She was a little nervous, quivery, and she appeared to be exerting a tremendous force of will to overcome her shyness. "I was standing on the street, and I heard every word. I've been reading this book"—she thrust it out again—"and I want you to know you're doing everything right."

The book was *The Loved Dog: The Playful, Nonaggressive Way to Teach Your Dog Good Behavior*. A dog-training manual.

The woman standing just a few inches away didn't look crazy. And anyway, in Anacortes crazy people don't walk around engaging strangers in conversation like their cousins on the big-city streets. I guessed her to be in her mid-fifties, and her strawberry-blond hair was gathered in a loose, low ponytail. She wore a tank top, shorts, and a fanny pack. She seemed sweet and earnest, like someone taking a risk to do a good deed.

"You're doing everything right," she repeated, as if urging me to stay strong.

It didn't really matter that she was holding a dog-training manual or somehow comparing my son to a wayward pet; she was being nice. And that just happens to be the worst thing to do when I was having a rough day with the kids. I instantly crumpled and began sobbing. She moved toward me, but in my peripheral vision I saw Joshua jump out of his seat and usher her away. When I looked up again, she stood in the doorway of the restaurant, waving her book in the air like a signal flag and yelling, "You're doing everything right! You're doing everything right!"

"I'm okay! I'm okay!" I shouted back, as if across the ocean.

I figured that my brother had told her I was having a rough go of it and that now probably wasn't the best time to talk. So after I choked out a few more tears, wiped my face with the coarsest of paper napkins, and swallowed a bite of pizza, I asked him what he said to her.

"I told her to go away . . . now," he answered curtly.

I was stunned.

"Then what?"

"I opened the door. She looked up at me and said, 'Oh, I understand.' And she left."

I stared at him. Such harsh words and behavior were totally out of character for my gentle brother, and it became clear in that moment that his nerves were as ragged as mine. But I could also see that he was trying to protect me. I rarely cry in front of him; as the Big Sister, I try to keep it together in every situation so that he'll think of me as a strong person. The truth is that I cry all the time, and crying is no big deal at all. I cry when I watch the movie *Madeline* with my kids and Madeline tells Lord Covington that his dead wife will always be with him. I cry at the sight of hummingbirds at our outdoor feeder. I cried once while watching a papal mass on television because the simple grandeur of the ceremony moved me.

At home, Scott had my habits pegged. Hearing me sniffle partway through a particularly heart-wrenching commercial for baby wipes, he would ask, "Really?" He didn't even have to turn my way, because he could predict that I was already wiping my eyes with the heel of my hand. He would reflexively click the remote until he found an innocuous sitcom, trying to save me from my emotions. But tears rarely wreck me. Crying is usually just a quick summer storm giving way to a perfectly ordinary day.

"That wasn't very nice of you," I told Joshua, still dabbing at my eyes.

He ran out the door to find the woman. He returned a few minutes later, after he apologized to her and told her she was a good person. I went searching for her after that too. I sensed that she had wanted to tell me something else. She seemed to know what I was going through, after all, and how much I needed to hear the words "You're doing everything right."

Besides, this being Anacortes, I knew I would see her again. (I often crossed paths with the anti-Semitic taxi driver, much to my chagrin.) And when I ran into her at the post office or wherever else fate would bring us together, I didn't want to pretend I didn't know her, or awkwardly look the other way, or cross the street. She had tried to be kind, and the least I could do was thank her.

She hadn't wandered far from the restaurant at all. I spotted her peering into the window of a store, clutching a wadded-up tissue in her hand.

"I'm so sorry," I called out as I approached her. She walked toward me.

"It's just been an awful day," I admitted. "But you were so nice to reach out. I know what you were trying to do. I appreciate it."

She held up the book again. That damn book! The dogginess of it all kept intruding on our moment.

"You were kind, you were not threatening, you didn't intimidate," she said. "You did everything the book says you should do."

She gave me a hug, and I hugged back. She smelled like a mom: like clean, generic drugstore shampoo. She held me like a mom too. "Your brother told me your husband is away," she said, embracing me for another moment before letting go. "I hope he comes back soon."

"I do too," I said, tearing up again as I faced her. Was I gazing in a mirror? A tear rolled down her cheek.

"I was a single mom too," she said. "For my son's whole life. He's thirty-three. He's a hurricane hunter down south. It kills me to think about it."

I didn't know anything about hurricane hunting, except for the obvious. "It must be very dangerous work," I said.

"It is," she replied. "I worry about him all the time. It's just him and me. That's how it's always been. Him and me. It was hard, but we did it. And he turned out great."

When she saw Ethan and me battling it out, she must have seen a reflection of herself and her son: the years, the regrets, the joys all rushing past like time-lapse photography. I wondered if during those decades she was raising her son alone, she wanted someone to tell her "You're doing everything right." The more I thought about it, the more certain of it I became. With those few words, she adopted me into the ranks of Anacortes's single moms on principle and in solidarity, and I felt honored to be included.

*P*too, *ptoo,* as my grandmother Beatrice would say, pretending to spit to the left and the right as she pantomimed the vestigial Jewish tradition of warding off the evil eye. "God forbid. *God for-bid you are ever a single mother.*"

Of course, I am not a single mother, and I understand only a fraction of the hardship and heartache that single moms experience. But as I focused increasingly on Scott's upcoming deployment, the inevitable became more unreal. I did not understand how I could possibly cope on my own with the kids for such a long period of time.

As many other squadrons on base deployed month after month, I watched dozens of my friends hug their husbands good-bye. At the time our squadron was preparing to leave, some of the wives in other squadrons were already halfway through deployments, comfortably in their groove and counting down to homecoming. Some still woke up every morning expecting to hear the sound of their spouse in the shower. For others the departure was so fresh they appeared at the gym or the supermarket dazed, like bomb victims wandering around in search of shelter. I asked these Navy wives—who were about to become the only people on Earth who could understand what I was going through—for their secrets. I asked for tips. I asked how they were doing.

Ronnie's grief was more public than most, since she broke down sobbing in church the Sunday after her husband Sam left for deployment.

"We were in our regular pew, but I sat in Sam's place," she recounted one morning, as we ran side by side on the treadmills at the gym. "The homily was about the Good Samaritan, and our priest kept relating it back to service members. I just couldn't help it. I cried. People kept coming up to me, and I kept crying. I couldn't stop. I couldn't get it together."

Carrier aviation is an inherently risky business. In nearly every flying tour Scott has lost friends and colleagues to mishaps. But in the context of the Iraq war, with ground soldiers experiencing far higher rates of casualties, Navy spouses in my community are generally grateful that our husbands fly on and off a boat. Other than the time they're in the air, they're fairly far removed from the

action, out of the reach of IEDs, suicide bombs, snipers, and the
other dangers that lurk in the field. But there are land-based naval
aviation squadrons in Iraq and Afghanistan too. Many on our base
deployed to those locations as members of expeditionary squadrons
or carrier-based squadrons that filled gaps in the schedule while the
carriers were undergoing maintenance. In the hierarchy of what
we wives wish for our husbands—given that they're headed to a
war zone, no matter what—the wives I know typically hope for
a boat squadron, then a land-based squadron in Iraq, and last, a
land-based squadron in Afghanistan. For reasons having to do with
perceived, mostly anecdotal, security threats, sending one's husband
to duty in Iraq seemed generally preferable to Afghanistan during
the time frame of our tour. Ronnie's husband had just left for
Afghanistan.

"How are the boys taking it?" I asked. Ronnie and Sam were
parents of a thirteen-year-old, a ten-year-old, and a one-year-old.

"Very up and down," she said, puffing with exertion in a manner appropriate to her situation at home. "The baby doesn't know,
and he doesn't really care. He sits at the kitchen table stuffing his
mouth while the rest of us push food around on our plates." I immediately thought of Esther, who seemed indifferent to Scott's absences until Flat Daddy made his grand entrance.

"Sam had an idea to help the older two, but it didn't turn out
the way he planned," Ronnie continued. "He bought some poster
board before he left and wrote down sayings and some inside jokes
between him and the boys. He taped up the posters in their room,
all around their bunk bed and on the walls. He did it just before he
left, so they'd find it afterward, after we dropped Sam off at the
squadron." I sensed where this was going.

"When the boys got home after the good-bye and went to their
room, they came running back out, screaming. I thought there had
been an accident. They couldn't stop crying long enough to tell me
what was wrong."

It was the quotes, Sam's effort to remind the boys of their closeness, their connectedness, despite the miles. But the boys were raw after watching their father fly off. Ronnie peeled the posters off the walls as fast as she could.

"You know Susie DeVol, right?" Ronnie asked, dabbing at her forehead with a towel as I struggled to match her pace. Susie's husband had deployed on a different carrier about a month before; their daughter, Lara, is ten years old.

"Susie's husband had a photo taken of just him and Lara. The morning he left he placed it on Lara's nightstand so she would find it when she went to bed. She fell asleep just fine, but in the morning, when Susie woke up Lara for school, the picture wasn't there. Susie asked her what had happened to it, and Lara refused to say anything at all. She totally clammed up."

"Oh, no."

"Susie waited until Lara went to school. She started digging around and found the picture under Lara's bed. Lara had taken it out of the frame and drawn tears on it with a magic marker. Tears and quivery lips."

My heart hurt, and it had nothing to do with running. I looked down. The digital red numbers on the treadmill panel blurred. I willed myself to keep going, one foot in front of the other. *Just keep moving forward, and it will be okay,* I told myself.

14

Tell Me Your Secrets

My curiosity about how other families handled the vexing question of remembering Daddy without fixating on his absence became increasingly acute as the deployment date approached. Our Flat Daddy still slept alone in the guest room. But before Scott left for the summer, a lightning flash struck me in the aisles of Radio Shack, in front of a talking picture frame. The idea was stunning in its simplicity: You slide a photo into the frame, press a button, and record a message. I bought one for the kids, so that they could hear Scott's voice anytime he was away. I would have bought more, because the clerk mentioned they were being discontinued, but one was all they had. And what a good thing that turned out to be.

I unveiled the talking picture frame to Ethan and Esther the morning after Scott left. "Daddy's present to you," I explained in the falsetto voice that mothers use to make the bizarre sound normal.

Ethan knew what to do. He pressed the button. Then came the message that would haunt me for weeks to come. It was harmless enough, the first go-round: "Sweetie pies, this is Daaadddy. I love you! I miss you! Byyyyyyye." Ethan and Esther must have played the recording twenty or thirty thousand times that first day, but I didn't mind. Scott's voice warmed me like a fleece blanket on a frigid night. I smugly congratulated myself for having found a good solution to a hard problem.

The congratulations turned to curses when I realized that the button wasn't the only trigger for the disembodied voice. Some evil genius had made the picture frame motion-sensitive and light-sensitive too. So whenever I walked within five feet of the thing, Scott started talking. Whenever I turned a light on or off, Scott started talking. Whenever I reached for the television remote, Scott launched into the same message, over and over.

"Sweetie pies, this is Daaadddy. I love you! I miss you! Byyyyyyye."

"Sweetie pies, this is Daaadddy. I love you! I miss you! Byyyyyyye."

"Sweetie pies, this is Daaadddy. I love you! I miss you! Byyyyyyye."

After a day or two, the deep tones of my beloved's voice screeched like nails on a blackboard. But I couldn't record over it; that would have been wrong. The frame belonged to the kids, after all. I couldn't get rid of it, and I couldn't move it to another room, because it would have continued to vomit its mantra each time a shadow crossed its path. It was like the telltale heart: chattering away, inescapable, demanding to be heard, begging to be found.

Flat Daddy redux. Flat Daddy's Voice.

One night after the kids had fallen asleep, I tiptoed into the garage, talking picture frame in hand, and I placed it on the shelf above Scott's tools, his face to the wall. *Sorry, honey,* I thought. I usually rushed in and out of the garage as fast as I could. For the next few months, until the batteries ran out (I never thought to remove them), I heard the disembodied voice only when I turned the light on. "Sweetie pies, this is Daaadddy. I love you! I miss you!

Byyyyyyye." I then threw our trash bag in the can as fast as I could, and turned the light off. "Sweetie pies, this is Daaadddy. I love you! I miss you! Byyyyyyye." Then hurried back inside, squaring my shoulders against the aural assault.

Normally I would have called Martina, arranged another Village Pizza date, and unloaded on her while trying to determine, yet again, how she managed during McGowan's IA. *Tell me your secrets* was always on the tip of my tongue. I figured Martina's breakdowns took place privately, but she never admitted to it. It fit her personality. Unlike most of the Navy wives I know, she's not a hugger, and she's uncomfortable with effusive displays of emotion.

I preferred Martina's way of coping to my own. In the weeks following Scott's deployment later that fall, I tended to break down in the middle of Esther's dance class or on the playground when other moms innocently asked me how I was holding up. It was embarrassing because I couldn't explain that I wasn't sad about Scott's being gone (yet) and that I didn't miss him (yet). I just felt overwhelmed and scared, especially during that first month.

Martina's lips never quivered, her eyes never welled up. She was mad at the Navy, and she was mad at McGowan for leaving, especially toward the end of his IA tour. When he first broke the news of the IA to Martina during the previous year, she assumed he had been involuntarily selected. As the year passed, Martina began to pick up clues that this was not exactly the case. By the end of his time in Iraq, she discovered that he had actually volunteered for the assignment out of a sense of duty to an EOD unit there that was short-staffed.

But I couldn't call Martina. After McGowan returned from Iraq, orders came through for him to staff the new U.S. Africa Command in Stuttgart, Germany. The Department of Defense had high hopes for AFRICOM, a brand-new office responsible for U.S. military operations in and with fifty-three African nations, and the assignment was a reward of sorts for his time away. Though it would be rigorous as any start-up enterprise, he would be home every night by six and would not be required to travel. However, Martina didn't want him to take the orders because she had heard that the DoD classroom curriculum overseas was a year behind most stateside schools, and she didn't want her kids to suffer academically upon their eventual return to the U.S.

Orders are not options, as we so often heard. So a few weeks after McGowan's homecoming, packers arrived. Martina scheduled the family to leave on a Friday; they were going to take a month of leave and vacation on the West Coast before flying to Germany. I called her that Thursday. Still so un-military, I was determined to say good-bye, to slap a coda to our extraordinary year together. Her outspokenness wasn't the only thing I treasured about our friendship. She had come through for me heroically that spring when my beloved aunt died, tragically and too young. Although Scott was technically at home, his squadron was immersed in a cycle of critical qualifying flights, which made it impossible for him to take a few days off to care for the kids so that I could join the rest of my family to mourn. I felt absolutely wretched about my aunt's death, and the thought of not being able to attend the funeral brought me to my knees. I had just finished explaining to Martina why I couldn't go when she interrupted me.

"I'll take them," she said, referring to Ethan and Esther. "Get off the phone with me and call the airlines."

"I can't," I said. "I have to be away for four days. It's too much."

"They're in school Thursday and Friday," she insisted. "I'll take them to Montessori in the morning, pick them up in the afternoon, and bring them back to my house. Scott can pick them up at my place whenever he's done. I'll just set two more plates for dinner. The kids can sleep over if they feel like it. We have plenty of room, we're all set up for it. If Scott has to fly during the weekend, I'll just keep the kids here."

"It's too much," I repeated. There were weeks I didn't want to spend two days in a row with my kids, no matter how passionately I adored them. I certainly couldn't ask that of Martina.

"I'm telling you I'm happy to do it. Go book your flight."

"I don't know." The truth is, it had never occurred to me that I had any friend close enough to make such an offer.

"Alison, stop this. I can't listen to another word. This is just one of those times you have to let people help you. I want to help you. Just say yes so we can be done with it."

"Yes," I said. I went to the funeral and sat *shiva* with the rest of my family. (In Jewish tradition, *shiva* is the mourning period that begins immediately after the funeral of a loved one.) And during the next two years of our tour, as I did my best to help squadron families through their own difficulties, the well-known words of Havelock Ellis proved prophetic: "One can know nothing of [anything] that is worthy to give unless one also knows how to take."

M artina already left," McGowan said, as I explained that I was calling to say good-bye.

"Oh." I was surprised. Actually, as his words sunk in, I was stunned she hadn't phoned to let me know.

"She decided to get a head start, so she put the kids in the car before naptime yesterday and drove through the night. She phoned from Sacramento this morning. She's going to stay there with her sisters for a few days. Then I'll join them."

"I'll just e-mail her when you guys get to Stuttgart," I said. "Tell her I'll catch up with her soon."

Since McGowan's return our families had gathered together

several times, and during one week, when McGowan sent Martina
to a fancy spa for her birthday, I met him at the park with the kids
nearly every afternoon. He was a watcher—quiet and observant—
so by then he knew me well enough to sense my disappointment.
He tried to cushion the blow, but I mentally kicked myself for
sounding like a lovesick teenager. The simple truth was that I
craved closure to our year together. Martina had introduced me to
an alternative way of living the life of a military wife, and it had a
profound effect. We'd pledged to keep in touch while she was overseas, but I'd made those kinds of vows with military-wife friends
before. The fact that we had husbands in the Navy was sometimes
thin gruel, too watery to feed a friendship. Despite what we'd
shared, I wondered if that would be the case with Martina.

Something about her last-minute leave-taking sounded suspicious, and that sense lingered after I hung up with McGowan. "You
need to talk through everything with Scott before his deployment,"
she warned me a few days before her departure, almost offhandedly.
"McGowan and I didn't do the work before he left for his IA, and
we're paying for it now. *Big-time.*"

I wasn't quite sure what that meant, but it sounded ominous.
Hanging up the phone with McGowan, I visualized Martina at the
steering wheel, staring at the road in front of her. She'd spent all
year waiting for her husband to come home, but since their reunion
she had seemed more unhappy than I'd ever seen her. And now they
were traveling separately.

15

My Sweetest Friend

Mommy?"

"Yes, my love?"

"When is Daddy coming home?" Ethan asked.

"In about ten days."

"Why did Daddy go away from us?"

"He didn't want to, but he had to do his job. He hates to leave you guys, but he has to sometimes."

Silence.

"Mommy?"

"Yes?"

"If Daddy doesn't want to go, why doesn't he turn around in his airplane or turn around in his aircraft carrier and come home?"

"He can't."

"Why doesn't he just tell the people, 'No! I don't want to!'" Ethan jumped up off the couch to proclaim his mock opposition, standing with his legs apart and holding his arm out stiffly as if initiating a sword fight.

"In Daddy's job, you can't say no. You have to do what they tell you."

Ethan found the idea of never saying no so mind-boggling that I could almost see the gears in his brain grinding to a halt. He stayed silent for several moments. Then he sat back down on the couch.

"Mommy?"

"Yes?"

"When I am a daddy, I am never, ever, ever going to leave my children."

"Really?"

"If people at my job say I have go to away, I am going to say, *'No!'* and turn around and come home and never go back there again."

"I hope you have the kind of job where you can say no, sweetie."

"I will, Mommy. I promise."

M y civilian friends found my Navy tales dark and fascinating. More than one wondered not only how the kids and I coped but also what could possibly make it worth it. "Why don't you go back to your parents' house?" one friend asked me. "Just wait out the rest of the tour there. Scott's never around anyway. Let your parents take care of you and hang out with your old friends."

Why are you making it hard for yourself? was the implied question. My friends cared about me and worried about my isolation. Returning to my parents' house seemed reasonable, though I never seriously considered it. When I thought about the other squadron families, the pull to help ease them through their own troubles was almost magnetic in its intensity. I wasn't expected to be a counselor or a therapist, or even a friend. The wives of squadron commanders are trained to provide squadron families with guidance that will help them navigate the abundant resources made available by the Navy, the military, and the dozens of nonprofit groups devoted to service members' families. For every life-cycle event or domestic crisis, there are multiple organizations to call upon. Several agencies exist solely to help the families of deployed service members.

There are so many resources, in fact, that it's hard to keep track of new programs and funding sources. Information is continually funneled to command spouses and the squadron ombudsman, a full-time volunteer position held by a spouse. Our lead ombudsman during deployment, Devin, is the wife of an enlisted sailor. She had completed training that was far more extensive than mine. When a crisis hit, she and I often worked together to focus on our best options and make the calls for help, but she had at her fingertips the knowledge we needed most, and she knew all the players.

The ombudsman is officially appointed by and reports directly to the skipper. So Devin also helped bridge the chasm between the enlisted troops and the officer corps, delivering enlisted families' concerns directly to the boss. The "front office" then worked to solve the problem, jumping ahead many steps in the typical sailor's chain of command and saving precious time in a crisis. Often, wives of enlisted sailors trust the ombudsman as one of their own and approach her with problems they would hesitate to discuss with anyone else. During our squadron's deployment, for example, Devin picked up a stream of late-night phone calls: one from a frantic young mother on the verge of shaking her baby, another from a woman reading aloud a just-delivered eviction notice, another from a sailor's wife who was drawing up divorce papers because the DNA test on their baby confirmed what she had long feared.

I always wondered, in the semidark caverns of consciousness, if my efforts really helped squadron families or if the belief that I helped simply gave me a sense of purpose. Those families always got along fine (or not) without me, and I'd be gone after a few years, anyway. If they didn't really need me, was it simply that I needed them? I didn't want to be a hall monitor and certainly not an annoying do-gooder.

My new-baby visits helped me realize it wasn't about doing good; it was about building a community of people who experienced the same sort of military-family issues that my kids and I did. That's how I found myself zigzagging across Navy housing one afternoon, useless directions in hand, sauce from a still-steaming lasagna spilling onto the backseat.

H i, I'm—" I held out my hand, but Shari's portable phone was cradled between her shoulder and her ear and a sleeping newborn was nestled in the crook of her other arm. "I'm talking to my mom," she mouthed, as she led me into her house. She was still wearing her oversized Seattle Seahawks nightshirt even though it was late afternoon. As I stood in the foyer I looked around at the scores of butterfly decals decorating the walls and ceiling. Shari lived in Navy housing, and because of her husband's years of service she qualified for one of the newly constructed homes, a stylish, spacious bungalow that was a far cry from the shacklike enlisted military housing of old.

I had never met Shari, but our ombudsman called me the day before to say that a squadron sailor and his wife had given birth to a baby boy. The family had recently relocated from another Navy town, and they didn't know very many people yet. I asked for Shari's number, and when I called to ask if I could bring her something, she welcomed the offer.

She remained on the phone and held out the baby to me. I took him eagerly. Cradling an infant was pure pleasure, and I kissed him on the head as he snuggled into position. With her (now) free hand, Shari motioned me inside the family room. A Johnny Cash music video, his rendition of Nine Inch Nails' "Hurt," was playing softly on a wide-screen TV that dominated the room. The baby stirred, and as I stood in front of the television I rocked him in my arms.

Johnny Cash, gaunt and withered by illness, sat on the edge of a table. It seemed like a concert for one. I stared at the baby, who was only ten days old. I didn't know his first or last name. He hadn't opened his eyes since my arrival. *What does your life hold, my sweetest friend?* I asked him silently.

Johnny Cash died soon after filming this video, the crawl line informed me.

Shari moved into the kitchen, assembling a sandwich as she continued chatting with her mom. I didn't mind at all. I hadn't held a newborn for such a long time. I felt utterly relaxed, standing in front of perhaps the largest television I had ever seen, rocking a stranger's child. Johnny Cash continued crooning his dark lullaby, which put me in a dreamy state of mind. The baby opened his eyes. I know infants can't focus, but he seemed to look right at me. I don't know how to explain it, but I fell in love with that child in that moment.

"Sorry," Shari mouthed from the other side of the room, pointing to the headset as if to indicate that her mother wouldn't let her get off the phone.

"It's fine," I mouthed, and I meant it. When she hung up the phone around the same time that Johnny Cash ended his song, I was the one who was sorry.

"He's a sweet baby," I said, handing him back when Shari held out her arms for him.

"He's my miracle," she said. "Doc told me I could never carry another one to term again after my first. I lost one after that, when he was a month old. A boy." It took me a few beats to realize she was telling me that her last baby had died. "And with this one, I got real sick. That's why they kept me in the hospital an extra week. They were worried about this." *About what?* I started to say. That's when she pulled up her nightshirt, revealing an oozing black caterpillar of a scar crawling vertically from her pubic area up her belly.

"It got infected, so Doc stitched me up all over again and

pumped me full of antibiotics. I just cried and cried. I wanted to take my baby home more than anything."

I blinked. And blinked again. The scar looked alive. It seared itself into my consciousness, burning away all memory of language.

"You got a sweetheart there," I finally said. "Can I hold him again?" She handed him to me and motioned me to sit next to her on the couch.

"What's his name?" I asked. Simple vocabulary returned, and I was grateful as a pious pilgrim.

"Gabriel Joseph. For the boy I lost, my angel in heaven."

I nodded. Even to my unchurched ear it sounded like a hymn. As Shari and I sat together on the couch, I learned a little more about her and how she, her husband, and older son were faring in their new Navy home. She asked me a question or two about my kids. I remembered how tiring it is to entertain visitors after giving birth, so I excused myself as soon as I could. I left the lasagna on the table and a gift next to the door. Walking through her makeshift butterfly sanctuary, I thought for a moment that I saw their tiny wings fluttering, the air pulsing with excitement. It was magic, but not that kind. The enchantment was in getting to know someone so quickly, without barriers. Shari, in her nightshirt, stripped away the superficial. I climbed into my car and waved good-bye as she stood shadowed behind her screen door. What mattered most was the baby, the scar, and the story behind it, and she shared all three intimacies without hesitation.

When I sketched the baby-visit scenes for my civilian friends, it never came out the right way. They always ended up screeching in horror or laughing hysterically. But there was no punch line. There was no serrated ironic edge in the telling. I liked doing it. I liked hearing the stories of the women I would see at event after event during the next two or three years. I liked comparing our kids' development and hearing how they fared in school. I liked watching babies learn to crawl; I liked seeing them smear their first birthday cake across their tiny mouths. I liked all of it.

So I stopped telling nonmilitary folks the tales I knew they wouldn't, or couldn't, understand. I stuck to the stories with built-in hilarity, which were not hard to come by. Especially when I shared my difficulties befriending some of the other Navy wives—like Millie. Although we'd never met, I'd heard about Millie for years because her husband and mine had struggled through flight school together. Leo and Scott saw each other infrequently over the years because their careers diverged, but now Leo prepared to assume command of the base's Naval Reserve squadron. Millie, like me, would become the skipper's wife.

I had already experienced firsthand the generosity of the other skippers' wives on our base, all of whom looked out for each other while taking care of their own squadron's families. These CO wives—women of different backgrounds but generally close in age and similarly seasoned in terms of their military experiences—made up my built-in peer group. We confided in and counseled each other when problems arose; planned fund-raisers, homecomings, and other events; worked in partnership on behalf of base families; supported each other through deployments; and gathered socially.

On the basis of first reports, I was optimistic about Millie. "She's great!" I heard from the other CO wives who knew her from previous tours. "She's so much fun!" "You'll love her!" Given my own lack of expertise about the military and how to survive deployment, I needed as many friends as possible to turn to for advice. So Scott and I arranged to meet Millie and her husband for dinner.

When Leo and Millie walked into the restaurant we'd chosen, Millie waved at us and then dashed over to a television hanging near the bar. She smiled broadly and gave us two thumbs-up as she checked out the score, then ambled back to our table and sat down. Tall and lean, she carried herself with easy grace and confidence, a vestige of her days as a competitive swimmer.

"Hey, ya'll!" she said. "It's great to finally meet you!"

We tried to make a connection. But Texas A&M was playing football that night, and since I'd never known an Aggie fan before, I didn't realize what that meant. In our case, it meant that every two minutes, in the middle of a conversation or question, Millie jumped up, ran over to the television, and either pumped her arms in the air and ran back to the table to report the score or hung her head as she relayed tragic news from the gridiron.

"If the Aggies win, I have a really great day," she confessed back at the table. "If they lose, it's hard for me to get up the next morning. I'm a really normal person, I promise. Just not when it comes to Aggie football."

"So do you still have family in Texas?" I asked, trying to pick up where we had left off after the last time Millie jumped out of her seat.

"Everybody's there," she said. "That's home. It's so hard to be away from home, isn't it?" she asked. "But since both sides of the family are within a block of each other, it makes holidays very tricky. We've learned some excellent— *Hey! What in the Sam Hill is that ref thinking?*" She bounced up again and ran screaming to the television.

Millie's down-home appeal attracted me. She was friendly, sincere, and smart, and I later learned that she had interesting insights and experiences galore to share. She just couldn't squeeze them out between Aggie touchdowns. But I didn't care that Millie seemed unusually attached to her college football team. The military brings together people from an unimaginably diverse cross section of the United States, and that same phenomenon reverberates in the parallel universe of the wives too. Though I didn't expect to meet someone just like me, I hoped, desperately, for a friend. I hoped to find a way to make the tour more fun than it had been up to that point. So, first impressions be damned. Determined to learn a lesson the military had been trying to teach me for years, I allowed myself to presume that there was more to Millie than what greeted me at the restaurant.

Of course there was, and it took the form of a deep reserve of wisdom and humor that I would come to value immensely in the trying days ahead. Much later, I discovered that I was one of Millie's shady Navy tales too. Toward the end of deployment, we laughed hysterically about our first evening together as she recounted how she initially described me to her mom: "She hates football! And she barely even drinks!"

I probably told my non-Navy friends most of the bad stuff and not much of the good stuff, simply because the horror stories make better copy than the serene days at Beautiful World. And there was no way to explain that Scott made it worthwhile even though he was rarely around. All marriages move from the general to the particular, and this was our particular, eccentric truth, the love child of circumstance and compromise: For most of that tour we lived separate lives, tethered together only emotionally. That "only" was everything. It's not that we had transcended any need for physical proximity, but through a leap of faith, we landed on the solid ground of each other's interior landscape. Only the essential mattered. Only the authentic resonated. I knew that Scott was out there somewhere thinking of me too and that his dreams of our reunion and our future mirrored mine. His gratitude for my efforts to support him and the deep connection between us that grew stronger throughout our long separations carried me through.

The mythic intermingled with the mundane. Because, of course, there were bleak moments too: Days I mourned being stuck at home coloring with two little kids, and nights I felt shackled after seven p.m., when I faced mountains of dirty dishes and piles of clean laundry. But although I was always waiting for Scott to return, I never felt like our relationship was on hold. It was, in fact, the opposite of stagnation. Facing the grief of separation was much less work, and ultimately far more rewarding, than avoiding it had ever been. Each time the emotional tsunami cleared, revealing Scott on his side of the world—thriving despite the loneliness—and me on my side—thriving despite the loneliness—I found myself surprised that the waves of loss had not washed me away entirely. Instead, those dark currents scrubbed away everything extraneous, until all that remained was the gleaming, sun-bleached spinal column of our relationship. It held us both upright, separately but simultaneously, solid and eternal as a fossil.

I finally understood what it meant to be married and continue growing as individuals. We had pledged to do exactly that in our *ketubah*, the marriage contract Jews sign in a traditional union. All weddings promise strength and happiness; ours was no different. But the text whose echoes still ring is a passage I transcribed from Edith Wharton's *The Buccaneers*, which I was reading during the time of our engagement. The lines are even truer today than when I first copied them:

> *In her heart was a deep delicious peace such as she had never known before. In this great lonely desert of life stretching out before her she had a friend—a friend who understood not only all she said, but everything she could not say. At the end of the long road ... she saw him standing, waiting for her, watching for her through the night.*

16

The Feast of Crispian

One evening just a few weeks before deployment, our squadron officers and their wives gathered in a private room at a waterside restaurant in a nearby town. Seagulls shrieked outside and a picture-perfect sailboat floated against the flaming-orange setting sun. It wasn't any ordinary dinner. This was a Dining Out—a formal Navy event I had not yet experienced.

I should have suspected that the evening would be somewhat unusual. Scott had spent an hour searching the house for a gavel before we left. He also carefully wrote out scripted notes he could surreptitiously hold in his lap. When we arrived at the restaurant, officers and wives whom we had known for the whole tour greeted Scott with the strange title of Mr. President. The evening would provide many similar surprises.

One of the squadron officers, tonight known as Mr. Vice, loudly declared, "Officers Call!" All of the guests filed to their table settings, which were marked with name cards bearing exquisite calligraphy. A slightly muffled version of "Anchors, Aweigh" played from a boom box as we all found our seats. Shortly thereafter, Scott delivered a short speech to introduce the guests, including three former squadron aviators who had served during the 1950s and 1960s. Until that point, I still imagined we were just enjoying a nice formal meal.

Oddly, Scott's comments and welcome were concluded by a loud order to "parade the beef." At this call, another officer began cavorting around the room with a giant platter of meat, followed by several garishly dressed restaurant workers, including a fiddle player and a singing minstrel. Thus began one of the strangest and most wondrous meals I've ever had.

As I discovered, Scott's role that evening was President of the Mess, and it meant he was responsible for enforcing decorum and discipline. (A keen wit, a fine sense of repartee, and a dose of energy and class go a long way.)

Mr. Vice, I learned, was shorthand for the Vice President of the Mess. Most of the evening's fun revolved around fines and punishments levied upon "offenders" of the evening's Byzantine rules. Mr. Vice played an important role in identifying violations such as tardiness, uniform discrepancies, or taking leave without the permission of the president.

The identification and punishment of violations were usually greeted with collective glee. Scott used his gavel to keep order and mete out appropriate sentences, usually a request for the offender to tell a joke, sing a song, or drink from one of the two (alcoholic or nonalcoholic) "grog" bowls.

After the parading of the beef, Scott struck the gavel three times and the room came to order and attention. It was time for the official toasts. Two strikes of the gavel, and all the officers and guests stood, raising glasses of port. (Toasting with drinking water, I learned later, implies you wish the person so honored to die by drowning.)

PRESIDENT OF THE MESS (aka Scott): "Ladies and gentlemen, the Commander in Chief." Two raps of the gavel, and all stood for a muffled rendition of the national anthem played from the hidden boom box.

ALL: "The President of the United States of America." People sipped their port. Scott struck the gavel once, and everyone sat.

COMMANDING OFFICER: "Ladies and gentleman, missing comrades." Scott struck the gavel twice, and everyone rose.

ALL: "Missing comrades." People sipped their port. Scott struck the gavel once again, and everyone sat.

OPERATIONS OFFICER: "The Secretary of Defense." Scott struck the gavel twice, and all officers rose.

ALL: "The Secretary of Defense." People sipped from their glasses of port. Scott struck the gavel, and the officers sat.

A few of the wives leaned into their husbands, smiling, and the room relaxed as a long sequence of formal toasts continued.

The tradition of the Dining In, which was created for members of a specific military unit—and the Dining Out, which includes wives and guests—reaches back to the eighteenth-century British Army, whose formal dining practices were replicated in the colonies since our ragtag Continental Army had few other role models. Some historians detect even deeper roots in Roman military banquets, the stylized victory feasts of the Vikings, and the practices of sixth-century British monasteries, though I doubt the burlap-robed friars of yesteryear enjoyed quite as much revelry as today's military officers.

Exotic origins aside, the Dining In/Dining Out ceremony was reconceived by the American military during World War II, as our military participated with the British military's Officers' Mess. (Though both the Navy and Air Force call this social affair the Dining In, the Marine Corps and the Coast Guard refer to it as "mess night" and the Army terms it "regimental dinner.") In its American incarnation, this highly scripted evening embodies what John Paul Jones (1747–1792), father of the American Navy, referenced in the infamous phrase "an officer and a gentleman":

It is by no means enough that an officer of the Navy should be a capable mariner. He must be that, of course, but also a great deal more. He should be as well a gentleman of liberal education, refined manners, punctilious courtesy, and the nicest sense of personal honor. He should be the soul of tact, patience, justice, firmness, kindness, and charity.

In the Navy, the Dining In/Dining Out is the perfect opportunity for today's men and women in uniform to demonstrate that they are gentlefolk as well as officers, as facile with a glass of port wine raised mid-toast as they are at the controls of a jet. Until that night, I had not had the opportunity to witness that side of service.

One of the junior officers proposed the last of the series of formal toasts. Peter Sanders, a new squadron member, pushed back his chair and stood up. His wife, a young woman I hadn't spent much time with, gazed adoringly at him. She seemed wide-eyed and innocent as a first-grader. I remembered hearing they were high school sweethearts from a farming community in Minnesota.

LIEUTENANT SANDERS: "Mr. Vice, I have a point of order."

MR. VICE: "Proceed."

LIEUTENANT SANDERS: "We deeply appreciate the women who grace our table tonight, the wives of the squadron, who make everything possible for us. . . ."

He was drowned out by the officers' cheers of "The wives!" "The wives!" as Scott quickly pounded the gavel twice and held up his glass.

PRESIDENT OF THE MESS: "Ladies and gentlemen, the wives."

I felt yet again that the military was a foreign country and that I had left my guidebook on the plane. I heard murmurs from a corner of the room, and then Jimmy Wering, one of the younger officers, stood up.

LTJG WERING: "Mr. Vice, I have a point of order."

MR. VICE: "Lieutenant Wering, proceed."

LTJG WERING: "In recognition of the pleasure provided to me and many others this past Sunday and on many other Sundays, I propose to begin the informal toasts by honoring the Dallas Cowboys Cheerleaders."

Scott struck his gavel twice. We were sitting close together at the head table, and the pounding of the gavel was starting to give me a pounding headache.

PRESIDENT OF THE MESS: "Ladies and gentlemen, the Dallas Cowboys Cheerleaders."

More toasts followed, along with dinner, pranks, a great number of inside jokes, brandishment of a Nerf water pistol, formal farewells to squadron members about to begin tours elsewhere, and an embarrassing tale told by an alarmingly drunk officer about his girlfriend's sexual preferences. Officers are encouraged to tell stories at the Dining Out, after being recognized in the sanctioned manner, and I had idly wondered what cast those narratives might take. I felt so mortified on behalf of the drunken officer's date that I wished the evening over before it really began. Then Caleb Lowell stood up.

LIEUTENANT COMMANDER LOWELL: "Mr. Vice, I have a point of order."

MR. VICE: "Proceed."

Caleb, one of the senior pilots in the squadron, reminded me of Scott. He was a mensch, as my grandmother would say, a good man who always tried to do the right thing. It showed in his kind, penetrating eyes and the permanent parenthesis etched around his mouth.

LIEUTENANT COMMANDER LOWELL: "You all already know I was that alien specimen, an English literature major at Annapolis," he began. "But what you don't know is that at the end of my interview to get into the Naval Academy, my dismal performance forced my interviewer to admit he wasn't sure if he would recommend me or not. I panicked. Annapolis was my only goal in life."

Caleb let that sink in, since others surely identified with that statement.

"So I told him there was one more thing I wanted to say. Early on in high school, I memorized a passage from *Henry V* that expressed why I had always wanted to join the military. I have to admit, as I recited the passage to my interviewer in my desperate attempt to make it into Annapolis, I didn't know what the hell I was talking about. But I do now. As we head into this war, I have faith that by working as one, we can do the job we're trained to do. And when we get out of there, we'll really have something to celebrate."

Then, without a pause or a single misplaced punctuation mark, Caleb, in his freshly pressed, white dress uniform heavy with medals, recited Shakespeare's passage in its entirety:

This day is called the feast of Crispian:
He that outlives this day, and comes safe home,
Will stand a tip-toe when the day is named,
And rouse him at the name of Crispian.
He that shall live this day, and see old age,
Will yearly on the vigil feast his neighbours,
And say 'To-morrow is Saint Crispian:'
Then will he strip his sleeve and show his scars.
And say 'These wounds I had on Crispin's day.'
Old men forget: yet all shall be forgot,
But he'll remember with advantages
What feats he did that day: then shall our names.
Familiar in his mouth as household words
Harry the king, Bedford and Exeter,
Warwick and Talbot, Salisbury and Gloucester,

Be in their flowing cups freshly remember'd.
This story shall the good man teach his son;
And Crispin Crispian shall ne'er go by,
From this day to the ending of the world,
But we in it shall be remember'd;
We few, we happy few, we band of brothers;
For he to-day that sheds his blood with me
Shall be my brother; be he ne'er so vile,
This day shall gentle his condition:
And gentlemen in England now a-bed
Shall think themselves accursed they were not here,
And hold their manhoods cheap whiles any speaks
That fought with us upon Saint Crispin's day.

I'd never heard it recited aloud before. The speech is heart-wrenching in its dignity, its sense of unity and quiet pride. I wanted to hold my head in my hands and lose myself in it, but this wasn't the place. Caleb let a few moments of silence pass when he finished, and then he sat down. He had transported us from a raucous U.S. Navy dinner in 2007 in a tiny corner of Washington state to a sober English military feast in 1415 in northern France and back again: millennia of service for the greater good, however the greater good was perceived at the time.

Hearing Caleb recite Shakespeare, I gained a dawning awareness of the concept of service, of both its sacrifices and its rewards. "My husband's in the service," I'd said casually, dozens of times since we married, without really understanding what it meant. Scott toiled in service of something almost ineffable, though he was impelled by qualities I found irresistible: integrity, honesty, the good of the group. Many of his colleagues in the squadron shared those same impulses.

I was still learning about the Dining Out, which manuals warn "is not a party in any sense; it is very similar to honors, for its purpose is to solemnly pay tribute to all of those intangibles for and by which the military unit stands." But I discovered something about my own husband that night, and about the men and women who derive such a deep satisfaction from working on behalf of the country. The abstraction of service materialized into an idea I could almost touch, and it all took place within the centuries-old format of the Dining Out.

Stern warnings aside, it was fun. Great fun, actually, after raunchy jokes receded into memory. If I had been a visiting anthropologist, I could have penned volumes of penetrating field notes. But I wasn't an anthropologist, and I had no desire to set myself apart. I was one of the tribe, and I enjoyed it—at last.

I was glad to see Peter Sanders's wide-eyed wife, Amber, enjoying herself too. The Dining Out marked her group debut; Peter had transferred into our community of jets after the Navy retired the surveillance plane on which he'd been trained. Such a change requires moving to a new base, making new friends, and learning the new cultural norms. So I imagined Amber would have had ample reason to be nervous, but it was just the opposite, actually.

"The Navy just feels like home to me. It doesn't matter where we are," she confided after dinner, as a few of the officers and their dates started dancing. She stood next to me so we could hear each other over the music. We leaned in so close that I could see chrysanthemums printed on the chopsticks that crisscrossed her chignon in a jet-black X.

"We got married a few weeks after graduation and then took off to Hawaii. The day after we returned from Maui, Peter told me he had signed up at the recruiting center. That was that. I didn't mind. Really," she insisted, reading my shocked expression. "It was the best decision he could have made. People in the military are so nice. I felt comfortable right away."

I nodded. People *are* so nice and so welcoming in military communities. I felt like a jerk for not appreciating it more.

"We both grew up in a small town, and we wanted that for our own family," Amber explained, smiling, as if each word was glued to the next in a speech she recited from memory to every new acquaintance. "Now we have that. Peter always wanted to fly jets. Now he does. I started volunteering at church and joined the bowling league on base. Bowling is really great. Hey, we could use another person on our team." Her looked changed in a flash as her wide eyes shrunk narrow as a predator. Or had I imagined it? She still smiled warmly. "You should really come," she urged. "We need more squadron spirit. My old squadron was really close. Now *those* girls knew how to have fun."

She pulled the chopsticks out of her chignon, shook out her hair, and twisted it up again. As the chopsticks slid into place, they reminded me, suddenly, of spears: thin, sharp, and able to pierce their prey leaving barely a mark of evidence.

During the next few days, I thought a lot about Amber and Peter and their sense of immediate comfort in the military. Something vague about the Dining Out nagged at me too, as if a name I was trying to recall lingered on the tip of my tongue. It had something to do with the tempo of the evening, the call-and-response nature of the script, the ease with which everyone stood up and sat down at the same time, and recited their lines in unison.

Finally, I remembered a book I had stashed on a shelf when we moved in. Amazingly, I found it on my first try: a careworn, beloved copy of *The Book of Common Prayer* inscribed with Scott's great-grandmother's name. (Scott's paternal grandparents were Episcopalian.) I opened it randomly and read:

> *The people devoutly kneeling, the Minister pronounces,*
> *Minister: The Lord be with you.*
> *Answer: And with thy spirit.*

Minister: Let us pray. O Lord, show thy mercy upon us.

Answer: And grant us thy salvation.

Minister: O Lord, save the State.

Answer: And mercifully hear us when we call upon thee.

Minister: Endue thy Ministers with righteousness.

Answer: And make thy chosen people joyful.

Minister: O Lord, save thy people.

Answer: And bless thine inheritance.

Stretched within these taut lines was ritual that reinforced commu- nity. The same certain knowledge of what to say, how to say it, when to say it, and why it's important—the shared effort to honor a com- mon, higher cause—created the rhythm that coursed through the Dining Out, even in the midst of the high jinks. I've long regarded the military as a secular faith, and now more than ever it seemed like a working man's religion. Perhaps that familiarity is what drew people like Peter and Amber to it, small-town churchgoers raised with the unshakable belief in something bigger than themselves and an understanding that individuals can't go it alone.

It's no surprise that the twenty-first-century Dining Out carries the cadence of prayer, or a whiff of worship, regardless of the faith of the officer giving the invocation. After all, it piously wound its way out of sixth-century monasteries. Then again, perhaps *piety* was the wrong word to apply to an evening that included the slurred boast ". . . and then I went down in my girlfriend's lap" from the drunk officer whose date forced herself to smile as the rest of the room looked down at their plates. But September pressed upon us. The Jewish New Year beckoned, our second in Anacortes, and reli- gion weighed heavily on my mind.

17

New Beginnings

September 2007

Dearest Ethan, sweetest Esther,

I didn't have time to write your annual birthday letters this past spring, but tonight is the birthday of the universe, as I explained to you a few days ago. Rosh Hashanah, the start of the Jewish New Year, begins at sundown. The table in the dining room is set with our white holiday cloth, your great-grandparents' china, my wedding crystal. The kitchen is a mess, brisket and chicken and kugel in various stages of completion spilling over onto the counters. The scent of matzo ball soup is in the air, my mom's recipe, a hit every time. She made it during her visit here last month and froze it for us. I defrosted it last night and set it on the stove an hour ago. Its salty perfume is wafting into the family room, where I'm writing to you from my favorite corner of the couch. I don't want another milestone to go by without words for your baby books.

Your dad left this morning for his last detachment before

the coming seven-month cruise. "Cruise" used to sound so
glamorous to me, like a Love Boat *excursion to a glamorous*
port, but now I know that in the Navy it refers to long deploy-
ments on the carrier, and it's lost that luster. He'll be gone until
just after Yom Kippur. He'll return for a month and then leave
for the long trip.

When I found out your dad was going to be gone for the
holidays again I was sad, angry, and confused. I didn't want to
repeat last year. I asked the base chaplain to put another notice
in the base newspaper so I could offer hospitality to Jewish sail-
ors and officers. Then I called a few Navy families who'd at-
tended our Hanukkah party and the Purim megillah reading
on base and invited them over for Rosh Hashanah dinner. They
all accepted, along with a young Marine pilot who's new in
town. They sounded so grateful and happy, I felt ashamed to
have been sulking about my situation.

So here's one piece of advice for the new year: When you're
sad, when you're lonely, reach out to someone who may be feel-
ing the same way. Offer them whatever comfort you can. After
all, our actions transform not only our own lives but also the
lives of those around us, whether or not we are close to them and
whether or not we even know them. A rabbi told me once that
it's as critical to take great care with small good deeds as with
obviously important big ones because actions have consequences
we cannot always anticipate and sometimes not even contem-
plate. So, be the one with the emotional resources to give, to
make, to do—not necessarily a holiday dinner but something
meaningful both to others and to you.

I keep thinking of my mom cooking her dinner tonight, of
the friends and family driving over, their own covered dishes
bumping along in the backseat. I can smell my parents' clean
house with its windows open, early autumn leaves outside giv-
ing the air a woodsy tang. The moody, dark orange setting sun

slowly seeps into the dining room as Dad hands kippot to men gathering around the table. Mom, in the kitchen, samples her matzo ball soup. She pulls the round challah out of the oven and covers it with an embroidered cloth as twilight falls. I wish I were there. I wish you were there to see it, so it could be your memory as well as mine. It doesn't seem fair that you're stuck with a mom like me, making memories out of defrosted soup and a store-bought tart. Making the best of it, instead of making an occasion of it.

Mostly, I wish I could be more introspective about the new year, focusing on what I want to change about myself in the months ahead. I want to read you one more book at night, instead of rushing downstairs to my time alone. I want to look at you when you're asking me a question, instead of continuing to type on my laptop. Instead, I'm fixated on the fact that your dad flew out this very morning, that my extended family is gathering without me, and that I'm hosting my first big holiday dinner solo. But I have faith in new beginnings, and Rosh Hashanah has never let me down.

Speaking of not letting me down, I don't know what this year will hold, but I am certain the two of you will continue to amaze me. Esther, you first: Just the other day, as we sat next to each other at dinner, you curled your short little arm around my shoulder and leaned in so close that our heads touched. I put my arm around your tiny shoulder too. I felt like we were never-say-good-bye campers posing for a snapshot. You get it. I don't know how, but you get it. My mom always reminds me that the moment she gave birth to me, my grandmother told her, "Now you have your best friend." When I gave birth to you, Mom walked into the recovery room and smiled, and I knew why. "Now you have your best friend," she said, and we both wiped away tears.

Ethan: I wish you wouldn't fight with me so much, but

that's just where we are right now. I know you get it too, though. When you were arguing me with me the other day about lunch, I just couldn't stand it anymore. I was operating on no sleep, we had been battling for days, and I was sure that the afternoon would drag on endlessly. You were roaring toddler epithets, raging as you tossed toys across the room and ripped magazines to shreds. You eyed your little sister as if she was prey.

"Stop," I begged, and then, before I knew it, I was crying. I didn't run into the other room; I didn't turn my back so you wouldn't see. "You have to stop," I sobbed. Like a man, you looked shocked and scared at my display of emotion. Then, like a man, you held both arms out to me. I don't know who was holding whom as we embraced.

"We have to be nice to each other," I implored, trying to control my voice. I didn't want to say, "It's just the three of us now, we're all we've got," but that's what I was thinking. I don't know what to expect from deployment, but that I know for sure. I love you both, and I wish for you a happy, healthy year. We're going to be very different people at the end of it.

PART TWO

‖ Deployment ‖

There is nothing like youngsters to keep one young in spirit, though on the Navy wife and mother falls the greater part of the responsibility in raising the family. She, in most cases, must make the important decisions in regard to their rearing, their schooling, the building of their characters; it is she who plays the role of strict disciplinarian. The children learn to take her for granted, but Father is that rare and honored individual whose infrequent visits are red-letter days in the lives of his family.

—*The Navy Wife*

18

By the Waters of Babylon

One afternoon shortly after Scott deployed, a package arrived in the mail. It was addressed to me, but I didn't recognize the handwriting. I unwrapped it carefully. A small gift box lay inside the larger one, and snuggled within the packaging as cozily as a Russian nesting doll was the tiniest box of all: a sterling silver pillbox engraved with my initials. I opened the accompanying note from Martina.

"My secret, revealed," she wrote, a scribbled smiley face letting me in on the joke. "Here's what you'll need to get by. Good luck with the deployment!"

A pillbox. I smiled. Actually, I laughed out loud. That laugh—not the pillbox but the laugh—was her real gift to me. Scott was gone. I stopped wearing makeup, since I still cried my face clean every day. I could barely meet the glance of other parents at Montessori school drop-offs because their concern for me was so intense it almost hurt. I kept my head down at the supermarket to avoid the gentle inquiries of well-meaning neighbors. I was liable to crumble upon contact.

Other military wives seemed to handle deployment far more

bravely. One friend whose husband left for six months hosted a coffee-and-muffin party for dozens of other military spouses the morning of his departure. Another friend launched a do-it-yourself home renovation before her Bagram-bound husband drove past our town limits to catch his airlift. Many service wives of the past, especially those of the last century who were unemployed and lived on base together, organized unit-wide bowling teams, bridge groups, or theater parties before their husbands' planes disappeared behind the clouds.

But when our deployment began, our squadron wives, though genuinely friendly with one another, were as scattered as stars. Many spouses spent their days shuttling children around, their schedules as complicated as commuter train timetables. Several spouses worked full-time, so balancing professional and family lives left them too exhausted to attend many social gatherings. None of the wives in our officer group lived on base, and our homes were up to sixty miles away from one another. One new bride chose to bunk with her parents on the East Coast during deployment. Another spouse, an active-duty Navy pilot who flew for a different squadron, continually deployed to hot spots across the globe.

I later discovered that the younger wives in our squadron leaned on one another heavily at the start of the deployment. The early bonds I forged with several of the women in our group comforted me tremendously throughout the many months of our squadron's absence, and by the end of deployment, our squadron spouses had become so intimate that we shopped together for homecoming-eve lingerie. For my own personal crises and all-around support, however, I depended on other CO wives. These women, whose husbands commanded other aviation squadrons on base, shouldered many of the same responsibilities and shared many of the same challenges that I did. Many of the wives had known each other for almost two decades as they followed their husbands to postings around the world. I was a relative latecomer, but they welcomed me immediately as one of their own. During the first rocky months of deployment, they understood my state of mind better than I did, and they knew precisely what the first day would hold.

In the hours after Scott left for deployment, I followed my usual routine. I showered, dressed, fed the kids, and drove them to school. But I dreaded returning to our empty house, knowing that Scott's absence would be a heavy presence for the foreseeable future. As I pulled into my driveway that morning, negotiating with myself over whether or not to divert, I spotted a beautifully beribboned bag on the porch. I parked the car—a small triumph. I walked toward the front door and kneeled down to pick up the bag, which overflowed with candy and chocolate. The card—signed by another CO wife, a caring woman who always reached out to me—read as follows:

> *A stick of gum . . . to remind you to stick with it,*
> *Hershey's Kisses . . . to remind you of a Sailor who loves you,*
> *A paper clip . . . to help you hold everything together,*
> *A Tootsie Roll . . . to remind you not to bite off more than you*
>   *can chew,*
> *A Starburst . . . to give you that burst of energy for those days*
>   *you'll need it,*
> *A Snickers candy bar . . . to remind you to laugh every day,*
> *A Nestlé chocolate bar . . . for when you feel you are in a crunch,*
> *A rubber band . . . for when you feel you are stretched to*
>   *the limit,*
> *A penny . . . for your thoughts,*
> *An eraser . . . because we all make mistakes,*
> *LifeSavers . . . to help keep you afloat,*
> *Marbles . . . when you feel as if you have lost your mind,*
> *And . . .*
> *Kudos for all you do!*

Later that day, other military girlfriends called, dropped off goodies, and extended dinner invitations for the kids and me. I started to understand that the fast familiarity among military spouses exists not only because service members' families move so often and are forced to bond quickly with others but also because military spouses are particularly sensitive to the pain of a long separation undertaken voluntarily, frequently, and with the whisper of potential tragedy audible every sleepless night. They know, as my care-package friend did, to leave a gift at the door but not to ring the bell—because the recipient probably can't face anyone.

My long-married military acquaintances assure me that the seventh, eighth, or ninth deployment is as hard as the first. "I tried to avoid the grief once by taking the kids out of town a few days before my husband deployed, so we'd be leaving him rather than the other way around," my friend Isabelle told me. "But the monster was laying in wait, and it attacked me as soon as I got home. You just have to grieve every single time."

So, chocolate notwithstanding, I grieved the day Scott left. I wandered aimlessly from room to room, sobbing my way through the house. I felt shell-shocked, unable to process the fact that he was actually gone and that responsibility for the kids' physical and psychological well-being lay solely with me. It wasn't that I missed him or was lonely; I hadn't had time to experience longing or loneliness yet. I just found myself completely overwhelmed by the job requirement. Though I have a high tolerance for emotional complexity—for rich, complicated narratives in my own life as well as in others'—sending my husband to war and taking on family life alone was bigger and more serious than I was prepared for. I didn't know how to make it funny or relate the story via cute anecdote.

That alone seemed tragic. After all, I considered myself part of a generation that thrived on two aesthetic ideals: quirkiness and irony. Before I married into the military, I thought that most issues were best considered with a light touch, a sense of humor, and the good-natured coyness that characterizes some of the segments on public radio's *This American Life*. I came of age musically in the company of David Byrne's disarming, nonthreatening strangeness. I cut my literary teeth analyzing the short stories of Lorrie Moore, whose characters' well-meaning attempts at humanity make their eccentricities that much more appealing. I became an amateur film critic screening the movies of Wes Anderson, whose lovable oddballs are presented without a wink and a nod, advancing the ironic ideal one step further. Irony isn't presented on a platter anymore; you have to internalize it fully to participate in the cultural offerings of the day. But there's no irony in sending your husband off to war, and there's nothing quirky or cute about taking care of kids by yourself during their father's deployment. I struggled for a perspective worthy of the old me, for some way out of the deadly seriousness of my situation. If ever something begged for a light touch, this was it.

I remembered the night Scott paced my apartment, explaining that he couldn't ask me to give up a world I controlled to ride the roller coaster of military wifehood. "It's not for you," he had insisted. "It's not your life or who you are, and you'd resent me for getting you into it."

He was right, partly; back then, it wasn't me. But after five years of marriage and two kids, it was my life because he was my life. As the deployment began, I transitioned into the final stage of my identity as a military spouse. I didn't resent Scott; far from it. Just as he felt his way blind around every nook and cranny of my career dreams, my hopes, and my personal goals, I was intimately familiar and conversant with his. I recognized that our new life had its advantages, anyway. During the past few months, I had developed a quiet crush on Anacortes. In addition to its natural beauty, my kind neighbors, and the many well-run local facilities and programs, the region revealed itself to be far more socially diverse than I had first thought. The presence of two major oil refineries, along with

Anacortes's robust marine industry, enabled me to meet families from England, Australia, New Zealand, the Netherlands, Lebanon, and many American cities.

I learned my way around the region as I played tour guide for a steady stream of friends and family from the East Coast, and seeing the islands through their eyes kept my own perspective fresh. My sister-in-law, who visited with her husband and two small children, met many locals during their excursions. "This place is *Top Gun* meets *Cocoon* meets *Hair*," she pronounced one night, marveling at the cross section of naval aviators, retirees, and aging hippies who call Anacortes home.

Gradually the geography of Anacortes, which earlier had shut me in with the finality of a crab trap, floated open. The kids and I became day-trippers on the local ferry system, riding out to Guemes Island to eat at Anderson's General Store or to Friday Harbor, where we dripped ice cream on the pier while watching an American flag flutter in the breeze. On one ride home from Friday Harbor, Ethan insisted on standing on the bow of the ferry so he could spot seals cavorting in the water. But his attention soon shifted to a knot of teenage girls from a church group sitting cross-legged on deck, singing gospel songs with their eyes closed. The harbor wind whipped their long hair across their faces, but they didn't seem to notice. At first Ethan stood just close enough to listen to their soft harmonies, but with each song he inched closer. By the end of the ferry ride, the girls had adopted him. He sat in the center of their circle, and they sang directly to him:

> *By the waters*
> *the waters*
> *of Babylon*
> *We lay down and we-ept*
> *and we-ept*
> *for thee, Zion.*

In the late-afternoon sunlight, with waves breaking all around us, their music was a physical presence, yet another force of nature all of us exiles gave ourselves over to.

Regardless of these new experiences, which expanded my sense of myself and of America too, the wrenching apart of our family remained a profound trauma. When I think about that time— November, my own cruelest month—a threatening granularity hovers over it, haze-gray, like the color of an aircraft carrier or the sky before a storm. Our storm cut a swath of loss so deep it took months to dig ourselves out.

19

American Trinity

It's hard to believe, even now, that in five years together Scott and I had never talked seriously about why he joined the military and why he became a career officer. We touched on it when we were dating, but he said something dismissive like "I wanted to fly planes" and "I needed a way to pay for college." Both reasons were true, though neither captured his real motivation.

Lying in bed the night before he deployed, aware that we had truly run out of time, we felt helpless. We held hands under the blanket. Neither of us could sleep, so we small-talked our way through the pain, chatting about the feast we'd gorged on that night and chuckling over the piggish absurdity of trying to combine Thanksgiving, Hanukkah, the Passover seder, and both kids' birthday celebrations into one final meal together. Our late-night conversations had always been quietly exhilarating, a reminder that the flame still burned bright despite the mounds of dirt that the chaos of our lives heaped upon it. But I felt no exhilaration the night before Scott left. Our whispers were not the urgent tones of a husband and wife rediscovering each other but the shaky murmurs of a couple unsure of how much more heartbreak they could endure.

Not that heartbreak, however deeply felt, would interfere with Scott's mission. Military officers excel at compartmentalization. I knew that the minute he walked out the door the following morning his mind would zero in on his flight crew's upcoming brief, and I was grateful for that.

"So are you ready for a new career?" I finally joked, trying to lighten the mood.

"At least I believe in what I'm doing," he responded. "More than ever, actually. The longer I'm in it, the more I understand what my purpose is."

That was new. I woke up a little. I'd been talking to Scott with my eyes closed, but now I opened them. The room was pitch black, and I experienced the sudden shock of blindness.

"What do you mean?"

"When I first joined the Navy, it was to fly. Serving the country was secondary. It was a nice bonus, and I needed to be part of something bigger than myself, so it was the best possible solution for meeting my personal and professional goals. Over time, the desire to serve became overwhelming. Especially during promotions and reenlistment ceremonies. Have you ever thought about the oath of office we use in the military?"

"No. Should I look it up?"

"Definitely. Every time you get promoted you reaffirm the oath. I've been promoted four times, and each time the words become more meaningful to me. You swear to support and defend the Constitution of the United States. Not a person or an institution or a branch of government, but the entire machinery of government. The individuals in power can change countless times during the course of service, so I see a military career as a means to reinforce the stability and continuity of the whole system."

"Is that why you don't get as upset as I do about politics?"

Despite my best efforts to take the long view, politics is still personal. I yell at the television news, mutter angrily at politicians giving press conferences, and rest my head in my hands while reading war coverage in the paper. *If our squadron and so many of our friends are going to fly in this conflict for three-quarters of a year*, I bluster to myself, *it better be for a good reason.* I know that these squadrons, just like every unit in each branch of the military, tackle no task halfheartedly. None entertains any thought of personal gain. I depend on members of Congress and policy makers to take their own job just as seriously. When they don't appear to, I can't help but rage against them and the system that shelters them.

"I think that's where we differ," Scott responded cautiously. My eyes adjusted, and the outline of his figure next to me came into focus. He laced the fingers of both hands underneath his head on the pillow as if he were relaxing on a hammock in the middle of the day. "It's hard for me to get quite as worked up as you do sometimes. I know there have been lousy presidents, inept congressmen, incompetent admirals and generals, but these are the exceptions. The founders created a system that has withstood the test of time, hundreds of years now. Any problems seem temporary compared with the long-term successes produced by the Constitution."

I struggled to remember the words of the Constitution. All I could come up with was the phrase "unalienable rights" and the American trinity: life, liberty, and the pursuit of happiness. Scott must have read my mind. It's one of his talents.

"The Constitution is actually a very practical document. The founders laid out a grand new vision in the Declaration of Independence with phrases like 'life, liberty, and the pursuit of happiness.' But the early states were unable to come together to fulfill this vision."

Ah. Of course not.

"The Constitution supports those grand ideas by laying out the machinery which has kept the wheels of government turning. So I like to imagine that what I do in the military—in a very small sense—supports the government's operation. It's not theoretical at all to me. Without people to support and defend the Constitution, America wouldn't work because government wouldn't work. So that's how I contribute to this experiment. To me, that's what's worthwhile about staying in the military."

I fell in love with Scott all over again that night, and it wasn't because he was leaving for deployment in a matter of hours. During the course of my life I had allowed myself to become comfortable on a perch of privilege, unaware of the fragility of the edifice supporting it. I remained entirely at ease with my ignorance of huge swaths of the American experience. Before marrying Scott, I had always been comfortable with what I knew, so the volumes in my mental library were old friends I returned to over and over, reaffirming often stale ideas with every rereading. The word *duty* always smelled musty and old-fashioned to me. Pages proclaiming the worth of individual sacrifice for the greater good were yellowed with age.

Clasping hands with the military sent those volumes tumbling to the ground. Just as modern-day military strategists refer to the "unknown unknowns" to point out an unanticipated uncertainty, my own life as a military spouse strayed so far from the course envisioned that I claimed no knowledge of what lay ahead for us. Only the most basic certainties still applied. Here they are, as I counted them in the dark: I was married to Scott, and we had two children. That was all I could depend on in the world of unknown unknowns.

And because of who he is—the person he revealed himself to be in five years of marriage and the person he showed himself to be during our midnight conversation the night before deployment—it was enough. More than enough, actually. That thought liberated me, and I was ready to run down the aisle all over again. But it didn't make it any easier to send him to the boat for seven months. Because there's the military, and then there's the war.

I n theater, eloquence lies in the unspoken. An entire story can unfold in an actor's hesitation. An arrested gesture conveys true motivation. The possibilities in the air make the room swoon.

"How do the wives feel about the war?" my civilian friends often asked.

"I don't know," I responded, over and over. "We never talk about it."

That was us: cast members in the theater of the absurd. Our troupe of wives was living on a remote island off the tip of the northwest coast as our husbands shipped off to Iraq and Afghanistan. We certainly understood the military's requirement that service members remain politically neutral in public—a prerequisite to the success of the American system, underscored in that election year in a forceful speech by Admiral Mike Mullen, chairman of the Joint Chiefs of Staff, warning military members and politicians to keep their distance.

Intellectually, most people realize that married couples can have different political views, but some unspoken undercurrent chilled the potential for political discussion among the spouses I knew. Perhaps opening the door to a political conversation or debate about the war, even with a peer, might be seen as inappropriately partisan. I personally craved some acknowledgment among the wives that we military families lived in the eye of the political twister, but it seemed that no one would even acknowledge the tornado spinning above us.

In my former life, my friends and I discussed politics continually. Many of us shared similar views, so these conversations were predictably satisfying, but of course the debates and discussions were much richer with those whose views diverged or who favored other candidates. (Since we loved to bait each other, we actively sought out those with different opinions.) The irony, of course, is that in my former life, I was far more comfortably detached from the policies under discussion. There was nothing riding on my opinion, however eloquently or persuasively I thought I expressed myself. It's easy to stake a position with words when those words carry no consequences.

As a military wife, the stakes are sky-high. I'm equally unable to affect change as an individual, but now I am—we are—affected by politics and policies in the most intimate, direct way. It's as if voters at the polls are pulling a lever that asks: "Should our squadron and our friends' squadrons deploy again? If so, for how long, and for how many years into the future?" I wanted to discuss all of this with my peers because the nuances of America's situation in Iraq and Afghanistan are precisely what make the conflict worthy of sustained, thoughtful discussion. Though I lay awake at night with serious concerns about American conduct and policy in the Middle East, my close-up with camouflage has taught me the value of seeing the world—and this war—in finely graduated shades of gray.

I understand that my political beliefs are important only to me. I dare to think they count precisely because other people's opinions, and the resulting actions, reach out and grab us by the throat around every dark corner. But just as Scott believed deeply that the military's role was to support and defend the Constitution—not a person, not an institution, not a branch of government, but the entire machinery of government—he and his colleagues understand that military leaders must never allow political preferences to interfere with readiness or morale. During the course of our tour, I gradually began to grasp why families don't venture into this arena, either.

"Political differences would shatter the community, don't you think?" my friend Isabelle suggested, when I asked her about it. She'd been at this life far longer than I and was even less likely than I to have become a Navy wife. She'd been born in Manhattan to American parents, devoted Francophiles who shuttled her between

Paris and New York until she chose for herself which nation to claim, landing at the Sorbonne for her undergraduate degree. There she met an American naval officer, a Fulbright scholar and recently minted Annapolis ensign who was studying international relations, and she followed him back to the United States. They waited several years to marry as she launched her career at Microsoft and reestablished herself on American soil. Finally, they tied the knot. And she, who navigated the most stylish arrondissements in the French capital and the coolest neighborhoods in Seattle, bought a map of Millington, Tennessee.

Isabelle never dreamed she'd be a Navy wife—an American Navy wife, especially. But she'd adapted in just the right way for her during the years since she and her husband had married. Perhaps it was because her natural instincts, unlike mine, were to stay quiet in a conflict. She never publicly expressed opinions she would later regret. (She swears she learned this the hard way after several costly social gaffes.) Though she feels strongly about many things, she thinks her words through, stringing them together on a sentence like pearls clicking softly into place.

"You mean there's so little that unites us as military spouses already, we can't go looking for more problems?"

"I think that's it," Isabelle nodded. "When I hear someone spout a political opinion I violently disagree with, it gets in the way of future conversations. We share so little in common, but we all have to be friends here. There's no room for dissent."

Luckily, that wasn't an issue for Isabelle and me. She is the only friend in the entire Navy with whom I discuss politics, and we know each other's points and preferences as intimately as our own. We'd danced around politics endlessly the first few years we'd known each other, dropping hints and offhandedly mentioning a politician's name here and there. One or the other would respond with the roll of an eye or a thoughtful expression meant to hide our excitement. We were like teenagers afraid to admit a crush. When

we finally came out to each other, during our husbands' tours in
D.C., we celebrated with a big breakfast at the most decadent diner
in town. I still remember that heaping plate of chocolate-chip pancakes and the hours it took to eat our way to the bottom of the stack.
It happened to be the morning after the 2004 elections, and aside
from the sugar rush, I was exhilarated to finally have a Navy friend
to hash it out with.

We marked another big transition that morning. Isabelle, to
whom I'd bid good-bye twice before when one or the other of us
had left our husbands' previous postings, was packing up again. We
knew we'd meet again sometime soon—that's just how it works in
the Navy. So we finished our pancakes, licked our forks, and clinked
them together. That was it for us for the next year and a half. I
didn't see her again until she walked through the open front door
of our house in Anacortes holding a box of Godiva in one hand and
a bottle of Champagne in the other the day we moved in.

20

The New Normal

I carried my camera with me everywhere in Anacortes and had filled four photo albums before it seemed like any time at all had passed. I documented our time in Washington state as if it were just another trip about to pass into memory; I was a tourist in Anacortes, in some ways a tourist in my own life during that period. I regarded our time there as Scott's tour of duty, and *tour* connotes something brief, with a built-in expiration date. The thing is, Scott's orders landed us there for three years. Over a year had already passed. I knew I was supposed to be living in the present, and yet I felt I was already practicing saying "Oh, that happened during our time back at Whidbey." But it didn't feel like a vacation; living there during that early period often felt like work.

I hungered for perspective, for some corrective lens to refocus my vision. I was hardwired to think of myself as a fortunate person, though stanza after stanza of screamingly positive self-talk didn't seem to be working anymore: "At least you have a husband you love!" "At least he's only going to be deployed for seven months, not a year!" "At least he's on a carrier, not on the ground!" "At least you don't have financial issues!" "At least your kids are healthy!" "At least you have a supportive family!" And the inevitable chorus, chanted in booming baritone, led by the thunderous voice of God: "Just think how much worse it could be!"

But at that moment life seemed pretty bad. Many people had warned me that all would go wrong the first months of deployment. They must have been clairvoyant—or experienced. In the weeks after Scott left, a tree fell in the yard following a windstorm, all three toilets backed up, Esther and I got locked in a bedroom when the doorknob fell off on the other side, all of the circuits in the house shorted, and the washing machine broke. Both kids got sick, of course, and threw up in bed for several nights in a row, which coincided with the demise of the washing machine.

The worst, though, was that once again Ethan suffered classic dad's-on-deployment symptoms: depression, anger, and withdrawal, a mockery of his best self. I asked him to draw his feelings, and he tore the pencil through the paper, ripping it to shreds. One morning I told him that I would write a letter to Daddy from him if he told me what to say. Here's what he dictated:

> *Dear Daddy,*
>
> *I wish you were home right now. I really miss you. I'm crying right this second, and I'm holding my shirt over my face. I wish you were home right now. I really really love you. Please tell the driver of the aircraft carrier to stop the boat.*
>
> *My dream was about you leaving home. You were in bed, and other people rang the doorbell and took you away, and me and Esther were pulling you back, and you had to drive away and we followed you but couldn't find you, and I cried and cried and cried.*
>
> *That is all done.*
>
> *Love,*
> *Ethan*

Ethan wasn't alone, of course. Although one Army-sponsored study concludes that "military children and adolescents exhibit levels of psychopathology on par with children of civilian families," it acknowledges that military children face "significant life challenges" not shared by their civilian peers. Boys with a war-deployed father may suffer especially frequent "emotional, behavioral, sex-role, and health problems," according to one particularly influential Army study.

Esther reminded me what a difference a year makes. The previous winter, as we had adjusted to Scott's long and frequent absences during workups, she seemed to barely notice that he had left. Her extreme affection toward Flat Daddy alone hinted at her memory of Real Daddy. But after Scott's deployment, she became very clingy, which is a typical response to deployment for young toddlers. For several weeks she refused to go to her babysitter's. She had always been one of those kids who ran to her friends and never even looked back, but after Scott's departure for deployment, she begged to be held, sobbing pitifully when I disappeared from view. Her well-meaning babysitter, an older woman who adored her, watched with great dismay.

"Have you talked to your husband about getting out of the military?" the woman asked one morning, as I tried to distract Esther with a toy. She had never tread on such personal ground before, and I couldn't believe my ears. I talked to no one about Scott's career plans. Among the more seasoned officers and their spouses, discussing one's aspirations is just Not Done. It's considered immodest, just as talking about salaries is taboo in other professions. I must have looked as shocked as I felt.

"Well, it's obvious he has to get out. Just look what it's doing to this sweet child," she insisted.

I've never been good at responding to a provocation. It's not that I think of the perfect thing to say later, as I'm driving away. I just never think of the perfect thing to say. *"Hmmmm,"* I mumbled, sliding Esther's arms back into the sleeves of her coat. I decided, in that moment, to take her home.

"The country needs healthy families," the woman said, meeting my gaze. A challenge. Sure, the country needs healthy families. Who could argue with that? The country also needs a military force to protect all those healthy families, I thought, offended. But it was impossible for me to engage. Scott had left a few weeks earlier, and I felt like a human pincushion. I carried Esther out. We were scheduled to return to my parents' house for another visit the following week, and after the new year Esther would be old enough to begin at Montessori preschool.

Part of me knows—knew even then, though I couldn't allow a pinhole of light to penetrate my camera obscura—that I said nothing in my own defense because there is no defense. Ethan and Esther, and countless other military kids, sacrifice a sense of personal security for America's national security. It's not fair. It's not right. And in our case, it wasn't going to change anytime soon.

Other military friends experience the same sorts of interactions with teachers, neighbors, and even priests, but this time, knowing we weren't alone didn't help. Reading and rereading Ethan's heartbreaking letter and reflecting on Esther's transparent insecurity, I felt bereft. Both kids were suffering. I felt guilty they had already spotted me crying, since military brochures press the point that it takes a healthy parent to raise a healthy child. I remained careful never to transmit a sense of fear to my kids and always stressed that although they were apart from their dad and everyone was sad about it, both he and they were safe.

The problem was how to navigate my path back to solid emotional footing. Scott had left our lives for seven months to fly in a war. In whose reality was that supposed to be acceptable? And more to the point: Why *should* I pretend it's normal? It was one of many

moments when it seemed inconceivable that our family could re-
constitute itself intact. We had such a long way to go, such an endless wait ahead.

But that was buying my ticket to the pity party, as some of my
military girlfriends called it. Other wives cheer on their peers during
deployment by chanting "Tigger! Tigger!" to remind them to emulate the cheerful character from the Winnie-the-Pooh book series
rather than the perpetually gloomy Eeyore. All of these exhortations
echoed in my head, calling me back to a more practical reality. Time
to move on. It may not have been normal, but it was our normal.
Or, as spouses in my circle had renamed the Navy's increasingly
unpredictable and demanding deployment schedules, "the new normal." The new normal required creative coping.

I quashed my negative thoughts that day and walked out to the
deck for a breath of fresh air. And then I thought I saw something.
I looked up in search of the eagles. They'd returned for a few weeks,
fishing for spawned-out salmon on the Upper Skagit River, and I'd
spotted two circling overhead earlier that morning as I drove across
Deception Pass. I remembered hearing that some of these majestic
creatures have a five-foot wingspan. I'm five feet tall, and my outstretched arms don't even reach five feet. It was hard to believe that
those eagles compared to me in scale. I smiled, vowing to stop thinking of myself as a short person and start regarding myself as a
tall bird.

No eagles appeared at that moment, but as I scanned the washed-
out winter sky I reminded myself that people can feel out of place
for any reason, any variety of circumstances. It's far from just a
military phenomenon. At one time or another, everyone believes
that the true life is being lived somewhere else.

It was a fresh start—one of many during Scott's deployment—
as I learned to live a life very different from the one I trained for.
It was a good life, and any time I stole away for a few moments of
reflection, I realized I liked the person I was becoming much better

than the one I had left behind. Just as pauses between notes create energy and emotion in music, just as the punctuation between words adds meaning and tone in prose, the spaces between our family's crises—those peaceful times in which I regained my equilibrium—built my new identity as the wife of a naval officer. And when that interior silence faded, I called BobbiJo.

BobbiJo seemed to have been ordered up straight from central casting: the trim, cheerful wife of a high-ranking Army officer and mother of two adolescents who has kept the family healthy and happy despite more than twelve moves and thirteen deployments during nineteen years of marriage.

The Army, the oldest of the American military services, has a deep tradition of taking care of military families. As a brigade commander, BobbiJo's husband had risen to command nearly one thousand troops, and BobbiJo was the star of an established, entrenched social scene wherever she went. Like many in that world, she still refers to her husband as an infantry soldier, and I'd bet big money that she sews her own curtains. Her soft, mossy drawl masks the depth of her insights and makes her flashes of anger as shocking as a dive into ice-cold water.

I've never actually met BobbiJo, despite years of phone calls and e-mails. A friend who heard her speak at a military wives' conference thought I would like her. I followed up with a hopeful note and then a call. When we talked, I didn't just like her, I hoped to become her spiritual daughter, or her mentee, or at least her once-in-a-while-when-it's-convenient friend. It wasn't quite a girl crush, because my motives were quasi-professional: job advice for the position of military wife, an informational interview.

BobbiJo was prepared to give. As I discovered, that's what she's always done as an Army spouse. A graphic designer by training, she has spent more than two decades donating her time, her energy, and her ideas to advocate for Army families. When I first called her, though, she was giving only to herself: She'd launched a self-styled sabbatical to reenergize following a difficult tour. Her husband had just completed a one-year deployment in Iraq, and during that time many of his soldiers had died in battle. BobbiJo, the boss's wife, comforted the widowed wives. There were twenty fatalities in her unit, nearly twenty grieving widows, in one year.

I'll always remember where I was on the frigid winter day that BobbiJo used the phrase "widow's basket." The words evoked such horror they rendered me speechless. During the year she helped comfort the widows and surviving family members in her unit, she assembled and readied these baskets in a small corner of her bedroom in Rose Barracks, housing on an Army base in Vilseck, Germany. Bavaria was beautiful, she assured me. But the contents of her widow's basket read like a hospitality kit in Hell:

Notebook for lists of thank-you's
Questions for the casualty assistance officer
Phone book
Points of contact for the unit
Tissues
Bottles of water
Tylenol and Motrin
Cell phone (so the family phone is always available)
Snack foods
Candy, coloring books, and crayons for the kids
Copy of the Army's Family Assistance Plan

BobbiJo pulled herself together for the spouses in her unit that year, but she admits that "it was difficult to deal with my own fear and maintain a calm presence. I compartmentalized my own grief and dealt with it after command." That led to her year off, which coin-

cided with her husband's one-year assignment to a military graduate school.

But she couldn't stay still for long. So she ran. As fast as she
could. Literally. "Long runs give me perspective," she explained. It
was possibly the understatement of the decade, since she became a
competitive long-distance runner. She'd raced in her first marathon
several years before, during a previous tour in Germany. "I wanted
to have something that was only mine," she remembered. "And that
was running. I drove into the Czech Republic on Mother's Day that
year and ran the Prague Marathon. So when we were coming off
our last tour, which was really wrenching, really difficult, I told
myself I'd use this time to reflect and recover. And race."

I never experienced anything like mass casualties in the squadron. That was, in part, why I sought out BobbiJo. Not because it
made me feel better to know that others had it worse but because I
saw the way she faced terrible traumas with equanimity. She always
set me straight, as gently and unobtrusively as she could, simply by
being a strong and humble person and an effective leader. She never
signed up for the job of Army wife, but she saw the need, and she
took it on with a big heart and a lot of smarts.

She wasn't a Stepford wife, despite her looks and her traditional
role. In fact, she was angry—upset about how the Army treated its
spouses and furious at the country too. "I worry about these girls
who are newly married and don't have a chance to build up their
marriage before these deployment cycles kick in," she fumed.
"Many of them are on their own, totally isolated. The country is at
war, and America is at the mall. These young wives don't know
what to think. It's a surreal existence."

BobbiJo loves the Army so much that she believes speaking
truth to power, even when it may reflect negatively on military
policy, is the only path to positive change. That's why she wanted
to get the real deal out there instead. "I grew up, literally, in this
role and in this lifestyle," she explained.

Her rant grabbed my attention. It echoed what I was just beginning to articulate for and about myself. "I feel like I've grown up so much already, just on this tour," I said. "And you've been part of the military for what—over twenty years?"

"I got married when I was twenty-three," she said. "I'm a totally different person than I was then, but that's not the point. I have been a lot of different women over the years. I started out young and idealistic. I had my own job. And then one day my husband just didn't come home. He didn't show up for dinner. I went to the post to find out what had happened. Well, the unit was on recall at the time, and at the moment I went searching for him, he was already jumping from an airplane into Panama. I had to become a stay-at-home mom. I had little kids.

"Then there was the tour when I got so restless I went back to school for a degree in architecture. Toward the end, I got pregnant by surprise. It wasn't a good time in our lives.

"Then I had a small business, advertising and desktop publishing. After we went to Germany the first time, there was no way to attract clients, so I taught soldiers remedial education to help them prepare for college entrance exams."

Now in her mid-forties, BobbiJo hoped to start working in graphic design again, but nixed the idea of a corporate job and the long hours that go with it. "I don't want my kids to worry about where both me and my husband are," she explained. "He's always getting into hot water. I'll do something else, something new."

That's exactly what she meant when she referred to growing up in her role as a military spouse. "You get to reinvent yourself with each tour. I value all these things," she added, "but I'm no different than my civilian sisters. These stages are indicative of any marriage." That's what I found most moving about BobbiJo's perspective. In the bizarre uniqueness of military spousehood, in all of its particularity (and peculiarity), she connected with women everywhere. She didn't isolate herself or believe that few can understand what we military wives experience. She believed her emotional growth was representative of all women's. She called other women her "sisters," minus the ivory-tower attitude of my former women's studies instructors.

This is why: As an Army wife, BobbiJo did, actually, live in a world of women, within which she created a well-run, warm, and productive mini-society. It's not exactly *Herland*; after all, if feminism is defined as a desire for independence from patriarchal authority, no one's going to find that in a military setting. I've thought a lot about feminism since I found myself, unexpectedly, assuming the most traditional role a woman can play, and when I reflect on my experience I keep coming back to the idea that feminism is about choices that expand women's lives rather than constricting them. Becoming a military spouse expanded my world, and the ultimate paradox is that I spent more time working within the domestic sphere than ever before.

BobbiJo was the first to demonstrate to me how to walk that line successfully, and she did it by following the less traveled path. She saw her life as an Army wife as the road to something bigger than herself, and the universe graciously expanded to fit her expectations. Her elegance of perspective inspired me to think about my life as a military spouse in a new way and influenced my own actions as the skipper's wife. At the start of each tour, for example, BobbiJo set out to form a community of women that could not only function but also thrive without men. (One military spouse has called it a "sorority of separation.") BobbiJo achieved this in part by creating strong ties to the civilian world. I followed her lead during our tour by scheduling events off base at every opportunity, by developing a relationship with the local Children's Museum of Skagit County (which generously waived its fees for our group's celebrations), and by reaching out to businesses in town that were eager to support the military.

This is a more radical idea than it seems, because some military wives barricade themselves in our insular environment. In fact, as I first learned in Japan, the world beyond base is referred to by some as life on the "outside." But inside the locked, wrought-iron gates of the post, these women don't feel jailed; they're free precisely because everyone understands and follows the same rules. As the years pass, however, life on base becomes a hothouse where only a certain kind of plant will flower. It becomes uncomfortable to live outside the military community.

BobbiJo witnessed this many times throughout her husband's career, which showed no signs of petering out. In fact, after her one-year emotional sabbatical, the family was slated to relocate to an Army post in California. Her husband would take on the highly coveted job of Brigade Commander. BobbiJo would oversee the well-being of several hundred families. She hesitated to think about the responsibility, but one thing was certain: She would keep running. It was hers, after all.

"I can't live through the man," she drawled at the conclusion to one of our phone calls. "He does fine on his own."

BobbiJo's husband—"the man," as I now think of him—may have been fine. Mine seemed to have settled into life on the boat, flying six-hour missions that culminated with night landings on the carrier, marking up endless piles of paperwork, and sitting through numbingly long planning meetings. But one little soldier wasn't faring very well as we marched our way through deployment.

21

"People in the Navy
Kill People"

M ommy?"

"Yes, my love?"

I tucked Ethan into bed. We had already read books, drank water, kissed, hugged, and discussed plans for the following day. I plotted my path toward the door, eager for nighttime peace.

"I can't see Daddy anymore when I close my eyes."

"What do you mean?" I kneeled by his side.

"I used to be able to close my eyes and see Daddy. Remember? Remember when I used my magical powers and saw him on the deck?"

This was urgent. It was an emergency, actually. In the time since Scott had left for deployment, Ethan's tumble off the emotional precipice had gained grim velocity with each new day. It mirrored his first episode of distress the year before, which had resolved itself gradually after the visit to his grandparents. This time, I saw the pattern clearly. Ethan lay on the couch, nonverbal and barely moving. After a week, his lethargy turned to fury. He took it out on Esther and me, hitting and kicking us. He stopped eating, consenting only to one plain hamburger bun per day. (I didn't know it at the time, but he was in the first stage of a monthlong hunger strike.) Nightmares terrorized him, but he refused to describe them to me when he woke up screaming.

"You can do it again," I urged. I heard the desperation in my voice and tried to control it. "Close your eyes, and you'll see Daddy. Just try. I know you can do it. Please try."

"No," he said simply, without rancor. My four-year-old sounded as resigned as an old man withering in a web of disappointments. "I lost my magical powers. He's not there anymore."

I solved the mystery of Ethan's nightmares around the same time that I finally cracked Martina's code.

It's not that I ever wanted to hear that she had fared badly during McGowan's IA. Given our experience as a family, it was difficult for me to understand how she had managed so well, but I had believed her. Kids are different, and family dynamics vary dramatically. Surely, if every military family had the same troubles we did, I would probably have heard about it.

So Martina's e-mail gave me a lot to think about. I had just written to her about our latest crisis: A five-year-old friend of Ethan's on a play date at our house saw a photo of Scott in uniform and told Ethan that "people in the Navy kill people." I tried to intervene, but the little boy insisted it was true and told Ethan that if Scott didn't want to kill people he could fly airliners from city to city instead of military jets.

My scalp tingled with fear. It was the moment I had long dreaded. From the time that tour began, I had been obsessed with controlling the manner in which I would tell Ethan about the war, or if I would tell him at all. I felt secure, since he was surrounded by three-, four-, and five-year-olds at Montessori, which stressed the virtues of a "peaceful community." But the little boy at our house that day was the child of civilian parents who openly discussed their antiwar feelings with their son.

I changed the subject, but it was too late. Ethan's nightmares resumed that very evening.

Martina wrote me back right away. She expressed sympathy for Ethan and heartache for our family. But she and McGowan, as it happened, were busy trying to save their marriage. As she e-mailed from Stuttgart:

> *It really is a rocky road especially because guys spout phrases like "I couldn't do it without my wife, who keeps the home fires burning." Blah. Blah. Blah. Every time I hear that crap I feel really pissed off! It's just so flippant with nothing behind it. The difficulties of deployment and the IA have touched the core of who I am. It's changed me, and I'm beginning to think it's permanent. Maybe I shouldn't have ignored my own feelings all through the IA, but it was how I coped. I just put my head down and plowed through. I don't let myself cry or any of that. I didn't break down until after McGowan returned and we unpacked everything in the new place. It's a delayed reaction, but I would never have gotten through the IA otherwise. My doctor said it's pretty normal; people just do what they have to, to survive a difficult situation, and may not deal with the underlying emotion and stress until it's "safe" to. I just wish a Wives' Club could talk about this stuff instead of napkin colors for the next social event. Especially for those young wives who think that because these problems are not discussed, no one else is feeling the way they are. Everyone is!*

Medical journals and military publications devote more and more pages to chronicling the emotional cycle of deployment. Authors always include "postdeployment" as an important stage, and I began to understand why. There may be resentment at having been "abandoned" for more than half a year. Spouses—like Martina—

may consider themselves the true heroes (watching the house, paying the bills, and caring for the children) while soldiers cared only for themselves. At least one study points out that stress is more likely to be reported by the stay-at-home parent than by the deployed soldier. Kids have even shown an "anniversary reaction," displaying significant anxiety up to a year later triggered by the possibility of separation.

When Ethan's nightmares finally tapered off, he seemed happy again—outgoing, funny, focused, and at peace for the first time in ages. But Martina's e-mail demonstrated that the end wasn't quite the end. Deployment doesn't neatly wrap itself up after the spouse returns. Once the last crumbs of sheet cake are swept away and the banners are folded and stored for the next group, serious family issues may return faster than anyone anticipates. After all, time at home for service members is getting shorter and shorter. *The Washington Post* tracked down Pentagon data showing that among 808,000 parents deployed since September 11, 2001, more than 212,000 have been away twice, and about 103,000 have gone three or more times. This inevitably affects children, since more than a third of active-duty military personnel are married with children, and an additional six percent are single parents.

Repeated and unpredictable deployments are spouses' biggest gripe with the military, according to one nongovernmental survey of Army spouses. Ronnie, my treadmill buddy, was a good example. She had only recently welcomed her husband, Sam, home from his six-month deployment, and yet he was due to redeploy in a few months for another half-year stint in Afghanistan. When I asked her about it, her mouth flattened into a horizontal line, and her eyes went dark.

Our squadron's future following deployment remained unknown. It was simply too early to know if a second cruise was looming for us and how soon after the first it would come. Luckily for me, I ran into Amber at the commissary, and she had all the answers.

I spotted the chopsticks first. Red this time, they gleamed like roadside flares from the other end of the candy aisle. Esther, nap-deprived in the front of my cart, swayed with exhaustion. But Amber beckoned to me excitedly, so I weaved through the other shoppers and maneuvered over to her. She'd announced at our most recent spouse group meeting that she and her husband were adopting a baby from Guatemala, and I hadn't yet had an opportunity to congratulate her.

"Our bowling league made it to the base championships!" she shrieked.

"That's great!" I had no appropriate bowling vocabulary. "Congratulations on all of your good news. I'm so happy for you and Peter."

"I just knew our squadron could do something great. We get our trophy at a ceremony next week. Will you come? This is the perfect opportunity to show squadron spirit," she reminded me, with those narrowed eyes and that suspiciously warm smile. The adoption seemed so far from her mind, I wondered if I had dreamed up the entire incident. I wished, again, that my amateur ability to read people's intentions had survived our transition into the military.

"Of course I'll be there," I answered.

"We're really going to have to stick together," she counseled. "Looks like we're in for another year without our sweeties. Another Thanksgiving, another Christmas, another Easter. I bet Daddy's going to miss another birthday," she singsonged as she knelt down and began tickling Esther under the chin.

Esther buried her head in my stomach, and I patted her hair for a moment while I figured out what to do. I felt like Amber had sucker-punched me. I had no idea what she was talking about. A second deployment right after this one? Scott never mentioned anything like that. As a junior officer, Amber's husband didn't spend his time reviewing official carrier schedules, but maybe he had found out something and had passed it along to her.

My most high-schoolish instincts kicked into high gear. I didn't want Amber to know that I was ignorant of any potential future deployment. She reveled in her role as information broker, and I refused to give her the satisfaction of seizing this nugget first. I smiled neutrally and said good-bye quickly as a dark cloud descended on me. Why is Scott keeping things from me? I wondered on the drive home. Doesn't he think I deserve to know? Doesn't he trust me? Why would the squadron let one of the junior wives in on something so sensitive? Doesn't he think I can handle it?

By the time I pulled into the driveway, our marriage was on the rocks, our kids were father-deprived delinquents with dead-end jobs, and I was drinking a bottle of wine for every teaspoon I mixed into the chicken marsala. Never mind that I couldn't stand to touch raw chicken. *Hello love,* I e-mailed as coolly as I could.

It's been an okay day, though I was somewhat disheartened to hear of the squadron's schedule—and to hear of it secondhand. I just can't stop thinking about being on my own another year, though we're not even a quarter of the way into this deployment. I know how busy you are, but drop me a line when you can so we can talk about next steps. I might take the kids back to my parents' house for a while. Everyone's telling me that's what I should do, anyway. I hope you're having a good day. I love you and miss you very much.

Agonizing hours passed. It was impossible to tell what Scott was doing at the time I sent any e-mail. Sometimes I might receive an e-mail reply within minutes. Other times, the ship's e-mail systems went down for hours or even days. On other occasions, he could have just catapulted off the carrier for a six-hour flight over Iraq, and I wouldn't hear back from him until the following morning.

Unexpectedly, the phone rang. "Remember I told you to beware of rumors?" Scott asked, barely pausing for hello. I couldn't remember the last time I had heard him so angry. His voice was gravelly from the effort of keeping his voice down. "This is exactly what I was talking about," he continued. "I don't know what you heard or who you heard it from, but I can promise you it isn't true. *I* don't even know our schedule. You see how destructive this is?"

"You're not going away again?" I asked. A few shining rays poked through my mood.

"It's too early to know. All I can tell you is that I haven't come across anything to say that we will or that we won't. Honey, I promise I will keep you up to date." His voice softened. "I just hate to see you get this upset over a rumor. I know what this must have done to you."

"So what's Amber talking about? She sounded so definite."

"It happens in every squadron I've been a part of. The spouses who are left behind talk to the other spouses who are left behind, and they gather up bits and pieces of information and string together a story that sounds plausible but has no basis in reality. This is the kind of rumor that absolutely destroys morale, both on the boat and on the beach. I've seen where this can go. It's not good, and it's going to happen again, so I need you to be ready for it."

"So should I tell her it's not true?"

"Just tell her that as soon as there is definite information, we'll pass it along. If you don't hear it from me, don't believe it. Okay?"

The dark cloud cleared. The sun shone again.

"Hon, I gotta go brief for a flight. I shouldn't even be on the phone right now, but I thought I'd see if there was a free line. Promise me you won't fall for this again?"

I promised. And as the tour dragged on, even more bizarre stories about the squadron's schedule circulated in an adult game of telephone that was far from fun. I remembered Scott's words and stood by what I knew.

22

The Navy Wife

Years ago, around the time Scott and I married, I began searching for books by military spouses. *There has to be a secret*, I thought, *or at least someone who will tell me what to do.* I didn't unlock the mystery, but I love the titles of these books: *With Powder on My Nose: Adventures of a Military Wife*; *Household Baggage: The Moving Life of a Soldier's Wife*; the plaintive *Help! I'm a Military Spouse, I Get a Life Too!* and the lighthearted *A Family's Guide to the Military for Dummies.*

When I read Jacey Eckhart's *The Homefront Club: The Hardheaded Woman's Guide to Raising a Military Family*, I was so taken with Eckhart's tell-it-like-it-is tone, describing how the crap that rains down on military spouses usually turns into a flood of biblical proportions, that I vowed I would buy copies for all of the wives in our group. They loved it too.

During Scott's deployment, reading other women's accounts of their lives as military spouses allowed me to place myself in a historical continuum that gave context and meaning to my experience. Throughout his command tour, for example, I felt for the first time the gulf that separates military and civilian families. It's not as if I expected to look around the mall and see people sobbing, but there was—and still is—a seriousness missing from American cultural life, a seriousness that wartime demands, given its devastating effect on so many families. But Main Street and the military are working at cross-purposes. The country has not been asked to make serious sacrifices since 9/11. Even my closest civilian friends seemed to be watching the Iraq War as if it were a low-budget movie in limited release, whereas I sat dead center in an IMAX 3-D theater, grasping the armrests and holding on for dear life.

So it was a comfort to read in Elizabeth Bacon Custer's 1885 memoir, *Boots and Saddles*, that when she left her husband's Army post in Dakota for a trip east, she had a similarly surreal experience in her civilian community. It was "during a summer when our regiment was fighting Indians," she wrote, "and my idea was that the whole country would be almost as absorbed as we were. How shocked I was to be asked, when I spoke of the regiment, 'Ah, is there a campaign, and for what purpose has it gone out?'"

Some things never change, especially the good things, which is lucky for me. In one book about military marriages I met Elizabeth Blair Lee, whose husband, Phillips Lee, joined the Navy in 1826 and advanced to the rank of rear admiral. When the Civil War began, Phillips's years of shore duty came to an end, and he headed off to sea. As he departed, Elizabeth promised herself, "Well we will know how to appreciate a home together in peaceful times even more than ever."

That is a sentiment I struggle to describe to civilian friends. One who listened patiently until she understood my perspective now insists that Scott and I have the most romantic marriage she has ever encountered. Scott and I are deeply at peace with each other, both when we're together and when we're apart, and I think it's because our marriage was born of war. Our priorities have been clear from day one: We make the most of every minute we share. As Elizabeth

Blair Lee so eloquently put it, we understand how to appreciate a home together simply because we so rarely get the opportunity.

T he older, out-of-print how-to manuals for military wives, many of which I've picked up at estate sales over the years, are the real knee-slappers, especially *The Navy Wife: What She Ought to Know About the Customs of the Service and the Management of a Navy Household*, first published in 1941. It was written for someone just like me—the mid-century incarnation, that is—with no family ties to the military and no particular instinct for that world. Its tone is practical and helpful, like that of a best friend, and like a best friend, it is breathless in its excitement for the new adventure the reader (i.e., the freshly minted Navy wife) is embarking upon. It begins quite logically with her invitation to visit the U.S. Naval Academy and coaches her through the first stages of courtship with her midshipman:

> *The hops [at Annapolis] begin shortly after nine o'clock. By nine-thirty all the guests have passed through the receiving line and the dance is in full swing. Your very best evening dress is appropriate, but do not go in for exotic, extreme styles. The girl in the simple dress of good material and youthful, becoming design is often the belle of the ball.*

The book culminates, of course, in the tips our fair heroine will need as a young Navy bride. In the past, all Naval Academy graduates were required to defer marriage for two years after graduation for financial and professional reasons. But once they're married, the practical advice follows: how to adhere to naval traditions and customs, how to pay bills on time as the family is continually transferred to new locations, how to adapt to living conditions at each of the naval bases in the United States and abroad, how to host required social gatherings on a paltry Navy salary, what to do when you show up at a port call and your husband's boat has been diverted to an entirely different location. Guidance on nearly every conceivable event is covered, from homecomings to funerals to state dinners at the White House. Inappropriate conduct is proscribed in severe terms, lest a misstep ruin a husband's prospects:

> *A wife's carelessness in financial matters or disregard of social proprieties not only reflect upon the character and intelligence of her husband, as evidenced by his selection of a wife, but also produce a state of anxiety and disappointment which cannot but divert his mind from his work, thereby reducing his efficiency and beginning the wrecking of his career. Those who are old in the service can name many once promising, efficient young officers whose naval careers were early blighted by the actions of unworthy wives.*

As well intentioned as these old books are, it's all too easy to make fun of them, especially in their outmoded assumptions about the marital relationship. (Today's offerings are appropriately au courant, such as the practical, helpful *Navy Spouse's Guide* and the sober, black-jacketed *Military Widow.*) Since the military is a microcosm of American society, it would be unreasonable to expect much from these dated volumes beyond the traditional schizophrenic mid-century view of the sexes. A wife was required to stand at the center of the family, running the show with competence and confidence, and yet step silently and submissively aside when the patriarch arrived to assert his will. This dynamic was exaggerated in a military relationship, since the service member really did deal with life-and-death situations that required his wife to run the family in his absence yet make way when Big Daddy returned to assume his rightful place in the household hierarchy. And when Big Daddy came home, wives were indeed on notice:

> *Being an aviator's wife is a big job, and it is highly essential that a flier's wife understand and be cognizant of the importance of her husband's career. In every way possible she must keep up his morale. Flying is a highly specialized career; it takes more than just the ability to fly. The aviator's actions at the controls must be instinctive, quick, and subconscious, but his judgment in an emergency must be perfect. To do this, he must have a happy, congenial home life.*

That's where outdated assumptions begin to blur into today's reality. Shards of advice from *The Navy Wife* still sting, and it becomes obvious why some military couples maintain fairly traditional roles. Flying is a tough job. I've never once heard an aviator complain, but it is exhausting and nerve-racking. When Scott was at home I saw it in the furrows etched into his forehead and in the gray threading his black hair. Lives are at stake, and I imagine that the responsibility of running a squadron, especially a deployed squadron during wartime, is crushing. So before Scott left for deployment, I did my best to rise with the kids in the wee hours, to keep them quiet when necessary, to satisfy their whims so he didn't have to. That's an outgrowth of my respect for him and the person he is rather than my assignment as a Navy wife. But I'm not sure that our family looks much different from the military families of yesteryear.

I draw the line at compulsory cheerfulness, though. "In a letter to your fiancé or husband be careful not to unburden your soul or to write needlessly of unhappiness or misfortune," urge the authors of *The Navy Wife*. Many of my friends still practice this epistolary evasion so that their deployed husbands won't worry about the home front. I wish I could too. I'm sure Scott's second Iraq tour at the start of Operation Iraqi Freedom would have been less stressful if I hadn't continually e-mailed him updates on my preterm labor. I'm sure his third Iraq deployment would have proceeded more smoothly if I hadn't e-mailed him with the news of the fallen tree, the day in the ER, the stopped-up toilets, the missing keys, Ethan's hunger strike, Esther's smashed finger, and the other crises that rolled through our lives like a continuous thunderstorm.

But I asked Scott before he left for each detachment and deployment how much he wanted to hear of our domestic dramas. "Tell me everything," he said each time. "I want to come home and pick up where we left off. Besides, if it would make you feel better to write to me about it, then I want you to feel better. It's the least I can do."

I don't know how military wives of previous generations managed, shouldering the responsibility for a husband's career success on one side and the family's emotional well-being on the other. After Scott deployed, I lectured myself to stay strong, but I also depended on others to maintain my morale. My parents, mother-in-law, siblings, and my best friend took turns visiting to provide much-needed company. They stood by me, backing up supportive talk with solid action. Knowing they were there to lean on helped me get through some of the toughest days.

The choices presented to military wives now—spurred on by the decoupling of the military wife's traditional duties and her husband's career, more and better employment opportunities for women, and most families' need for double wage earners—gave me the freedom, paradoxically, to become deeply involved in the squadron. I didn't feel compelled to entertain when I didn't feel like it. I didn't feel compelled to do anything, which made it easy to choose activities that fit best with my interests. The volunteerism served my needs as well as the Navy's. In the process, being a military wife became attractive because it was the only thing I had ever done where I could stand out and fit in at the same time.

Earlier generations of books written for Navy husbands are equally thought-provoking, especially the old chestnuts, like *Service Etiquette: Correct Social Usage for Service Men on Official and Unofficial Occasions* (1958). With index entries like "Cream puffs, how to eat," followed by "Crest or coat of arms, on wedding or formal invitations," trailed by "Damages, apology for," and "Dental care, importance of," how could I ever resist?

Service Etiquette may have been written for service members, but I started referring to it early in our marriage, during our days in Japan. I craved information. Invitations arrived in the mail: first to a Navy wedding in Tokyo, then to a change-of-command ceremony, then to a luncheon hosted by a visiting admiral's wife. One day, Scott mentioned we'd be attending a "wetting down" for a few of the younger officers in his squadron, and I asked him to repeat it three times because I thought I had misheard. (It's a party to celebrate a promotion; the name owes its origin to naval officers' tradition of dipping a newly added gold stripe on their uniform in seawater. Apparently the process accelerated tarnishing, so "wetting down" the new stripe helped it match the old in short order.)

By reading these old books, I gradually came to understand how John Paul Jones's officer-gentleman had evolved over the centuries to resemble something of the international Renaissance man—a James Bond in service dress blues. According to *The Naval Officer's Guide* (1943), for example, at social events during a shore-based tour in a foreign country,

> *Your contribution may be as complicated as acting as interpreter and guide for a visiting VIP or his wife, or as simple as carving a tenderloin of beef or turkey, for the Independence Day reception, which your wife roasted in her own oven the day before. You*

may be able to take a part in an American Community play for
the benefit of charity or do a variety act for an Embassy party. If
the bar boy fails to show up for an Embassy function, get behind
the bar until the situation clears up. It will require a nice sense of
judgment and timing to recognize the need and to fill it promptly
and effectively.

The military's adherence to the principles of merit-based progress, and its by-your-bootstraps attitude, made it the perfect laboratory in which to build this ideal officer.

23

That Stupid Boat

Just as sailors and officers continually flew in and out of our lives, new wives came and went frequently as tours ended for some families and began for others. Our base seemed busier than Grand Central Terminal as families packed up and drove out of town while more minivans arrived, equally loaded down with boxes. I still felt like a greenhorn after twelve months at Whidbey, but in Navy parlance I now qualified as an old-timer. Other wives, new to base, sought me out for advice. Some who were uneasy with their role heard that I kept my name and my job, and figured I might be a kindred spirit. I listened to their anti–military-wife rants and encouraged them to pass the task on to someone else, but I didn't have the heart to join in the bitch session.

"It's *his* life," one of the newer wives entreated, looking for support. "It's not what I chose. Why should I have to go along with it?"

"You're right," I said. "If you don't want to, you shouldn't."

I wasn't sure if she knew about the unexpected, unlikely rewards of military spousehood and didn't care, or if she knew little about these details. When I tried to explain my own journey, though, she quickly dismissed me as someone who drank the Kool-Aid.

I sympathized. Just a few years ago *I* would have been the one bitterly complaining about unfair expectations and doubting the motives of anyone who tried to convince me otherwise. It was surreal. I wasn't different in any fundamental way from the person I had been when I walked down the aisle in my mother's lace dress. I hadn't compromised on any principles. My political views were unchanged. I felt, more strongly than ever, that it was important for military wives to work if they so desired as a way to maintain their identity and control their financial future.

The only difference was that in the time since our tour began I had seen how enormously squadron families, especially young enlisted families, benefit from the Navy's formal and informal support networks. Many of these families had few coping mechanisms and even fewer resources during deployment. I thought of the harried twenty-year-old wife of a sailor who spent all day, every day, with her toddler and her infant because she had no money to hire a babysitter. I thought of one of our officer wives on bed rest with preterm labor during her husband's absence. I thought of a wife who broke her ankle and had to care for her infant, her toddler, and her teenager by herself while in a cast and on crutches. I remembered one of the wives who spanked her three-year-old at the enlisted-spouse group meeting and called him a "turd," and the exhausted young woman who told me she was on the verge of shaking her ten-month-old son, who wouldn't sleep and wouldn't stop crying.

Even Pippi, whose good-hearted outrageousness had endeared her to me at the air terminal many months before, seemed to give up the fight. At that same spouse group meeting halfway through deployment, I spotted her toddler pounding on another boy's head as if it were a wayward nail.

"What can I do?" She glanced up at me as she halfheartedly

pulled her child off the other boy. She radiated defeat. "He's mad, and there ain't a thing left that works. I don't know what else to try."

Pippi, who favored snug T-shirts and low-slung jeans, wore a loose-fitting man's button-down over a pair of sweatpants. As she pushed her toddler toward the dessert table, I eyed her stomach. I didn't know how to confirm what I suspected.

"Are you getting support on that other issue?" I asked. Pippi had been cleared of any sort of child endangerment, and one of the base agencies now sent a parenting counselor to her house every week to assist her.

"Yeah. They've been real helpful. This nice lady comes to my house every Thursday. She's helping me figure out a good nap schedule for the kids, and she showed me how I can plan to get one thing done every day while they're sleeping. She even found some money in their budget to buy me a new vacuum cleaner. The house is a lot cleaner now. The boys haven't been getting sick."

"And how are you feeling?" I tried not to glance toward her half-hidden belly.

"Oh, this?" She smiled, for the first time since we'd said hello, and inched up her shirt. There was the baby bump.

I nodded.

"Kind of a surprise," she admitted, laughing. "You know, it's those damn dets."

Deployment takes its toll on all military families, but the stresses cost some more than others, and kids often pay the price. I never had any reason to suspect Pippi or any of my friends or acquaintances of mistreating their children, but one squadron family was the subject of an investigation by Child Protective Services, and I tried to stay aware of other families at risk. Multiple studies link deployment to increased risk for child abuse, and this weighed on my mind. According to one paper in a peer-reviewed medical journal, reports of child abuse and child neglect peaked among military families during one of the early main deployments of troops to Iraq. When major deployments began, reports of abuse of children age four or younger doubled; the abuser was usually the parent who remained at home. The study found that military families had lower rates of child maltreatment than civilian families before the active-duty service member deployed and that "increases in child maltreatment may also extend to families at risk of being deployed" and at the time of the service member's return from deployment.

Because of these kinds of findings—along with a series of wife-murders perpetrated by Army soldiers based at Fort Bragg in 2002—the military has placed a high priority on reporting abuse within families. Any sort of domestic dispute or child-related abuse must be conveyed up the chain of command immediately, and a series of referrals and interventions then take place, usually with the commanding officer's involvement.

My own observations are anecdotal and unofficial. I have nothing to compare my experience with and I certainly can't offer quantitative analysis. But I lost count of the number of times during our tour that a woman with a deployed husband told me she slapped her kid. "I never did it before, I swear," I heard over and over, word for word. "This is the first time. It just got to me."

I wasn't trained to tackle their issues, of course, but through a roundabout network I could offer families under stress a referral to resources in town or on base. Often, the squadron ombudsman and I discussed our concerns, and she reached out directly to the family. Together, she and I tried to be aware of potential crises, tackling them early to avoid disasters. To be honest, part of the concern was squadron readiness; after all, if a family at home is in crisis, the sailor at sea ceases to function as a productive worker, and the entire unit suffers. More pressing, though, was making sure our families operated as safely and constructively as they could under the circumstances.

As for our stressed-out family, the kids and I finally got our groove back around February, the deployment's halfway point. We told funny stories at the dinner table. Ethan and Esther performed hilarious skits that I summarized in my daily e-mails to Scott. We all slept through the night and hatched ideas for new and exciting weekend adventures. I felt, for the first time in ages, that the three of us were a team. Life was good. And the kids were going to see Daddy on TV.

Technology is amazing, and the way the military has exploited technology to help deployed troops and families communicate with each other was a revelation to me during Scott's deployment. I got the first e-mail about our video teleconference (or VTC) from the squadron's senior enlisted sailor, the command master chief, who worked hard to make sure all of the enlisted sailors signed up for slots first. (They had more limited access to e-mail than the officers, since many of them—metalsmiths, mechanics, electricians, and ordnance technicians—do not routinely sit at a desk or have easy access to a computer.) Once sailors signed up, the officers had their chance. And before the week was up, Ethan, Esther, and I found ourselves driving to base.

"You'll get to see Daddy on TV and talk to him, and he'll talk to you," I clumsily explained to them on the way over.

"I want him to come out of the TV," Esther objected.

"Why won't he come out of the TV?" Ethan asked.

"He's still on the boat, but you can see and talk to him and show him stuff. Ethan, what song are you going to play for him?" Ethan brought his violin along.

"I'm going to show him my plucking. I am really good at plucking," Ethan said.

"That's great. Esther, what do you want to show Daddy?"

"My new black shoes," she said. "And my new tights. They're just like a mommy wears."

"And I brought my planet puzzle," Ethan added. "I want to do the puzzle for him while he's watching."

"Okay, but we have to remember we only have ten minutes, then we have to let someone else have a turn."

"But I want him to come out of the TV," Esther repeated.

"I know, me too," I said. "I'm mad about it." That was my new strategy. Whenever the kids seemed to be angry about Scott's absence, I told them I was angry too. Ethan especially loved to see me pumping my fists in the air in an exaggerated pantomime of infuriated motherhood, so he picked up on it right away during our drive to the VTC.

"That stupid boat!" he exclaimed.

"Stupid boat!" Esther echoed.

"Daddy hates that boat, right?" Ethan asked. "He wants to be with us instead."

"Daddy wishes he could be home with you," I said. "But he's really good at his job, and they need his help. That's why we're so proud of Daddy, because he does such a great job."

"Stupid aircraft carrier driver," Ethan muttered, ignoring me. "I wish he would turn that boat around." We'd hit upon his favorite theme. No matter how many times I tried to explain to him that it wasn't the aircraft carrier driver's fault, Ethan always heaped the full force of his hatred on that poor helmsman, whoever he was. He craved a target for his anger.

"We're almost there, guys," I said. "Let's just remember to take turns talking to Daddy."

The VTC technician warned us there would be a couple-second delay in the audio and video feed, which she thought might confuse the kids. But it wasn't the kids I was worried about; I was far jumpier than I had anticipated. It had been such a long recovery since

Scott walked out the door that dark morning in November. I'd been feeling shaky since first hearing about the VTC, as if Scott had taken a step toward us only to back away again. But it was easy to push those anxieties away as my excitement at seeing him carried me forward. I spent so much time wondering about his life on the boat and how he coped. His e-mails to me were frequent, loving, and supportive but very short—just a few lines at most. Whenever I asked how he was doing, he simply said he was tired.

In times of stress, poetry has always helped me make sense of my situation, so I turned to my old standby to get a feeling for Scott's experience. I found *Here, Bullet*, a collection penned by one of the first warrior-writers of the Iraq war, an infantryman named Brian Turner. He didn't let me down:

> *At seven thousand feet and looking back, running lights*
> *blacked out under the wings and America waiting,*
> *a year of my life disappears at midnight,*
> *the sky a deep viridian, the houselights below*
> *small as match heads burned down to embers.*

Scott and his squadron mates were flying six-to-seven-hour missions nearly every night around that time, logging so many hours above the norm that they required written waivers and interviews with the air wing flight surgeons. I reread that poem, "Night in Blue," whenever I thought Scott might be in the air. I especially liked the middle section, because I remember how long it took for Scott to explain to me his impressions of the war after he flew in it the first time in 2003 and how disjointed and difficult those conversations were for him.

> *. . . What do I know*
> *of redemption or sacrifice, what will I have*
> *to say of the dead—that it was worth it,*

that any of it made sense?
I have no words to speak of war.

I knew the VTC would usher in no great revelations and no talk of war, especially. I wasn't quite sure what I would say. Life during deployment mirrored the enjambment of Turner's poem as events, impressions, thoughts, and questions ran from line to line, day to day, without a break or even a cue for a breath. None of that mattered, of course. I just wanted to see how Scott looked and watch him smile as he took in the kids' antics.

D addy, come out of the TV," Esther shouted as she ran into the conference room. Scott's face hovered on a monitor across the room. My heart leaped as it had on our first date, when I opened the door and saw him standing there, patiently waiting for us to begin the rest of our lives together. We seated ourselves around the conference table. The kids and I spotted ourselves in the picture-in-picture screen on the monitor, so we knew Scott could see us. There was the smile I'd been waiting for. He looked so handsome in his desert flight suit, though he seemed thinner and had more gray hair, especially around his temples. But he seemed in great spirits, and he reconnected with Ethan and Esther immediately as they scrambled to exhibit their special things.

"Daddy, watch! Daddy, watch!" They overlapped each other as Ethan plucked away on the violin, then hurriedly put it down, picked up a pen, and wrote his own name while Scott *ooh*ed and *aah*ed. In the months since Scott left, Ethan, then four and a half, had begun reading and writing, and he was excited to show off. He threw down the pen and grabbed his planet puzzle, frantic to fit it together under Scott's approving gaze and within the time constraint.

"Daddy, watch! Daddy, watch!" Esther, then two and a half,

sank deep into her seat so she could prop up and display her new black patent-leather shoes on the conference table. Then she stood on the chair and pulled down her tights to show Scott her "big-girl underwear."

At minute eight, the kids finally calmed down and turned to other curiosities in the room, examining the microphone and leaving Scott and me a moment to connect. We forgot our own rules, mistaking the delay for real-time pauses, talking over each other, then giggling and both insisting, "No, you go ahead," at the same time. It didn't matter. There was nothing we had to say that we hadn't already said in scores of e-mails, dozens of letters, and a few static-laden phone calls.

The VTC coordinator cracked open the door to the conference room. Even the kids knew what that meant.

"Daddy, come out of the TV! Now!" Esther insisted, a new urgency aflame in her tone.

"I can't, baby," he said sadly.

"We just got our one-minute warning," I told Scott.

Esther jumped out of her chair and ran toward the monitor. She wrapped her arms around it, pressed her cheek to the screen, and closed her eyes.

"Esther, where'd you go?" Scott called out. "I can't see you anymore."

"She's hugging you," I said.

24

Pancakes and Ice Cream

Mommy?"

"Yes, my love?"

Ethan, Esther, and I were driving around town a few weeks after the VTC. Both of them had been so happy since then. It was as if seeing Scott on the monitor had reassured them that he still existed even if we couldn't see him every day. I was relieved that our family had somehow healed itself. Four months remained until his return.

"What is our real home?" Ethan asked.

"What do you mean?"

"Is our real home Washington, D.C., and our pretend home Anacortes?"

"They're both your real homes," I punted. "You're lucky. You have two homes. Most people have just one."

"No," he said slowly. "I think Washington, D.C., is my real home."

"Why?"

"Daddy was there with us. Daddy is not with us at our Anacortes home. So it's our pretend home."

I know that nostalgia makes some places seem idyllic beyond logic or recognition, but the kids had been doing so beautifully that I didn't want to say too much in either direction or do anything to tip the balance we had finally achieved. The conversation unsettled me, though. It felt too early for Ethan to debate the abstract idea of home. He was too young to feel out of place. Even I hadn't figured it out. Far from it. Around that same time, I frequently recalled a comment Maya Angelou had made during an interview on a PBS program. "You can't leave home," she said. "You just take it and rearrange it."

That statement seemed to crystallize my aspirations in Anacortes: rearrange what home meant to me, so I could offer my kids the richest foundation for life I could possibly give them. It was rocky, arid soil, compared with what I grew up on in the old world of daddies who packed their children's school lunches the night before, carpooled every morning, walked in the door every night at five-thirty, and sat down for a family dinner at six-thirty. My past took place not on another coast but in another culture altogether.

"Home can be two places," I repeated to my son. It was a weak response to a profound question. Ethan had a right to whatever comforting thoughts his old house held for him—he was only four and a half, after all—but the idea of home is so troubling in a military context. Some of the Navy kids I knew had moved ten or eleven times already. I wasn't sure how many relocations our future held or how old Ethan would be when Scott retired and we settled in one place. I was already worried about how to tell Ethan that his new best friend, a little boy he bonded with after Martina's son Ronan moved away, was about to leave; his dad had received orders to a base in California.

It was one of many times in our life as a military family that I came up blank. *What would* The Navy Wife *say about this,* I wondered. As we pulled into our driveway, I remembered words of advice that BobbiJo, my favorite Army wife, had passed along during our very first phone call. "Unrealistic expectations will sabotage you," she stressed. "Life doesn't have to be perfect. Pancakes and ice cream for dinner is not a bad thing." So I ushered the kids inside, sat them down at the kitchen table, and reached for the Bisquick.

25

Rock Bottom

H ey, hon!"

My heart still fluttered when I heard Scott's voice on the phone. To make sure I never missed a call, I took my cell into the bathroom, the garage, the backyard, and everywhere else. On that particular day, my compulsion had paid off.

"Where are you, sweetie?" I always liked to picture Scott talking to me.

"We pulled into Jebel Ali last night," he said. The boat had just begun its four-day port call, the second of four scheduled breaks during deployment. Dubai is one of the principalities that constitute the United Arab Emirates, and the central city is renowned for its progressive and cosmopolitan atmosphere. Everyone on the boat loved it. Scott said you could walk down the street amid skyscrapers, Western-style restaurants, and luxury malls (one of which featured an indoor ski slope) and feel like you were in New York City.

I liked it because Scott called every day when the boat was in port.

"How's everything going so far?"

"Great," he said, enthusiastically. "The squadron really needed this. Everyone is exhausted. For me, it's still work, but it's nothing like last time."

During the previous port call, Scott had been tapped as the Senior Shore Patrol officer, which meant he was responsible for dealing with any trouble from the ship and air wing's five thousand sailors, the majority of whom were eighteen to twenty-one years old. They'd been cooped up on the boat for months with no days off, no alcohol, and no fun whatsoever, so Senior Shore Patrol was a job fraught with extra-special levels of difficulty. Scott slept far fewer hours per night on Senior Shore Patrol duty than he did flying on the boat.

"Tell me more about your first taste of freedom."

"Well, you know me," he said. "I would have been perfectly happy in solitary confinement. I got that new book you sent me and those DVDs, and I was looking forward to a few hours on my own. But some of the junior officers wanted to see the city, and since I got to know my way around last time, they asked me to come with them."

"So you had to play tour guide?" It was strange to think that Scott knew enough about Dubai to show others around—just one of many times I marveled at how different our lives were. We had so many adventures, so many new and transformative experiences, on our own.

"Yeah, but this place is fascinating, so I didn't mind. I took them to the Irish Village for drinks and burgers. A few of the guys sat in the courtyard, and they met some girls from Dublin who live here. One of my single guys fell for one of them, so he begged me to drive everybody to a disco. That's how we ended up at Rock Bottom."

"What's that?"

"A dance bar, that sort of place. We all went to help one guy hook up. You know, we have to provide wingmen for support. Unfortunately for him, nothing panned out in the romance department. So there I am, dancing with her friends, these three Irish girls, and one says to me, 'Are you married?' Of course I said yes. 'Don't you miss your wife?' she asked. I said, 'More than you could ever imagine.' Then she wandered off. I guess it was a bad pickup line." He laughed.

It was a great pickup line as far as I was concerned, but the truth is I stopped hearing anything after "So there I am, dancing with these three Irish girls."

So this is what jealousy feels like, I mused, once tsunami-force waves of irrational rage had subsided.

"Tell me more about those Irish girls," I said carefully.

"They were—" he stopped himself, picking up on my tone. "Honey! Don't tell me you're jealous."

"A little," I conceded. And then it passed as quickly as it came. I realized how ridiculous I sounded; after all, Scott didn't want to be apart any more than I did. "I can't remember the last time I danced with you, and here are three girls you're boogying on down the road with." I did allow myself to whine. It merited a whine.

"You can be mad I spent the evening with strangers I care nothing about, and not you," he allowed. "That's fine. But don't be jealous of those girls. I'm perhaps the worst possible target for the single females in town. I'm a complete waste of time."

I trust Scott completely. I have since the moment we met. So when he asked, the night before he deployed, if it would be all right to leave his wedding ring at home, I didn't hesitate. (Safety regulations prohibit aviators from flying with jewelry, and he worried about losing his ring every time he took it off.) Together, we placed it in my jewelry box, next to my charm bracelet, for a cruise-long slumber. I didn't give it a second thought. It's hard to imagine spending as much time apart as we did—with trainings, detachments, and deployments—if one didn't have complete faith in one's spouse.

But it's not just a question of whether service members have opportunities for diversions. During Scott's workups and deployment I saw how easy it would be for married couples to become estranged in a dozen different ways. After all, we spent more time apart than together. I worked hard to keep him up to date, though I did keep some things to myself—like the occasional visits from Gone Mom, when I found myself watching the kids' mouths move without processing the words. I didn't tell Scott about the day I discovered the kids were eating with chopsticks because I had been too tired to unload the dishwasher and no clean flatware remained in the drawer.

Overall, though, I probably went overboard conveying the details of our day-to-day lives to Scott. I transcribed many of the kids' conversations, mailed him our neighborhood newsletter, even forwarded all forty-nine Christmas cards we received that year. Perhaps some of these special efforts were motivated by articles I'd come across since marrying into the military, like one Army study showing that the number of active-duty officers and soldiers getting divorced rose sharply with deployments to Afghanistan and Iraq. In one two-year period toward the start of the war, Army officers' divorce rates were up seventy-eight percent. At that time, Army officials blamed the combined stress of combat, long separations, and difficulty readjusting to family life as key reasons for the surge in divorce rates, which has not been replicated in any study since then.

The stresses on deployed service members can certainly be extreme. Though Army deployments differ substantially from Navy deployments, and there is no way to translate those findings to our community, these data set off a mental alarm that I couldn't ignore. There is no shortage of stories about the joys of a port call, after all. Women in ports are the stuff of legend.

What kept us going is that we both knew home port was the ultimate stop. I woke up every day with the best attitude I could muster (though sometimes *best* was simply *not horrible*) because I wanted to give Scott someplace wonderful (though sometimes *wonderful* was simply *intact*) to pull into. He never asked me to, and that's exactly why I worked so hard at it.

26

A Draft of the Heart

As our squadron reached the deployment's halfway point, we commemorated the milestone with several events, including a pizza and bowling party and a bus trip to Seattle. These celebrations lifted our spirits at a time moods plunged low.

Our squadron's officer wives also scheduled an evening out to toast how far we'd come. We met at a restaurant in town. When I arrived, our twelve spouses were already seated around two leather couches at the bar, relaxed and friendly. I'd grown to think of many of them as my little sisters, and I worried about them just as I fretted over my own siblings. I knew whose cysts required biopsies, whose husbands weren't e-mailing often enough, whose diabetic cat had only days to live. The wives worried about each other too, calling me if a fellow spouse seemed depressed or worn out. Though they never looked to me to solve their problems for them, they often included me in the discussion, which I appreciated. From a scattering of stars, we'd gradually knit ourselves into a constellation, transmitting a pattern of light and meaning through our closeness and cooperation.

Even Amber had begun to let me in a little. She had called one night earlier in the deployment to tell me she had suffered a miscarriage. No one except her husband had known she was pregnant, she said. The miscarriage, which had struck at the end of her first trimester, was her sixth.

"I'm just glad I didn't get sepsis this time," she said. Her voice sounded hoarse, either from crying or from exhaustion. "I had to call an ambulance when Peter was deployed before, and I lost the baby. I was out cold by the time the EMTs arrived."

Amber and I spent an hour on the phone that dark winter evening. All she wanted, she said, was a baby. She thought about babies all day and dreamed of babies all night. I felt terrible for her. Though I had delivered Ethan without my husband present, I couldn't imagine losing a baby without my husband present. So I listened as sympathetically as I could, hoping the two of us could start fresh. But I had a hard time feeling that our relationship was built on mutual trust. Something about her predatory glance during the Dining Out still chilled me.

The spouses' warm smiles from the couch assured me that on this night, at least on the surface, all was well. The large glasses of Champagne in front of them glittered like seas of diamonds. My own drink was gone before I could even recall its taste on my tongue. Maybe that's why I stumbled into a discussion of politics. Amber just happened to be perched next to me.

"I mean, they're never ever home, and it's an election year; you'd think we would be talking about candidates and who stands for what," I sputtered. "It matters to us most of all. Why don't we ever discuss the issues?"

Amber had a two-glass head start, so we weren't exactly walking parallel paths in the conversation.

"I know," she said, nodding so vigorously the chopsticks in her chignon nearly clattered to the ground. Officer wives tend to agree aggressively. "I don't care if Peter deploys six more times, the military needs him more than I do."

I sobered up fast, quickly grasping the wisdom of not talking about current events. I flashed back to Isabelle's observation that political differences might shatter our fragile community. In this crowd, politics is so personal that it seems we must talk about it— until we do, when it becomes clear that it's too personal to talk about at all. The next day, I called Martina.

"I *hope* you didn't let them tell you, 'Hooray, you're halfway there, you're almost done,'" she mimicked.

"Yeah, that's what they said," I admitted. Actually, we all said it. It's axiomatic among military spouses, who regularly transform lemons into lemon meringue pie: Halfway is nearly there. Halfway is when you start trying on outfits for homecoming. Halfway is when you landscape the yard. Halfway is when you struggle to shed that last five pounds. It's the only deployment-related milestone of any consequence, and we cling to it like a newborn to the breast.

"Halfway is *not* almost there. Don't fall for that crap."

"Oh, I know. Sometimes it feels like we have a million years to go. Actually, four months is a million years, isn't it?"

"Of course it is," she said. "I wanted to punch every single person who told me that when McGowan was on his IA."

"Well, I didn't punch anybody," I said, replaying for her my conversation with Amber.

"At least you're not a house divided," she responded. "McGowan and I go round and round on politics. He won't admit it, but I know he tells himself, 'Somebody's got to do this job, it might as well be me.' I know he thinks the sacrifice the kids and I make is worth it. Just the other day, I said to him, 'I know the Navy is number one for you.'"

"What did he say?"

"Oh, he denied it. But I told him, 'You choose it every time. You choose to stay in the Navy, which means you choose to leave us. What other message is there?'"

"And?"

"He said, 'My family is the most important to me.' But I know him. He believes in all those ideas, in truth, in freedom, justice, democracy, all that lofty stuff. I tell him I don't give a shit about any of that. I just want him home with our family."

There it was. Martina, my teacher once more, laid bare the thought I'd been playing whack-a-mole with from the moment the tour began. Every time it popped up, I slammed it down again.

Perhaps conflict between family life and a service career is inevitable. As one sociologist has written, both the family and the military are "greedy institutions," competing for the loyalty and commitment of its members. But I didn't want to believe that military service was for other people and not us. We weren't better, or smarter, or more capable than anyone else, and if we were, that just meant the military needed us even more. I couldn't think of an organization more complicated than the military, tasked with a more relentlessly difficult job (in peacetime *and* wartime), or in greater need of critical thinkers. I couldn't think of a group that conferred better opportunities upon high school graduates with no money for college, or families without health insurance, or small-town inhabitants with few job prospects.

Still—why the hell would someone with other good options, like my husband, choose military service? Many curious and well-meaning relatives, friends, and acquaintances asked us this question. I glow with embarrassment when I remember that I myself quizzed Scott on it numerous times when we first started dating. Only now can I appreciate the superhuman level of patience it required for him to explain, rationalize, and defend his choices. Now it seems crazy to me. Why should he have to defend his choice to voluntarily work on behalf of his country? This strange dichotomy points to the severity of the cultural chasm separating America's military and civilian communities. That's why, nerd that I am, I did a happy dance when I found *AWOL: The Unexcused Absence of America's Upper Classes from Military Service—and How It Hurts Our Country*. "The last draft in America is a draft of the heart," the authors write, pointing out the way that spouses, parents, and grandparents are drawn as unexpectedly as I was into the extended military family when a loved one volunteers for service.

Though the military is consistently cited in Gallup polls as the institution in which Americans express the greatest level of confidence, Gallup also reports that barely a majority of Americans would support their child's decision to enter the military; a "substantial proportion" would suggest their child try a different occupation. Similarly, studies from the aptly named Project on the Gap Between the Military and American Society found that leaders in the larger society were four or five times more likely than military leaders to say that they would be "disappointed if a child of mine joined the military."

This finding is certainly in line with my own experience. When my mother first heard that my new boyfriend Scott was a Navy pilot, she urged me to log on to JDate and update my photo.

College-age children are heeding their elders' wishes as well as their own desires. In 1956, 400 out of 750 in Princeton's graduating class entered military service. In 2004, Princeton led the Ivy League in the number of graduates entering the service with nine members. In 1956, 1,100 Stanford students enrolled in ROTC; today there are 29, and all are trained off-campus, earning no credit hours from Stanford, as *AWOL* notes.

Statistics like these are just snapshots. They are sometimes useful, sometimes misleading, and can often muddy an observation that's already as clear as the ice-blue water of a swimming pool. I knew the truth of the situation simply by looking around. You don't need to observe with the acuity of a novelist to register the shade of someone's skin, the number of tattoos inked across their back, or the language a sailor speaks among friends. Military service, or the lack of it, has become a class issue, or it is perceived to be one, which is in effect the same thing.

On that tour, my civics lesson was ongoing, my citizenship

skills continually challenged. But the bottom line was the same. I'd screamed the identical words into my pillow, late at night, as Martina had just said out loud: *I just want him home. Nothing else matters.*

Was Martina my personal Greek chorus, giving voice to secrets that shamed me into silence? Was she my bad angel? Was she still, as I believed early on, my teacher?

I dog-paddled in the gulf between "I don't care if he deploys six more times, they need him more than I do" and "I don't give a shit about any of that, I just want him home." Neither shore seemed reachable. Neither seemed desirable. But I had endless time—alone, as usual—to find my way.

27

The Happy Family Photo

Mom!"

That was Esther. From the moment she turned three that spring, she never spoke if she could shout, never walked if she could run. She formed quick opinions about the clothes she wore, the food she ate, the outings we took. And five months into the deployment she discovered that she too had something important to say about it.

"Yes, little love?"

"I want Daddy!"

I polished off the usual reassurances—the ones I'd been reciting for months to Ethan—and prepared to make them sound shiny and new all over again. Maybe this time they would even work. But then, to my surprise, Ethan put down his Lincoln Logs, walked over to Esther, and gave her a hug.

"You miss Daddy?" he said soothingly to her, more like a father than an older brother. He was about to turn five and had been testing out a certain gravitas as the big day approached, but I had never expected this.

"Yeah," she whined, snuggling into his embrace.

"You know what to do if you're sad about Daddy leaving?" he asked.

"What?"

"You just look at a picture of Daddy and you feel better. Want to try it?"

"Yeah."

I remained half hidden in the kitchen while Ethan took his little sister by the hand and led her to the cabinet that holds our photo albums. Together, they sat down on the floor and pulled out album after album, paging through them in the most wildly destructive way possible as they assigned each photo its own hilarious caption. I wished I had had a pen to record their words, but I was frozen, afraid to move and interrupt the scene unfolding in front of me.

If Ethan comforted Esther over Scott's absence, I thought, he must be faring pretty well himself. He must have landed in a solid place emotionally. He must have overcome the hardest part. He must have emerged from this trauma intact. *Right?* I kept asking myself. *Right?*

I had never explained to Ethan that my own brand of coping during the deployment relied heavily on staring at family photos, but any visitor to our house probably guessed it immediately. Or simply assumed that I was the biggest narcissist in Anacortes.

Where gazing at Flat Daddy in his flight suit failed to soothe and listening to Flat Daddy's voice sent me diving for cover—where watching family videos ripped open old wounds and left the kids and me aching for days—family photos placed around the house created a soothing, comforting background that healed us so slowly, so quietly, that for months I barely even registered their power.

One picture became emblematic of the deployment, a photo snapped during a previous fly-in. Perhaps the memory of that happy reunion gave me the hope I needed to move forward each day. It was taken by my friend K.C., a former Navy wife now in her early sixties, who became a photojournalist during her husband's many tours abroad. Now that the family had retired to Whidbey, K.C. offered her services to squadrons at an embarrassingly low fee because, she said, it was the least she could do to pay the Navy back for years of adventures. Besides, she said, she couldn't pass up a homecoming. A fellow softie, her eyes welled up at the thought of families embracing on the flight line.

So she showed up at one of our previous fly-ins, following an unusually long set of workups the August before deployment. That brilliant summer day promised great riches: The sky was Tiffany-box blue, and there was no end to it. Scott climbed down from the cockpit and embraced the kids and me. In the picture he is holding Ethan; I'm standing next to him, grasping Esther between us, and she's gazing up at her dad with pure joy in her eyes. We're all smiling real smiles, radiating happiness, shining like the sun.

I printed a copy of it when K.C. e-mailed me the photos she took that day, and I sent it with Scott when he deployed. But after he left, I made another print—a big one—and I hung it up on the wall opposite my bed. The first thing I saw when I opened my eyes each morning, it made me feel better instantly. So I made another print, also a big one, and placed it on the hall table between my room and the family room, so I could look at it as I walked into the main part of the house. I imagined that Scott held my hand as I started each day. I couldn't help but notice that the family room, where I spent most of my time, remained bare. So I made another print, medium size, and framed it for one of the shelves next to the fireplace. *There,* I thought. *That's better.*

That led me to the kitchen: another print, another frame. I leaned that one behind the sink, so I could gaze at it as I washed dishes or prepared dinner. Since I was on an ordering binge anyway,

I printed up another one for the refrigerator, and I placed it low, so the kids could touch it.

The kids! I ordered a few more pictures. I framed the family shot and centered it on the wall separating Ethan and Esther's bedrooms so they could start their day with it too. That left just the office. *Well, I've gone this far,* I thought, as I ordered two more copies. That one landed on top of Scott's desk. For good measure I pinned one to the bulletin board too.

I've heard that one of the beautiful things about aging, for women especially, is that you stop caring about what others think. Sure, eight copies of the exact same family photo placed strategically around the house is extreme. I get that. I understand that my decorating style won't land me on the pages of *House Beautiful.* But my Happy Family photo sheltered me from the storm, and I craved shelter more than ever.

28

COWs and Other Mammals

As Anacortes thawed out after a long winter, I looked for the one inarguable sign that spring was approaching: the status of the board in front of Island Adventure, a whale-watching outfit based on Commercial Avenue. "Gray whale spotted today," the board read one afternoon in early March. At the end of March, the sign boasted a half-dozen whale sightings; by the time tulips blanketed the Skagit Valley, Island Adventure began to guarantee its tours; and when school let out for summer, the parking lot teemed with eager whale watchers.

But in late March, when Scott's change of command took place on the boat and he assumed the role of commanding officer of the squadron, the talk among our squadron wives was not of whales. We spoke, instead, of cows. COWs, that is, because apparently I was to become one soon. In the shorthand-obsessed military, the term "commanding officer's wife" was affectionately abbreviated with the acronym COW.

Other squadrons celebrate their incoming COW with great pomp and circumstance. I'd heard of COW parties in which the new skipper's wife dressed up in a cow costume for the duration of the celebration, and I'd spotted more than a few front yards decked out with cow-themed items. Our squadron was a bit more low-key. I received a few funny cards from our wives ("Herd there's a new cow in town" was a favorite line), cow-shaped cookies, and cow baskets filled with goodies. I woke up one morning to plastic cows grazing on my lawn. But although I appreciated the thoughtfulness, care, and camaraderie, I'd long disdained the COW-party phenomenon. Like many other traditions among Navy spouses that might seem ridiculous to outside observers, it is just impossible to understand until you are on the inside. Halfway through our command tour, I was still groping around blindly.

"Did you see Ronnie's yard?" I had asked Millie, just a few weeks earlier. Ronnie's husband had just assumed command of their squadron.

"Was it COW-tastic?" Millie asked, smiling. She perched on a counter stool at my kitchen island, where we were planning our participation in a base-wide fund-raiser on behalf of college scholarships for military kids.

Millie and I had begun to work together on a few projects, baby steps toward a recovery from our rocky getting-acquainted dinner. I began to think that she was right: she did appear to be a normal person when it came to anything other than Aggie football. She had provided thoughtful advice on how to squelch the simmering bitchery between two squadron spouses and had accompanied me to visit a colleague with a child in the hospital. Determined to show me some fun, she even drafted me into her monthly poker game, though I warned her beforehand that I hadn't flipped over a playing card since losing at Go Fish in third grade. But we were still feeling each other out.

"I found it embarrassing," I admitted. "It just looked silly, all that cow stuff everywhere. I can't believe she was happy about it."

"That was nothing. You need to knock down the door of a few COW parties," Millie said. "I've been to some that would peel your socks off your feet, literally. The wives changed into cow-patterned stockings as soon as they walked through the door."

"I just don't get why the wives are being congratulated on their husband's promotion," I complained. The thought of COW parties always put me in an irritable mood. "I've had very little to do with Scott getting to this point in the Navy. He worked hard to be successful long before I met him. It all just seems very retro to me."

Before she spoke, Millie glanced down for a moment, a gesture I would become familiar with during the next year and a half. I would come to look forward to it, the flash of insight following a few beats of silence.

"I think it's exactly the opposite of retro," she said, looking up. "You know how hard you work for the squadron. Some of these CO wives have been giving it their all for the last sixteen, seventeen years. They've put up with a lot, I can promise you that. These gals used to do all the work without anybody thanking them. Now at least they get the recognition they deserve. Their husbands may not even appreciate them, but the women they're on the phone with every night sure do."

Point taken. "But does it have to involve a cow costume?" I pleaded.

"Well, that's just plain ol' fun," Millie laughed, her southern twang plucked straight from an old country-music record. Every once in a while, when she decided I was a lost cause, she played hillbilly and ended the conversation.

For naval aviators, taking command of a squadron is the hallmark of success capping a career that has lasted nearly two decades. For the commander and his or her family, it's a big deal. COs almost universally describe command as the most rewarding tour of their entire careers, and most are very reluctant to relinquish command when the assignment has been completed. Afterward, many begin Pentagon or major staff tours. This transition can be tough, as a commander at the Pentagon typically wields far less influence than the skipper who controls the daily lives of sailors. It's difficult to go from being the boss who makes life-altering decisions to assuming a position where selecting fonts for PowerPoint slides could dominate the day's events.

While in command, the CO has a remarkable degree of authority over the squadron itself (roughly two hundred sailors and officers in our case) and also helps shape events in the air wing (nearly two thousand sailors and officers) when at sea. If an officer eyes command of a larger unit (such as an air wing, a base, or the aircraft carrier itself) or hungers for an admiral's star, a successful squadron command tour is an essential first step.

When the squadron is at home, the change-of-command ceremony is a meticulously planned formal event, laden with meaningful naval traditions. I've attended changes of command for Scott's colleagues when I could because attendance is viewed as a supportive, collegial gesture, and it's fun to watch friends achieve their dreams. During the ceremony, the outgoing CO sits atop a dais festooned with patriotic bunting, surrounded by a sea of flags. The incoming executive officer typically serves as ceremonial commander of the troops, calling out orders to stand at attention for appropriate segments of the ceremony. The entire crew, in dress uniforms, stands behind the guests to witness the transition. Guests are seated in hundreds of folding chairs, with the commander's spouse and family members—who may have flown in from all over the country for the ceremony and congratulatory parties— gathered in the front row.

A chill runs up my spine during every change-of-command ceremony as the transfer of authority takes place and the incoming CO reads the official orders to the assembled guests. As with many naval ceremonies, the proceedings are scripted. After principals exchange salutes, the new CO steps up to the podium. "Troops, at ease," he or she immediately says, and even the guests in the front row can hear the sailors in the back relax their posture and exhale. There's electricity in the room, a sense that something new is in the air. Slates are wiped clean; it's a fresh start for everyone. There's a new sheriff in town.

From the start of my life as a military wife, change-of-command ceremonies were field lectures in my ongoing citizenship class. As all of the players on stage shift their roles, either assuming or relinquishing power, I can see clearly how individuals fit into squadron operations. When the guest speaker, often a senior officer in the chain of command, takes his place at the podium, it's apparent how the squadron's role fits into overall naval operations. As the band marches across the hangar, playing "The Star-Spangled Banner," and guests hold their hands over their hearts, I understand what purpose the Navy serves in America's understanding of the military—which, like medieval legends, is part myth, part reality. For once, the mythology and the reality coexist. The characters, setting, plot, and theme—sailor, squadron, Navy, country—all fit together.

The part that really thrills me, though, comes at the end of the ceremony. All faces turn to one of the airplanes in the hangar. A sailor standing by the jet pulls a string that's holding in place a large piece of paper taped under the cockpit. The paper floats to the ground. Under it, painted on the canopy rail, is the name of the new CO.

"That's your favorite part?" Scott asked, genuinely puzzled. He called from the carrier a few hours after his change-of-command ceremony had taken place to let me know that everything had gone smoothly.

"It's just so dramatic," I said. "You know I'm a sucker for the big gesture."

"I do know that," he said.

"So how did the day go?" I asked. I was disappointed I didn't get to witness Scott's ceremony, but from his earliest days in the squadron he knew he would have a bare-bones change of command at sea. This suited him fine. Being the center of attention always made him uncomfortable, and he had become especially disenchanted with the elaborate after-parties that had become de rigueur at our base.

"I think we set a new record. Seventeen minutes, start to finish."

"Wow. You must have been thrilled."

"I was," Scott said. "It was great. We did what we had to do, it was done, and we got on with our flying. I couldn't have asked for more."

"Nothing more?"

"Well, you, of course," he quickly amended.

"All I need is an invitation," I teased.

Living on the boat with Scott was an outlandish idea but not as outlandish as I had once thought. Although Navy regulations that went into effect beginning in 1802 forbade U.S. ships of war to carry women to sea or to house them on board, there were some exceptions allowed, and commanding officers did occasionally take wives or female relatives to sea with them throughout the early days of the republic.

Documents housed at the Naval Historical Center illuminate the case of one of many Navy families that traveled together: the wife and daughter of Daniel Todd Patterson, commodore of the USS *United States*, remained on board throughout the boat's 1832–1833 Mediterranean cruise. The Patterson ladies' presence was chronicled by one Midshipman Stuyvesant Fish, who wrote irritably: "The females have been already wished home a thousand times by every officer, as they have already given difficulty and will cause, eventually, the cruise to be disagreeable. They rule when the ship is to sail, already."

During the nineteenth century, several other cases of wives and female relatives on board naval ships were chronicled with disaffection by sailors. Births on board Navy ships were also recorded in journals of the period, because although regulations forbade carrying women to sea, women were allowed to come aboard when a ship was in port and sail back to the United States if a marriage had taken place abroad. If an American sailor married a local woman when the ship was in port, as happened frequently on the U.S. Navy's many Mediterranean tours throughout the 1800s, there was usually a christening at sea nine months later.

A captain's wife or female relative would never be allowed on a naval cruise now, though of course thousands of female sailors serve on Navy ships alongside male peers. After a 1978 court ruling, women began assignments on selected noncombatant ships, and another court ruling in 1993 repealed the combat exclusion law. In today's Navy, all communities are open to women with the exception of submarines and SEALs. But husbands and wives are not allowed to serve together in the same deployable Navy unit, and strict policies on fraternization discourage romantic relationships between sailors. The majority of sailors are single and between eighteen and twenty-four years old, however, and life can get lonely on cruise. Romantic relationships do develop, and sometimes nature takes its course.

Not all sailors stumble into pregnancy accidentally. Pregnancy is a surefire way to avoid going on cruise or to end a deployment, since pregnant women are prohibited from Navy ships. The environment simply presents too many hazards, and the Navy has dealt with that particular liability with a no-exceptions-allowed ruling. A few pregnancies—perhaps unplanned, perhaps not—can be expected among female sailors in the month before a squadron is deployed. For many, it's not about shirking responsibility; it's a simple case of logistical overload. For these female sailors and officers whose husbands are also in the military, and who may have other children at home, child-care requirements in the face of dual deployments can become simply unworkable.

"I can't see any other way around it," my friend Hallie confessed. She's the only military officer I've ever known who admitted to planning her pregnancy to avoid a deployment. I met her at a neighborhood park one lazy Saturday afternoon a few weeks after we moved to Anacortes, and we tried to coordinate our visits to the swings every weekend after that. I was immediately intrigued by the contrast between her quiet manner and her decidedly unquiet lifestyle as a Navy jet pilot. With a toddler and a five-year-old at home and a husband also scheduled to deploy soon, the couple decided it made more sense to have another baby—avoiding Hallie's deployment and assuring her of a desk job on base—than farm the kids out separately to relatives during the time they'd both be at sea.

Hallie knew that it was not an ideal solution, and she planned to retire from the Navy as soon as she could. But she held out hope, year after year, that armed forces administrators would find a creative way to help dual-military couples with children navigate their way through their careers. She'd fought too hard to join the Navy to give up without exhausting all of her options.

"My mom pushed me into joining the Navy," Hallie was fond of saying, "by telling me not to do it."

Hallie grew up in a military home. Her dad was an Air Force pilot who flew in Vietnam, but he retired when she was still young, and she spent most of her childhood and adolescence in Hawaii while her father started his second career as a civilian program officer at Pearl Harbor. Her mother, an old-school Navy wife who could have written any one of the books in my collection, hosted white-gloved teas as competently as she tutored her daughter in womanly wiles. Most of all, she urged Hallie to marry a naval officer.

"But I didn't want to marry one," Hallie recalled. "I wanted to be one."

Her mother wouldn't hear of it, and her father couldn't imagine how a female aviator would handle a crisis in the air. Hallie took her future into her own hands when she signed up for ROTC in college. I imagine her then, ten years younger, her green eyes flashing and her black bangs brushed back in a barrette, as she arrived home wearing her first flight suit.

She married a fellow officer she met at her first posting. They both loved to fly, but they weren't in the same squadron or even deployed on the same boat, since spouses are prohibited from serving together. Scribbles on their calendars detailed two competing sets of trainings, deployments, detachments, and long hours, with ever-increasing levels of responsibility as each was promoted. These stress-inducing squares promised nothing but separation. Five years of difficult child-care arrangements wore Hallie out and weakened her resolve to stay in the Navy.

Analytical to the core, she had memorized statistics that kept her going. There are 50,000 women in the Navy, she told me, serious and thoughtful, as we waited for our kids at the bottom of the slide. Nearly half the women in the military are married to other service members. And despite the all-too-real nightmare of dual deployments, women today weren't going to give up the chance to have kids, she believed, as earlier generations of female service members had.

"They've got to come up with a solution to this problem," Hallie insisted, as if I were the one who needed convincing. *They* were Big Navy, those who set regulations and policies in place, and it went without saying that we held no sway over Big Navy. Hallie understood that the government spent too much money on her flight training to make opting out a comfortable solution. That made it a moral as well as a logistical issue—a public as well as a private burden.

Other women in the Navy made different choices. Octavia, a pilot in my book club who was married to another pilot, employed a full-time live-in nanny to help coordinate care for their two young girls. A few days after her husband, Liam, deployed for eight months—his second long cruise during their time at Whidbey—she answered a phone call and was informed that a job at CENTCOM headquarters in Tampa, Florida, awaited her.

"Either I take it, or I don't advance any further," she explained to our book club one cold winter night. Octavia's open, trusting manner drew people to her, and the rest of us, perched on the couch or sitting on the floor, leaned forward. "There's no choice, really," she said, palms up. "I'm taking the kids. We're packing out next month. Liam will move into bachelor quarters on base when his deployment ends, and he'll live there for the rest of his tour. We'll be apart for another year after this. Hopefully his next posting will be somewhere on the East Coast, but I really don't know."

Hallie and Octavia stood out among the other military spouses in my orbit. As naval officers committed to their careers as well as their family, they struggled with a completely different set of challenges, more complicated than I could wrap my brain around. We all called ourselves Navy wives, but my problems paled in comparison with theirs, as they contemplated abandoning careers they loved for the families they loved.

When our book club meets now, I remember Octavia, palms up, as she prepared to move her family across the country, unsure of when she and the kids would live with her husband again. And whenever I pass a swing set, I think of Hallie, pushing her kids higher and higher in a cloudless sky, green eyes flashing, and dreaming of flight.

29

Everyday Fantasies

Dubai. The boat's second-to-last port call in the Middle East. Three months to go.

"If someone could look into my heart, they would just laugh," I told Scott when he called. He was able to phone every day while in Dubai, so we covered more than just the basics: the kids, the squadron, the still-sketchy homecoming details.

"Why?" he asked. I sensed he was in a contemplative mood, or maybe just lonely.

"Most people have big dreams, like vacations they want to go on or houses they want to buy. You know what I've been dreaming of?"

"What?"

"It's pathetic. Don't make fun of me."

"What?"

"I have these fantasies of you and me and the kids on a Saturday morning years from now, the kids wearing soccer uniforms, as we go grocery shopping together after the big game. A completely normal, unremarkable day. Or the four of us sitting around a table at a restaurant, sampling from each other's meals. Reading out loud our fortune-cookie messages and laughing. Just the most ordinary things."

There was a pause.

"Me, too," he said, surprising me.

"What do you mean?"

"I can't think of anything better than the kids climbing into bed with us on a weekend morning, just hanging out, watching cartoons in bed. When I'm back in my room alone after one of these incredibly long days, I think about it obsessively. Or giving the kids their baths at night. I never enjoyed doing it when I was home, but now that I'm so far away, all I want to do is watch them splash each other in the tub. And comb Esther's hair afterward. Remember how I used to do that?"

I did. It brought my mom to tears once when she discovered Esther perched on Scott's lap, waiting patiently in her one-piece footed pajamas as he carefully combed the tangles, strand by strand, from her long, wet hair. Esther never sat still for anyone except him. She ran from me as soon as she saw a comb in my hand. But for Scott, she could sit for hours as he smoothed the hair that reached all the way down her back, working at it so gently that she barely detected a single tug.

"I'm sure when I'm actually there I'll be annoyed with them or want time alone," Scott began, talking himself out of the vision. "It won't be as idyllic as I'm making it out to be."

"No," I urged, with an intensity out of proportion to the conversation. "It will be just as you imagine it. I promise. Don't let it go." I was speaking to myself as much as to him. After all, the Greek word for *homecoming*, which Homer used to refer to Odysseus's return, is *nostos*, etymological great-grandfather to *nostalgia*. Indeed, Scott and I yearned for the past in the very same moment that we anticipated our future reunion, the pain of that longing sweetening the joy of his eventual arrival.

30

"If It Were Easy,
Anyone Could Do It"

"Mommy?"

"Mmm?" I turned over in bed and rubbed my eyes. Ethan stood next to me, pillow lines creasing one flushed cheek. His hair poked out of his head at angles that would have made a punk rocker proud. He grinned. I glanced at the clock: a few minutes before six a.m. Cruel any day, but especially on a Saturday.

"Look out the window!"

"What is it?"

"You. Will. Not. Believe. This." He enunciated his declaration with the pitch-perfect emphasis of a suburban teenager. Actually, I didn't want to admit it, but I was that suburban teenager; Ethan had adopted all of my speech patterns during the deployment. *Note to self,* I thought. *We need a man in the house. Fast.* I remembered when one friend's husband returned from deployment and discovered that their toddler son, whom the wife had potty-trained during the husband's absence, delicately wiped the tip of his penis with toilet paper when he finished peeing. The husband was horrified.

"I'm too tired to get up. Just tell me what's out the window."

"It's snowing!" Ethan almost shrieked with excitement.

That got my attention. The calendar read late April; that night marked the start of Passover, a holiday whose origins lay in the celebration of the spring harvest as well as the Israelites' exodus from slavery in the land of Egypt. Our tiny Jewish community in Anacortes—the core group of friends who met at the first Hanukkah party I organized on base—was gathering together for a seder. We'd convened for every major Jewish holiday during the past year and a half, and I looked forward to another enjoyable evening with a group that had become comfortable and fun.

I found it hard to believe we would have a snowy Passover; that kind of thing just doesn't happen to a desert people. So, to Ethan's great delight, I got out of bed and wrapped a blanket around my shoulders. I slid my feet into whatever shoes were closest. Together, he and I unlocked the door to the deck and walked the length of its powder-white planks. We surveyed the backyard. The trees were covered in snow, the grass was blanketed in snow, and snow fell soft and wet on our faces. We glimpsed the high peaks of Mount Baker—glowing, postcard-perfect—through the early-morning mist.

"Hold me," Ethan said quietly.

As I bent down to lift him, a flickering above the trees caught my eye. I spotted a pair of eagles flying parallel, like train tracks up to heaven. My first eagles of the season. My eagles. It was spring in Anacortes, after all.

S ister!" Leah, our Passover seder hostess, greeted me with a hug at the door. She had introduced herself to me the same way on the first night we met, standing beside the latke table at our Hanukkah party. That night was also Leah's fortieth birthday, and the clump of Mylar balloons in her house shivered in a corner of the ceiling. I smelled the brisket, and I glimpsed three children's tables set up next to the dining room.

Ethan and Esther hugged Leah's kids, and then they and a half-dozen other children disappeared into the playroom. During the next few hours, they joined the adults to listen to parts of the seder and to pick at the meal. They spent most of the evening together, somewhere else, doing I'm not sure what. But they had fun, and they didn't cause trouble. I remember my own childhood seders exactly the same way, celebrated with a tribe of other children whose rituals I recall even today.

I allowed a few moments to praise myself for finding a way to give Ethan and Esther the Jewish basics, even in a place so kooky that it snows instead of blooms at the end of April. I needed that praise, for reasons that had nothing to do with Passover, or the seder, or religion of any stripe. Just a few days before, BobbiJo, my favorite Army wife, had read me the riot act. Nicely, of course. Sweetly. And firmly.

"I feel sorry for Ethan and Esther," I had told her, deep into one of our quarterly phone calls. "For this lifestyle. It's not fair to them. Being military kids seems like a pretty bad deal to me."

"My son just turned seventeen last week," she responded. I mentally slapped my forehead with the palm of my hand. Lack of sleep had worn my situational awareness down to the nub. Of course BobbiJo had children of her own, and of course I just implied she had done her kids a disservice. *Sheesh.* I didn't want to make it worse by apologizing or by saying anything at all, so for once I kept my mouth shut.

"My kids learned about loneliness and fear long before they should have," she admitted in her soft drawl. "They understood death long before they should have. But they're self-sufficient and open too. They're not afraid to be among people who are different from them. They understand other cultures and religions because we've lived in so many places around the world."

My brain hurts when I have to pry out an idea that's wormed its way into the core. Listening to BobbiJo, I sensed the familiar ache behind my forehead, telling me that such a shift was in process.

"We live in a global economy," she continued. "The sentimental ideas of the past, the hometown no one ever moved away from, the nearby job that lets you come home for lunch—that's just not the way it is. All the military kids I know are adventurers. They can jump into any situation, in any country, and make a fast friend. They adapt quickly to new environments. They don't cheat, they don't take shortcuts, and they don't depend on anyone else to do the work for them."

"You're right," I croaked out, thinking of older military kids I knew, who impressed me with their characteristic combination of worldliness and humility. They crisscrossed the globe but claimed no sense of entitlement. No one owed them a living; no one owed them anything at all.

"That's the person who's going to be successful in life, don't you think?" she asked.

"Yes, of course."

I would have said anything to make the situation better, but it was already better. BobbiJo didn't take offense, she simply told it as she lived it. And she was right. Increasingly often, Ethan and Esther quickly surveyed any new home, as they did at Leah's, and joined a nerve center of kids pulsing with activity. They came when I called them and rarely wanted to leave. Military kids aren't shy, and my kids had become military kids.

Seated around Leah's dining room table that evening, participating in the traditional retelling of the Israelites' escape from bondage and touching upon their subsequent travails, BobbiJo's final words to me that day seemed especially relevant.

"Always remember this," she urged. "If it were easy, anyone could do it."

I had not sketched my portrait of the tragic military child independently.

"I grew up invisibly in the aviator's house," the novelist Pat Conroy writes of his own life as the son of a U.S. Marine Corps fighter pilot. "We became quiet as bivalves at his approach and our lives were desperate and sad." Elsewhere, he continues:

> We [military children] grew up strangers to ourselves. We passed through our military childhoods unremembered. We were transients, billboards to be changed, body temperatures occupying school desks for a short time. We came and went like rented furniture, serviceable when you needed it, but unremarked upon after it was gone.

As a lifelong reader, I believe in literature, both its truth and its transformative power. Pages turn, and worlds unfurl. Words provide comfort and company, and in the absence of direct experience, I depend on others' words to teach me. I have no direct experience as a military child, just as most military parents don't. That's exactly why *Military Brats: Legacies of Childhood Inside the Fortress*, the seminal book on the subject of military kids, calls them a tribe separate and distinct from the families they are born into. "Military brats" (the preferred term, according to the author) constitute a group with their own characteristics, verbal shorthand, and outlook and carry a "Warrior legacy" synonymous with secrecy, stoicism, and denial.

The "fortress mentality" that for so long characterized military families may not endure in the current tell-all generation, which has reinforced the idea that secrets are rarely singular. But aspects of military kids' experiences render them foreigners to mainstream American culture. Military kids grow up engaging in behaviors that to them seem perfectly normal, like referring to their father by his call sign (Spanky, Stinky, Two-Cent, Lobster-Boy, Thermo, Fetus, and Fungus are just a few of my favorites), hanging out with a deployed parent via video teleconference, and describing their toys as "household goods," which I find endlessly amusing.

I grew to love my kids' unexpected accommodation to military ways. They casually and automatically pick up a pair of ear plugs on the way into the hangar, like seasoned mechanics. The acrid smell of jet fuel will always evoke happy homecomings for them.

Ethan and Esther don't yet realize that you don't always have to show an ID when you buy something, as I do on base, or that all cars aren't screened by security. They have no idea when we visit colleagues in Navy housing that the units are clustered and assigned according to rank. They simply assume that making a new best friend every year is a fact of life.

None of this is necessarily good or bad, but eventually, when my kids are old enough to pay attention, they'll realize there are two very different Americas. When Ethan, Esther, and I attend a movie at the base theater, for example, an American flag appears on screen before the film begins. The kids stand and place their hand over their hearts, as does everyone else in the auditorium, and remain standing as "The Star-Spangled Banner" plays in all its fuzzily recorded glory. Of course, Scott instructed me in this, one late-December evening the first week after we were married, as we waited for a movie to begin in the base theater in Japan. The lights dimmed, and the room quieted. But instead of previews, an American flag waving amid palm trees in an idealized, tropical summer breeze materialized on screen. It was an old reel (a reel!), sepia at the sides and skipping a bit. All conversation ceased, and the entire audience stood as one. I remained frozen in my seat. As Scott nudged me to my feet, I suddenly realized I had a role in the performance too. It was one of the most serious dramas I'd ever participated in, and I've never since forgotten the script.

I recalled this lesson especially vividly one day while leaving Base Medical with the kids after a routine doctor's appointment. It was late afternoon, and as we walked outside, I noticed a beautiful sunset bleeding into the orange horizon. Almost as if on cue, I heard the bugle call signaling the lowering of the flag throughout the base.

"Just stay still for a minute, guys," I whispered, as we froze in the parking lot and turned toward the flagpole. Two sailors stood at attention beneath it. They were assigned to pull it down, fold it, and bring it inside once retreat was over. We didn't worry about standing amid traffic, because drivers stopped their cars, got out, and stood at attention beside their doors.

At reveille at eight a.m. and retreat at sunset, all movement on base screeches to a halt to observe these traditions. I learned that at our base in Japan as well. I was out running on the track one morning when a mysterious bugler started playing and all the other runners slowed and then stood, panting. I couldn't place the tune, though it seemed familiar. I noticed that all the cars on the street had pulled over and that a few bikers had dismounted and were also standing still. I kept running, of course. I couldn't imagine what was taking place; it was so far beyond my experience that I didn't even hazard a guess. I noticed a few glares shot my way, but I just kept going, blithely confident that whatever was happening didn't include me.

"I'll explain it in a minute," I told my kids, who were fully consumed by the novelty of the theatrics in the parking lot.

"What is everyone looking at?" Ethan said.

"That flag."

"Why?"

Good question, I thought. At that moment I became a teacher rather than a student of the particular strain of civics the military had injected into my life. But explaining the flag to a kid is a little like explaining God. Each parent has his or her own approach, and I hadn't thought through mine yet. I just knew I didn't want to revert to cliché or dumb down such an important emblem, especially because, as a military child, Ethan would be asked to demonstrate a measure of respect to it over and over again, and I wanted him to understand why.

"Mommy! Why do we have to stand here and not move?"

"The flag is the symbol of our country, and if we stand here and watch quietly while they're taking it down, we show how much we love it."

I gave myself a B-minus. Actually, that was grade inflation. I deserved a C, at best.

"You mean our country, North America?"

"Just America."

"What about South America?" He was learning world geography at Montessori.

"Our country is just plain America," I reminded him.

"No," he said crossly. "That's not fair to North America and South America."

The sailors folded the flag into a small triangle. Suddenly, I felt very tired. Scott always phrased difficult concepts in a way the kids could understand, and out of his mouth, nothing rang saccharine or sentimental. He made these sorts of ideas meaningful, and the corresponding actions important, because he lives his job from the inside out. Standing in the middle of the parking lot, I missed him terribly. I found myself on his base, surrounded by flight suits that weren't his, and it seemed horribly unjust.

I breathed in deeply. "You'll have to take my word for it, sweetie," I said lightly. It was a rotten civics lesson. I held both kids' hands and crossed the street carefully as traffic inched forward. "It may not be fair, but it is America, that's our flag, and this is just what we do."

31

Diving into the Wreck

S o how long do you have left?" my mom asked on the phone one day.

"Two months or so," I answered, "but we don't have a solid homecoming date yet."

"No, not homecoming," she said. "Believe me, I'm counting down with you on my calendar. How long till Scott can get out of the Navy?"

That one took me by surprise. Scott and I talked often about what he might want to do after the Navy, but the conversations were purely theoretical. So many variables remained unknown, including potentially exciting and meaningful jobs in the Navy that Scott might be qualified for. Aside from that, Scott and I felt fortunate to have landed in a stable, secure, and rewarding job environment that also provided free health care and significant commissary benefits.

"Well, technically, he can get out when he hits twenty years of service," I said, cautiously.

"When is that?"

"When he's done with this tour, he'll be at nineteen years. So we'll have another tour after that."

"And then he can get out?"

"I'm not sure what we'll do," I said. "There could be some great jobs down the line. He'd love to stay in the Navy if there's a way for him to feel useful. Or he may not get promoted, and the decision would be made for him. It's a really fluid situation. It will be a while before we know one way or the other."

"I would think you'd be dying to get out," Mom said.

I could understand that impression, despite her respect for the armed forces as an institution. After all, my mother desperately craved my happiness, and she understood how difficult it was for me to live on my own with the kids. She and my father sacrificed much of their own time and money since we had moved to Anacortes, coming to help me as frequently as they could during Scott's absences and financing my siblings' mercy visits. It was the most concrete way they could show support for their own service member. In any case, they knew no way to parent other than unconditionally, enthusiastically, and unreservedly.

Those trips had saved me so many times, snapping the kids and me out of our slump. If I occasionally detected in my parents' actions an element of penance for their past, it only added to the richness of our time together. But I couldn't ask my family to keep it up for an indefinite number of years. It may take a village, but that particular village did not have endless resources.

"I don't know what we'll do," I repeated. "That's a tough one."

"Remember those early days, when Scott was so worried you would hate Navy life?" she asked.

"Yeah."

"I guess he was right all along," she laughed.

"I don't hate it," I said quickly. "I don't hate it at all."

"What do you mean? This deployment has been so miserable for you."

"It hasn't been easy," I admitted. I knew how impossible it would be for someone else, anyone else, to understand the swirl of emotions that encircled our military lifestyle.

"The deployment forced me to do things I never thought I could do," I finally said. "But I did them. And I've met a lot of incredible people in the process."

During Scott's absence, I developed my own term for the Navy: the University of Right Now. The deployment represented a major exam. Now that my final grades loomed, I wasn't about to downplay the hard work I'd poured into my courses.

"The Navy has taught me things I would never have learned anywhere else. It has a lot to offer," I added, feeling strangely protective.

Me, defending the Navy? That was a first. I asked myself whether I was bowing to the collective consciousness or to a version of communal reinforcement that affirmed the enterprise I had married into. I didn't think I had a confirmation bias—I'd spent too much time *rejecting* my own preconceptions of the military—but more and more, when I heard myself speaking about the Navy, it sounded like hive mind. I couldn't help it. I controlled the quest but not the results. I recalled Adrienne Rich's famous poem and her search for "the wreck and not the story of the wreck / the thing itself and not the myth."

My exploration of the Navy felt much the same. If I was going to discover the truth of our family's experience in the military— either to strengthen our long-term commitment or to ultimately choose a different path—I needed to focus ruthlessly in my pursuit of the thing itself. Past dives into the wreck had left me with bruised legs, scraped hands, and injured feelings. This time, though, I swam to the surface, gasped for air, brushed off my bauble—and discovered a treasure.

Only one group of people seemed to understand absolutely and perfectly my conflicting emotions about the military: other military wives. More and more, I called on my new friends when I was mad, or worried, or upset. It started out slowly. Once my published essays about our life as a military family began circulating, Navy friends on base read them. I'm certain that some people didn't like what I said, and I was comfortable with that; the process was liberating simply because I no longer felt I was faking it as a Navy wife. I couldn't hide, because my writing spoke for me. Before, I had been too shy to tell the truth of our situation. Fellow military wives insisted they were doing fine, and I wasn't going to be the one to interrupt a winning streak.

But a potent alchemy gradually transmuted the nature of my friendships with other Navy wives. As we sat together at restaurants, gathered at receptions on base, or ran side by side on the treadmills at the gym, they began to trust me with the golden truths of their own lives. As I looked behind the makeup I detected bags under their eyes too. Many of them were worn down just as I was. Operating as sole head of household during their own squadron's deployment left a few of them worried, sleep-deprived, and sick for months on end. Some of them discovered, just as Martina had, that their husbands had volunteered for overseas duty at times the family needed them most, and they struggled to tamp down their anger. Others worried about a looming IA, or found themselves depressed about moving and starting over again in a new town or a foreign country.

Despite these concerns, we, the officers' wives, considered ourselves lucky in comparison with many of the other military spouses I befriended. Military officers are usually college graduates with skills and experience that often make them highly attractive to civilian employers. Among many enlisted families I worked with in the squadron, the military wasn't one of several potential job options; it was often the only solid career path available.

Devin, our squadron ombudsman, had personally called the recruiter on her husband's behalf. Before he joined the Navy, her entire family—parents, aunts, uncles, cousins, as well as she and her husband—had worked shifts at a machine-parts factory in Idaho.

"After 9/11, they laid everyone off," she explained. We lingered together at the dessert table during a spouse club meeting, where I finally got around to asking her how she had landed in the military. Though she is barely thirty years old, Devin's world-weary eyes have witnessed some of the worst life has to offer, but her ready smile transmits the certainty that something better is sauntering right over to say hello. She's an old soul, probably because she spent her childhood in a series of RV parks around the country, where her closest friends were the retirees who returned at the same time each year. Devin's mother gave birth to her at age eighteen, and Devin had attended twenty-eight schools by the time she finished twelfth grade. She grits her teeth when questions about her childhood come up, but she still grins when she remembers the snowbirds who invited her into their RVs for hot chocolate and asked for her perspective on current events. She wonders what they would have made of 9/11. What she herself thought didn't much matter, she said; what mattered was what happened next.

"After the terrorists hit and the airline industry collapsed, our whole family was out of work," Devin continued. "There was no going to relatives for help, because everyone was in the same boat. So we pooled the money we had left and bought a tumbledown apartment building. The men in the family managed the construction, and the women handled the front office. We all stuck together. It worked out really well, and we had that place up and running in no time."

"So why did you leave?"

"I got pregnant. It was a while before I could see a doctor, but after my first visit he told me the baby had Down's syndrome."

"Oh my God."

"My first thought was 'We don't have insurance. I have to get myself in with the place that offers the best insurance in the entire country.'"

"The military," I mumbled, mostly to myself. Military medicine may have an uneven reputation, but its coverage for dependent families is comprehensive and free.

"Right. I had to do something to help our family, so I called the Navy recruiter. I didn't even have time to talk to Stu about it. When he walked through the door that night, the recruiter was sitting on my couch with the paperwork fanned out on the coffee table. I handed Stu a pen, and the rest is history."

Several officers I know joined the Navy after 9/11 out of a sense of patriotism. But 9/11 forced Devin and her husband to join the military, whether they wanted to or not, because no other job would allow them to dependably support their family—a family that was about to grow by one profoundly disabled child. But I had met Devin's daughter, a bright, bubbly, communicative toddler.

"Sarah's not—" I started to say.

"No, she's not," Devin smiled, radiantly. Triumphantly. "Not at all. The doctors blew it. But we like the Navy. We joined as a family, and we're committed to it as a family."

In fact, Devin's desire to become a squadron ombudsman bloomed from the seed of her pride as a military spouse. She thought through her role as a Navy wife with tremendous intelligence and care, and believed that serving squadron spouses and children supported the Navy's mission. It has not been easy for her: After boot camp, her family moved into a house on base that was unfurnished, drafty, and in dire need of a paint job. As an E-1 (the rank at which a newly enlisted sailor typically enters the Navy), Stu brought home a $500 paycheck every two weeks. It wasn't enough, Devin told me later, remembering that period with a faraway look. Her mother pitched in until they could catch their breath, financially.

"Are you worried about Sarah moving around so often, though?"

I asked. My conversation with BobbiJo lingered like an aftertaste, flavoring many of my questions to friends around that time.

"If we stay in the military, Sarah will have a much more stable childhood than I ever did," Devin reminded me. "Joining the Navy has helped us plan ahead in a way we never did before. It was the only thing that got me out of thinking past the immediate gratification of tomorrow." She was serious now, though her eyes twinkled, and in them I could read her entire history. I realized that a cookie-cutter wife could never withstand the heat of military life. "Now we think about our lives three years from now, six years from now. So we feel like we're doing this for Sarah as well. I'm going for the white picket fence. I want it all."

Millie, with her sixteen years of experience as a Navy wife, spoke especially openly about how she came to terms with the military, especially the agony of deployment.

"Don't get me wrong," she said, sitting across my kitchen table one night as our kids played together outside. "I hate deployments. Hate, hate, hate them. But deployments show you what you're made of, and they teach you how to be independent. I got married the day after college graduation, so I had never lived on my own," she said. "Deployments give me the confidence to know I can make it without Leo."

"How do your kids do?" Her girls were ten and twelve.

"It's rough. It's been different with every age, and it never gets fun, I can promise you that, but I'm really proud of one thing."

"What?"

"Deployments have given both girls a new perspective on me as their mom. They see me fixing the washing machine. They watch me drilling nails into the wall and haulin' the trash out every Wednesday night. It's a chance for them to watch me be independent, and I think it's good for them to grow up knowing you don't need a man to run a house. I'm really grateful I can give them that."

I tried to imagine our world through Ethan and Esther's eyes, and how they would process our experience of deployment.

"That's a good way to look at it, but I'm not quite there yet," I admitted.

"Just remember that the military is just like life, but with higher highs and lower lows. And a lot more planning." She grinned broadly. "You know, the whole Costco-sex thing."

"Um, what whole Costco-sex thing?" If she wanted to get my attention, she had it.

"Oh, you never heard of it? You have Costco sex before deployment, stocking up for six months. Then during the deployment you have Home Depot sex. That's doing it yourself." She winked at me.

Millie was the first person I ever met who openly acknowledged the sexual deprivation of military couples, which made me treasure her friendship even more. We laughed together about our strange, shared plight as twilight darkened the trees. A Prowler roared overhead. She and I fell silent, since there's no way to talk over a jet scorching the air.

"I love that sound," Millie said, after it flew off.

"You're kidding," I replied, though Millie and I were so different that nothing should have surprised me. "I hate that sound. I absolutely despise it."

It was her turn to look shocked. "Okay, explain," she said.

"I hear it and remember that Scott's not with me. It's a concrete reminder of why he's gone and what he's doing when he's gone. I want to forget, but the jets don't let me forget."

"Hmmmmm," she replied, carefully. She stared at the table for a moment, then looked up again. "For me, it's exactly the opposite. Hearing the jets is the one thing that comforts me when Leo's gone, because I know he absolutely loves being in that airplane. He hates being away from us, but he's doing something that makes him happy. So listening to the plane rip the air means he's somewhere out there, making the most of our time apart."

Millie and I smiled at each other. Since we'd grown closer, the differences between the two of us had evolved into a shared source of amusement. At times like this, we related to each other like friendly foreigners, eager to display our respective culture and explore each other's strange traditions.

"That sound is part of our marriage," she said, firmly. "I wouldn't give it up for anything."

"I get it," I said. "You're very Mama Bear about the Navy, aren't you?"

"It's just part of my coupon-cuttin', Spam-eatin' self," she laughed, dipping a nacho. "You know, we have a saying down in Texas. 'You can't get to know someone until you sit around their kitchen table.'"

There it was again, the mythology of the kitchen table, scene of so much family bonding. This time around, I was part of a military family. And to our surprise, and delight, Millie and I discovered that we were in the same clan.

32

"When Is It My Turn?"

Millie once mentioned that since she'd spent her entire adulthood married to the military, she didn't know how to be a wife without being a Navy wife. The Navy was intertwined so tightly with their marriage that she couldn't imagine what she would do after her husband retired, who their friends would be, or how they would fill their free time. Uncertainty lingered over our future too, but for different reasons.

Scott made it clear, early on in our relationship, that he was enthusiastic about a long tenure in the Navy, but that decision would rest with senior officers who handle promotions boards. Despite the difficulties of the command tour, I was beginning to see the benefits of a long-term military career. More important, I finally understood the purpose and importance of my husband's assignments and the kinds of contributions he could make. He and I both remained open to a stint of several more years, but a lot of *if*s freckled the face of these conversations.

The sheer number of future scenarios made planning nearly impossible. Like any of the officers in his position, Scott might get promoted and be able to live in one location for several follow-on tours. (Great for family life but highly unlikely; the Navy doesn't have much use for people who want to stay put.) The more likely scenarios promised continued disruption to a stable home life. Many at his rank continued to deploy for years to come, and, with alarming frequency, postcommand skippers from his community packed their duffel bags for one-year IA assignments to Iraq and Afghanistan. Scott could easily be next. There was no way to know what the Navy would need at the time his career would be up for review.

Then again, an interesting assignment in a desirable location abroad could also pop up anytime. As promised by the old recruiting call "Join the Navy and see the world," an overseas posting that served the Navy's requirements might give Scott a greater breadth of professional experience, help the kids to learn a second language, and allow all of us the privilege of experiencing another culture. Perhaps it was well worth staying in the Navy and weathering the inevitable long separations to engage in this sort of fulfilling work.

We continually asked ourselves the same question: What's the point at which a military career becomes too costly to our family? Like most of the Navy couples in our circle, our discussion of career options was ongoing and open-ended. In the middle of washing dishes or folding clothes, one of us mentioned a friend whose orders were finalized (for better or for worse), and the conversation took off at breakneck speed. Despite the number of hours devoted to the topic, these talks never gave us the illusion of control over our future. It's simply impossible to assume anything in the military, where even "final" orders can change at any time because of current events, national security findings, Department of Defense needs, or the most banal personnel issues. A fellow commander's sudden firing, an admiral's reconsideration of his predecessor's decision, an officer's broken arm—all of these events, which took place during our tour, changed the lives of Scott's colleagues, who, with their wives and children, shuffled to unexpected new assignments in the wake of someone else's crisis.

In any case, if Scott stayed in the Navy, the two of us would wield control over very few decisions pertaining to his career path. These deliberations remained in the hands of screening boards that determined if he was promotion-worthy. They fell to placement officers who worked out the timing of certain assignments. Family considerations typically play no role at all in these matters. We had no say, because the needs of the Navy are paramount, especially during wartime, when resources are stretched beyond the limit. Everyone has to sacrifice for the war effort.

We weren't the only couple among our peers that agreed to remain in the Navy at least until reaching the twenty-year retirement marker. As our friends on base served out their command tours and approached the long-sought (for many spouses) or long-dreaded (for many officers) ending, we witnessed more and more conflict among couples. To be precise: The men changed their minds.

"We had it all figured out early on in our marriage," confided Belinda, a longtime acquaintance. "David agreed to stay in twenty years, and I agreed to make the military and the kids my job during that time. Then it was going to be my turn. I could go back to work, real work, of my own choosing. I could pick where we were going to settle, find the house of our dreams, the whole bit."

David just marked his twenty-year anniversary in the Navy and began a new assignment, so I figured that that particular scenario had gone awry.

"What happened?"

"Somewhere in the middle of his command tour, he sat me down and told me he wasn't ready to give up the Navy. He started looking at opportunities, and then suddenly we were discussing paths that would guarantee another eight years, even ten years, in the Navy. I couldn't believe it." She shook her head. "It felt like a total betrayal."

I would have felt the same way. "How did you work it out?" I asked.

She paused and shook her head again, slow as a funeral bell. I'd known her since we moved to Anacortes. One of the few African-American officer wives in our community, she was a private woman; we'd never before had such a personal conversation. In any case, she didn't let much slip, but I glimpsed that day a wellspring of pain diverted for the good of her husband's career. "We're still working it out. It's not easy. We're taking it one day at a time. I just keep asking him 'When is it my turn?'"

I raised my eyebrows in a silent "And?"

"He can't answer me. He says this is just something he has to do for himself, for the country, and even for our family. I just don't get it, Alison, I don't get it. Haven't we given enough?"

I t's just like that poem," Scott said on the phone one day soon after that, during the carrier's last port call in Dubai, when I mentioned my conversation with Belinda.

"What poem?" I asked.

"You know, that poem by Lovelace. 'I could not love thee, Dear, so much, Loved I not honour more.'"

Every few years, Scott said or did something that completely surprised me, something I would have sworn, hand on Bible, could never, ever happen. This was one of those times. I barely remembered Lovelace from my undergraduate *Norton Anthology of English Literature*.

"The poem is about why he keeps returning to war and keeps leaving his wife. He basically says he wouldn't be a good husband if he weren't a good and loyal soldier first. I don't feel that way, but I know a lot of people who do."

"Like David?" He and Scott had sweated through their first tour together, and their careers were practically mirror images.

"Tons of people. It's not just that, though. Being in command can be really seductive because your authority is total, and it's unquestioned. You know your place, and everyone else knows it too. You've heard that retired military officers have an unusually high rate of suicide, right? It's partly because they've lost the certainty of where they rank in the hierarchy. They enter the civilian world, and no one cares who they are, how they think, or what their opinion is."

"So you're saying people stay in the military because their ego can't take the fall."

Scott sighed. He hated when I sacrificed truth for brevity. "I'm saying the military is a hard thing to give up, for lots of reasons, once you've been in command."

I thought of Belinda and David as I retrieved "To Lucasta, Going to the Wars," penned by the English son of a military family in 1649.

> *Tell me not, Sweet, I am unkind,*
> *That from the nunnery*
> *Of thy chaste breasts, and quiet mind,*
> *To war and arms I fly.*
>
> *True, a new mistress now I chase,*
> *The first foe in the field;*

And with a stronger faith embrace
A sword, a horse, a shield.

Yet this inconstancy is such,
As you too shall adore;
I could not love thee, Dear, so much,
Loved I not honour more.

33

Pippi

My laptop pulsed with impatience when I woke up. Devin's e-mail, which had been waiting for me for hours, was short and to the point: Pippi lay in a hospital bed after a car accident the evening before. Her two kids were bunking with neighbors who knew the family well and who could keep them indefinitely. That was a relief, because doctors warned that Pippi may need an emergency C-section; the crash had triggered worrisome contractions. Her pregnancy was only thirty weeks along.

Not Pippi, I groaned. The poor girl, a country song in the making, attracted more grief than anyone else I knew. The only thought easing her through cruise was the squadron's scheduled arrival in time for her husband to be present at the birth. Her mother had died the year Pippi married her sailor, and she'd delivered both sons during past deployments, squeezing the hand of the nurse on duty.

I waited until seven a.m. to call Devin on her cell phone. She answered from Pippi's bedside. Fortunately, the contractions had eased in the last few hours. Pippi remained connected to her IV drip because she was dehydrated, but she didn't require anything else.

"What can I do?" I asked Devin.

"There is one thing," she answered hesitantly. Devin always hurried to do a favor for anyone who needed it, but hated to ask anything of others. "I've already called Red Cross to notify the squadron of the accident, but we need the power of attorney and some other papers. Is there any way you can bring them over? The house is unlocked."

She read me the address. Pippi lived near base—not in Navy housing but nearby. After I dropped off my kids at school, I drove over, scribbled scrap paper in hand. I was completely unprepared for what I found.

Pippi's trailer is nestled in a notch of trees set back from the two-lane highway snaking through our part of the state. After missing it twice, I finally pulled up on a patch of gravel in front of the door, next to a Volkswagen with its hood propped up. I glanced around the yard. Plastic pots of African violets lined the front porch. The screen door was frozen wide open, as if Pippi had left in a rush moments earlier.

I jiggled the doorknob, let myself in, and flipped on a light. It took a while to make sense of what I saw. Two torn dog beds stacked in a corner convinced me that the chewed-up foam that littered every inch of the carpet had been there for a while. Mountains of dirty clothes, broken toys, discarded DVD cases, empty apple juice boxes, and crushed soda cans lined one wall, literally end to end. As I crossed in front of the bathroom, I noticed that a broken toilet seat balanced on the rim of the tub. In the boys' small room, their tattered and bare mattresses lay side by side on the floor. The kitchen, which I passed next, doubled as a diaper-changing station. The linoleum reeked of urine, and I strongly suspected the bulging trash bags in the corner held weeks-old dirty diapers. Empty wrappers—from energy bars, mostly—filled the sink.

I cared about the state of Pippi's house only to the extent that it illustrated the degree to which her interior world had shattered.

She was clearly unable to pick up the pieces. At seven months pregnant, with two difficult toddlers and a deployed husband, Pippi and her house were in crisis. I knew, given that her husband was a junior sailor, that it was nearly impossible to support a family on his paycheck or to hire anyone to help out. *This*, I thought, glancing around the trailer, *is what a military salary looks like*. I don't know if I was sadder or angrier, understanding for the first time that enlisted families, who sign up to sacrifice it all, are forced to live on nearly nothing.

By the time I reached Pippi's room, with the aquarium full of fish, belly-up in gray water, I could barely sketch her face in my mind. The house appeared so different from the woman I knew, who was ballsy and spirited, young and capable. I wondered what happened to the volunteer who had bought her a vacuum cleaner, coached her on the importance of a consistent schedule, and encouraged her pursuit of a GED.

As I reached for the power of attorney—in her nightstand, as Devin had directed me—I spotted a stack of unopened letters from a mortgage company on her bed. The hairs on the back of my neck froze. The house lay beyond Pippi's power or control, at least at the moment, but to lose it would be catastrophic. I took a deep breath just as I spotted two fat rifles on top of the bookshelf, a pair of pythons waiting to pounce. Enough. I wanted out.

I reached for the light switch on my way through the front door. That's when I noticed the paint chip taped to the wall. I squinted to get a closer look and then retraced my steps through the entire trailer. In each room, in a spot a few inches above the light switch, Pippi had affixed Benjamin Moore samples in shades of orange— Pumpkin Blush, Blazing Sunset, Orange Froth, Persimmon—on and on and on. Except for the paint chips, the walls glared bare, an ugly, thick, popcorn-plaster bare. Pippi obviously felt the same way, and planned great improvements for the place with colors that rivaled (or perhaps complemented) her hair.

The poignancy of the paint chips pierced me deeply. It meant that Pippi had never given up trying to coordinate all the elements of a better life, even if it meant layering a few coats of pride on top of the pain. I could relate, in my own way, because I comfort myself with home improvements too. I've been known to throw a few fabric swatches on my couch and dream up a big change on a bad day. Pippi's face materialized in front of me again, her wry smile and dancing eyes. I picked up the phone and dialed Devin's number.

The next morning I reported for duty on Pippi's front porch at nine. Devin and two other squadron wives who had arrived before me pulled cleaning supplies out of their flatbeds. The dewy grass smelled like spring. I noticed a few early blooming wildflowers among the weeds that pushed and bent themselves against the trailer.

Three more trucks crunched the gravel driveway, exhibiting the same quiet, controlled force as the women behind the wheel. One by one, we mustered our brooms, mops, and Swiffer Wet Jets against the screen door. The bottles of Lysol, Comet, 409, and other cleansers were arrayed at our feet awaiting the call to battle. Devin held a clipboard. This was her doing, of course.

"I don't know what we can do, Devin," I had said the day before, after she excused herself from Pippi's bedside to talk to me on the phone. "Are we allowed to break confidentiality and bring this to anyone's attention? Like an agency that could provide some resources?"

"We can't breach the circle of trust," Devin said firmly. Her signature line, I heard it during that tour almost as often as I heard Ethan and Esther ask me for ice cream. Her sincerity and commitment to the ombudsman program's principles rendered any debate fruitless. If spouses thought the ombudsman would betray their darkest secrets and deepest needs, they would never confide in her.

(The skipper is automatically included in this circle of trust, and because I worked so closely with the squadron during deployment, I was often included as well.)

"What are our options?" I asked.

"Let me see what I can do," Devin responded, slowly. "I may have an idea."

Later, she gently explained to Pippi that all of the other wives have hit bottom at some point during past deployments. I don't know what else Devin said, but she got the go-ahead from Pippi to call a few sympathetic squadron spouses. The next morning, Devin dispatched all of us to our duties. One of the wives, armed with a jumbo box of Tide, ferried piles of dirty clothes out the door, and when the towels, onesies, overalls, and nightgowns touched the ceiling of the cab of her truck, she headed to the laundromat. One team of young wives claimed they could conquer the bathroom, so with great solemnity, Devin handed them a bucket and a toolbox.

Each of us was assigned a room or a project. One of our officer wives brought her steam cleaner, so the carpets became her responsibility. Another arrived with a hand-me-down trundle bed and new sheets for the children's room. An aspiring vet among us handled the dead fish, then fed and calmed the two large dogs tied up in the backyard.

Amateur strategists that we were, we split the kitchen into action zones. Two senior enlisted wives—Filipina sisters who married sailors stationed at Subic Bay before the closure—had spent the previous evening cooking meals for Pippi's freezer. They dumped shelves of soggy Swanson's boxes and replaced them with pans of lumpia, pansit, pork adobo, and beef stew. Devin mopped the floor, wiped out the cabinets, and sprayed slow-moving ants into oblivion.

I placed myself on trash duty—selfishly—because it assured me of some time outside. Pippi couldn't afford the county's trash ser-

vice and had confessed that she left the children asleep after night-
fall to dump her garbage in commercial dumpsters. I didn't see
any other option, and the weeks' worth of poopy diapers didn't
leave a lot of room to debate the ethical dilemma. I loaded up my
minivan—once, twice, three times—and headed to base.

The McDonald's parking lot next to the Exchange was a high-
traffic area at any time, but the lunch rush left me particularly
exposed. A few sailors in dungarees glanced my way as I heaved
white bags from my trunk into the dumpster, but they pretended
not to notice. Another officer's wife spotted me from her booth inside but looked away quickly. I wore my fifteen-year-old UMass
sweatshirt, faded jeans, and running sneakers, attire far more casual
than usual for the base, where I was always sure to meet someone
I knew.

It's hard to overstate the shock of watching a skipper's wife
openly breaking a rule on a military installation. We are supposed
to set the standard for our squadron spouses and their families or, at
the very least, lay low and stay out of trouble. But the red capitals
screaming NO RESIDENTIAL TRASH would have made it tough to come
up with an excuse had I been questioned. I didn't care; all of us
working in the trailer that day felt like Pippi's crisis could have
been ours. I think our fervor to help her grew out of the knowledge
that we were only a deployment away from our own private piles
of shit.

At the end of a long day of adventures in trash, I waved good-
bye to the women still scrubbing their hearts out at Pippi's house
and drove the twenty miles back to Anacortes. I pulled into the
driveway of one of our officer spouses, a friend with whom I often
traded favors. With a newborn and a toddler at home, she wasn't
in a position to help Pippi, but she had volunteered to babysit Ethan
and Esther so that I could take care of business. She greeted me on
the porch, her eyebrows raised.

"Everyone came together," I told her, though she hadn't asked the question in words. "It was incredible. Seriously, I've never seen anything like it."

I wanted to say more, but I didn't know what. "I get it," I finally admitted. "I get how things are supposed to work around here." And I thought I did.

My friend nodded and called Ethan and Esther to the door. Together, we herded them into my minivan.

"Thanks again," I said, standing in front of my open car door. The emotional and physical exhaustion of the day started to seep into brain and bones. I could smell myself, and it wasn't the usual CK One. "I'm going to go take a shower."

"Here's something for you," she said, handing me a grocery bag. I peeked in. Four large Tupperwares, lids cloudy with the steam of a freshly cooked meal, were stacked like a tower. It was my turn to ask the silent question.

"I thought you could use a good dinner tonight," she answered, simply.

Maybe I didn't realize how tired I was or how deeply Pippi's sad situation had worked itself into my soul, but my friend's thoughtfulness left me on the verge of tears. As I climbed into my seat, waving good-bye, I understood that each military spouse—when they're at their best—is a link in a chain of kindness that always, eventually, hooks on to the person in need.

M any months later, after the deployment ended, I stopped by Pippi's trailer for a new-baby visit. After the scare of the car crash, she recovered with few complications; in fact, her daughter slid screaming into the world ten days late. Pippi's husband cut the umbilical cord. When I arrived with a gift and my usual pan of leaking lasagna, the place shone spotlessly, and the baby's father whistled happily as he hooked up Pippi's breast pump. The baby slept in a pink-ribboned bassinet. The toddlers seemed charmed by the new arrival and uncharacteristically calm.

As for Pippi, she stood at the stove, one hand on her already-slim hip, stirring a pot of chili. Its warm, earthy scent wafted through the trailer. "I'm gonna need some frickin' protein to handle this crew," she pronounced, smiling and rolling her eyes. She brought the wooden spoon to her lips for a taste and then kissed her fingers, chef style, peeking up at me to see if I wanted in on the joke.

I was relieved Pippi seemed to be tackling life with gusto, but I remained shaken by the degree to which I had misunderstood her situation, and even now I wonder if I failed her when she was drowning in the single-mom duties that accompany deployment. In those moments of self-doubt, I try hard to remember Buber's line "All actual life is encounter." Because I may not have accomplished everything I wanted to in many of my encounters with military spouses in need, but at Pippi's house, for the first time, I felt like I was finally living.

34

Counting Down

To: Friends & family
From: Nora L.
Re: Ten days and counting

Dear friends,

Many of you know that it was this time last year that Aaron began his one-year tour in Bahrain. Well, with training and travel the one year turned into fifteen months. For most of you the time has probably gone by pretty fast. I hear that a lot. We have felt every day of the fifteen months, but now we're finally counting down to the end. I thought you might like to count down with us. Aaron is as ready to come home as we are ready to have him home. It's been interesting and at times downright difficult, but it's over now. And that's all that matters.

Thank you for your prayers. Thank you for your e-mails and letters, and for babysitting and carpooling. I could not have done it without your help. You kept me company, and you kept me sane.

*Ten more days to go and we will hopefully have some
sense of normalcy around here.*

Love,
Nora

It was particularly satisfying, in a closing-of-the-circle kind of way,
to hear from Nora near the end of our first deployment, because she
is the first Navy wife I ever befriended. Our bond transcends logic—
as well as our many differences. She's a Seventh-day Adventist who
gave birth to her first child, a daughter, at age seventeen. Her
daughter also found herself pregnant at age seventeen, making
Nora a grandmother at age thirty-four, right around the time she
discovered she was expecting again—a boy, this time. I remember
the day I spent with her in Virginia Beach shortly after her son was
born. He and Ethan, both six months old, squirmed around on a
blanket on the floor in front of us as Nora and I shared tips for coax-
ing infants to sleep. During a lull in the conversation, she reminded
me of the moment we met, back in her old house on Whidbey
Island.

"How long had you and Scott been dating then?" she asked.

"Four months," I said. "I think we showed up at your house a
day or two before we got engaged."

"I knew you were getting married," she pronounced. "I knew
it the minute I saw how close he was standing by you when I opened
the door."

I recalled that moment vividly. We felt like newlyweds already,
proud and happy, announcing ourselves to the world.

"When did you know he was the one?" she asked, leaning
forward.

"He called me one day at my office." The answer was obvious
as the hands in front of my face, though I had never reflected on
it before. "We'd been together only a few weeks, during his time
at the test squadron at Pax River. He had injured his back that

morning and managed to crawl into bed, but he couldn't move. He told me there was a Diet Coke on his nightstand but no food. He couldn't even reach his prescriptions. He spoke in a whisper, because he could barely catch his breath between the spasms."

I remembered the churning panic that impelled me forward.

"I ran into my boss's office and told him I had to go. I drove the two hours down there without even packing a change of clothes first, and I stayed for five days. Nothing else mattered."

Nora's eyes welled up. She was a sucker for drama, just like me. That's why I love her, despite the fact that her world and mine have only the Navy in common. I've seen her just twice during the seven years we've known each other; most years we simply exchange Christmas cards. But when "ten days and counting" popped up on my screen, I cheered as loudly for her as I would have for my closest college roommate.

I looked forward to writing one of those e-mails myself. The USS *Truman* had just departed the Persian Gulf and was preparing to cross the Straits of Hormuz and steam its way through the Mediterranean on its way back to the Atlantic. Sailors counted the days until they disembarked at port calls in Rhodes and Marseilles. Sometime after that, as the boat crept toward the Florida coast, four Prowlers would catapult off the carrier, fly west over the vast American landscape, and cross the sky over Naval Air Station Whidbey Island with a geometric precision heartbreaking in its beauty.

Twenty-five days and counting.

M y backyard was my backyard, but it was also the ocean, a desolate, watery wilderness with rolling whitecaps and violent intentions. Three jets had crashed in it already, and bodies floated just under the surface of the sea. I stood on my deck and watched another plane buzzing above. Sputtering and unsteady, it looked like a sick bumblebee.

I ran inside and grabbed my portable phone. Be calm, I told myself. Be clear. I dialed 911 and enunciated my address. "Jets are crashing in my backyard," I told the operator, as I rushed back to the deck. But now the deck was also the bow of a carrier, and I looked over the water again, far below, to where men's bodies floated motionless as wax figures. Their facial features were too blurred to distinguish among them. Another jet went down just beyond, a nosedive into the deep, and I heard yet another above me, the deafening noise of the engine swallowing all my other senses.

I woke up.

It sounds counterintuitive, but the period in which the carrier heads home is actually among the most dangerous times of a deployment. The squadron flies its regular events, but the natural instinct of many is to let their guard down. After all, the deployment is nearly finished; the theater of operations is literally behind them. But on a carrier, all of the actors have to be hypervigilant at all times. There are still tailhook landings to be nailed, navigational systems to be maintained. A sigh of relief, writ large, spells disaster. It didn't happen to Scott's squadron, though it's exactly what happened to me. Emotional disaster, that is.

During the deployment, I had seen very few men in Anacortes. Maybe I wasn't looking; maybe I averted the eyes in my brain; maybe I was constantly glancing down at Ethan and Esther to make sure they didn't race into the street. Now that I woke up every morning anticipating Scott's imminent return, however, men were everywhere. There were fishermen home for a month's break from crabbing before sailing up to Alaska for salmon season, pitching baseballs to their kids in the local field. There were ER doctors from the hospital on their day off, accompanying their daughters to ballet. Two aviators living in nearby neighborhoods flew home from their own squadrons' deployments, and I watched the men and their wives strolling down Commercial at midday, enjoying the simple act of holding hands in the noon sunshine. I saw my reflection in their mirrored Ray-Bans as I waved and smiled weakly.

No jealousy bug bit me for the entire six and a half months of deployment. I hadn't been angry at the Navy—not once. But when the carrier left the Gulf, I let my guard down. As it steamed its way home, I steamed too—over our family's lost time together and all that Scott had missed. I penned ridiculous, tragic lists in my head. Since Scott joined the squadron, he'd been absent for entire seasons of Ethan's peewee baseball, peewee soccer, peewee basketball, and now a second spring of peewee baseball. Since last fall, he had missed Ethan's violin recital, both kids' dance performances, both of their birthdays, and countless holidays. The kids and I had journeyed to Seattle dozens of times and had flown to the East Coast for two vacations, creating memories he'd never share.

Ethan now operated my Mac PowerBook on his own. He asked brain-bending questions about the solar system I couldn't answer. Esther had moved out of her crib and into a twin bed. She had taught herself how to pedal her tricycle. She was thriving at Montessori and came home begging to peel carrots.

As for me, the essays I'd published about our life as a military family had met with enthusiasm and some (perhaps positive) controversy. A magazine I long dreamed of writing for e-mailed me to ask for an original piece. The scripts of the conversations that followed between the editor and me lay beyond my adolescent imaginings. My dreams are tiny things, of little consequence to the world but of great consequence to me, and so their fulfillment led to emotional fireworks of the most spectacular sort. But Scott wasn't around for any of it. He lived in my mind, as close to me and as far away as that implies. Countless times I had wanted to pick up the phone and share my excitement about the kids' progress and the direction I was moving in professionally. I couldn't call, of course, and there was often just too much to write about. On days when the most happened, my e-mails to him were the shortest.

So six and a half months into the deployment, the kids and I were flourishing by any objective standard. That was precisely the source of my anger, though it took me a while to figure out what to call it. I didn't want to be angry. Angry, after all, was helpless; angry was unfair; angry, most of all, left me confused. Because after more treacherous ups and downs than a creaky roller coaster in a small-town carnival, Ethan and Esther were absolutely fine. As the end of deployment wagged its index finger toward me, I finally breathed a sigh of relief. At the tail end of that sigh, though, I found myself enraged that Scott and I had forced our family to power through such an exercise.

I couldn't understand my own perverse reaction. Fury and grief flooded my system. My unbridled excitement over Scott's return was at complete odds with my belated anger over his departure. Regardless of my destination, I arrived brooding. My fury had no focus. I glared at loving couples dining alfresco at restaurants and yelled at any government official who appeared on television, even if it was just to announce a change in personnel. *Just be a happy person,* I begged myself.

All around me, spouses in the squadron scheduled appointments with their hair stylists, coordinated their homecoming outfits, and finished their fix-it projects. I did all of those things too. The other spouses and I planned the fly-in, with decorations and sheet cakes and welcome-home bags, with as much care and as many spreadsheets as we generated for our own weddings.

I found it impossible to pull apart what I was feeling. Martina's words echoed in my memory: *I just kept my head down the whole time McGowan was away,* she told me once. And later: *I was so angry. The IA changed me; it made me a different person. It's taken the whole year to get back to where we used to be.*

But Martina and McGowan recovered, at last. In our recent phone calls she sounded more relaxed and happy than I'd ever heard her. "I finally realized that my husband is not the Navy," she confessed. "It's obvious, now that I'm saying it out loud, but it took me a long time to figure it out. Once I did, I stopped being so bitchy to him all the time, and he started listening to me. I wasn't sure what direction we were moving in, but now we're a family again."

As a fellow Navy spouse, Martina always offered herself up as a cautionary tale, sharing her trials not simply as a buddy, but as a professional colleague whose lessons learned can benefit the whole company. I'm not sure if this trait is unique to military wives, but Millie shared confidences in exactly the same way. She and Martina, the yin and yang of my military-wife friends, were opposites in everything, but both gave me exactly what I needed: the benefit of their experience.

Martina's painful year demonstrated to me that I couldn't spare seven months of anger toward the military. I had to work through it before Scott returned. No way would I be mistaken for one of the harpies that confronted Odysseus on his journey home, a storm wind blowing our family's happiness into the netherworld.

Our ombudsman forwarded the group an article about post-deployment reunions, and I studied it more carefully than a graduate student. It was titled "Give It Time." *How much time?* I wondered. Then, in the next paragraph: "Many chaplains suggest one day of reintegration for each day of deployment. . . . Considering the many changes you've experienced, you may experience grief during your reintegration. You may grieve lost time with each other, missing out on what the other experienced, the loss of your former life together, or the death of a friend or comrade." That helped reset my perspective. Deployment doesn't compare with the desolation of death, though it is intolerable in its own way.

"One of the greatest needs for families is to make meaning out of this experience," the article continued. Since Scott and I hadn't yet had a chance to debrief on the deployment together, I started thinking about how I could make the last six and a half months meaningful and what I could do so that it would not simply pass into memory, unmarked and unexamined. The deployment had been so challenging (and continued to generate such a jumble of emotion) that I didn't want to forget it. Instead, I wanted to sculpt it into permanence. Whether it would be a monument or a memorial, I didn't know. But I needed to be able to run my hands over it, to scrutinize it from every angle, in sunshine and in rain, and to become familiar with each notch and imperfection in the carving. I knew only one way to do that.

I thought back to the way Scott paced my apartment years earlier, breaking up with me after endless discussion about Navy life. I remembered the night Ethan was born, when Scott called my hospital room from the USS *Kitty Hawk* following his six-hour mission over Iraq. I flashed back to the afternoon of his promotion to commander, my own pride reflected in his eyes as he stood at attention in a Pentagon conference room, reciting the oath of office. I saw my first eagle, and the afternoon sun shining off the snowy glow of Mount Baker. I felt Scott lying next to me the night before he left for cruise, and the heartbreak of the following morning. I realized, all over again, that despite the challenges, this tour allowed me to become the involved, physically present mother I always hoped to be.

Most of all, though—even more than the thunderclouds that crowded my thoughts toward the end of the deployment—I heard the chant that quietly but insistently worked its way into my consciousness: *We did it. We did it. We did it. We did it!*

The end was a beginning. I opened my laptop and started to write.

PART THREE

‖ Homecoming ‖

To a Navy junior his dad is a hero and his ship is the largest and finest on the seas. There is something very touching in hearing a group of Navy youngsters boast about their fathers and their ships. And when Father comes home—what a welcome he gets! No New England sea captain of the old days could have received a finer reception.

—*The Navy Wife*

35

Magical Powers

M ommy?"

"Yes, my love?"

"You said we have nineteen days left till Daddy comes home."

"That's right."

"That means tomorrow when we wake up there will be eighteen days left."

"True."

"I think I know what that really means."

"What?"

"It means the driver of the aircraft carrier heard what I told him."

That poor helmsman again, whoever he was. Ethan heaped so much hatred on him during the deployment.

"What did you tell him?"

"Remember when I asked you to close my door when you left my room?"

I did. Ethan was scared of the dark, and it was unusual for him to want the door closed after I said good night, but that's what he requested a few evenings back.

"That was the night," he said. "It was totally totally black in my room. The door was closed, and the window was closed. So in my brain I told the driver of the aircraft carrier to turn the boat around. I thought it and thought it and thought it. And when the thought got so big it bursted out of the room, it flew into outer space and landed on the boat."

"Daddy was always scheduled to come back now—" I started to say.

"*No,*" Ethan insisted. "*I thought it and thought it and thought it.*"

"Wow," I conceded. "Well then, it looks like you got your magical powers back, mister."

"Guess so," he said, shrugging, and then turning casually to the next thing.

Service members' return from deployment is often likened to astronauts' reentry from space. Conditions are so radically different that assimilation back into a formerly familiar environment takes days if not weeks. Knees will be wobbly. Appetites will waver but eventually return, with great ferocity.

As for us military wives gathering at the squadron's hangar bay the afternoon the jets flew in from deployment, knees wobbled, and appetites wavered. The kids and I arrived first, two hours early; I couldn't help myself. I watched our spouses filter in, surveying the blue and green balloons, the banners and flags, the platters of food that would remain untouched. Millie and her girls arrived just after I did, to support us, and then I saw Amber walk in with the rest of the wives. After that, several parents of the younger officers joined us. A half-hour before the fly-in, officers from other squadrons arrived to welcome their colleagues. By that time, the fly-in had swung into party mode. We hugged and squealed in anticipation, and I basked in the delight of having almost made it. I loved everyone. The beautiful wives glowed with excitement; the dazzling children charmed even the grumpiest sailor on duty.

"It's too bad about the surge," Amber said, sidling up to me, chic and elegant in a silky red blouse, black pants, and patent-leather heels. Red chopsticks speared her chignon in place. I fell for it. I wasn't on guard, and I certainly wasn't prepared for a bitch-off.

"What surge?"

"Oh, you know about the surge, don't you? I guess your husband didn't tell you."

My heart fell. I shook my head and spotted Millie at the other end of the hangar. She caught my panicked glance. She and I had discussed Amber's rumormongering many times.

"The most recent squadron back is always on surge mode," Amber explained patiently, as if talking to a small child. "They're the first out again in a crisis. Our guys are probably going to Afghanistan in a couple of weeks and then directly back to Iraq. Unless they go to Japan, which they'd do if something bad happens in North Korea. And you know, something bad is always happening in North Korea."

I'd never heard of surge mode. I didn't know how to respond to Amber, who smilingly waited for me to say something.

"Hey, girl!" Millie came to the rescue, a caped crusader in a crocheted summer sweater. She hugged Amber. "I've been looking everywhere for you. Can you do me a huge favor and chat up a few of those parents standing all by their lonesome in the corner? They're gonna love you!" Amber beamed and made a beeline to the parents' corner.

Millie, my friend, my ally, and my liberator, winked. She put one arm around me and leaned in. "We have a saying down in Texas," she whispered. "'Don't wrestle with a pig in the mud. You both get dirty, and the pig likes it.'"

I have often wondered what strange magic transforms a perfectly ordinary woman into a military wife and whether or not there is one quality shared by all military spouses, who are otherwise as different as any other random assortment of humans on the planet. In the last few minutes of our first deployment as a military family, waiting for Scott to land, I looked at the women around me and realized that if there really is one characteristic that unites us, it's not patriotism, not politics, and not religion. It's not even love for our husbands.

It's endurance. Military spouses can endure anything. Some do so quietly, like BobbiJo and Isabelle and Devin, and some do so loudly, like Millie and Martina and Pippi. Some do so happily, and some unhappily. But they endure because they can count on each other in nearly every situation life hurls toward them. They show up for each other's farewells, halfway dinners, and fly-ins. They bring heart-shaped pizzas to Valentine's Day parties, and red, white, and blue berry pies to Fourth of July picnics. They babysit one another's kids and construct widows' baskets they pray over. They clean each other's houses and cook a week's worth of meals for a sick friend. They arrive at events bearing scrapbooks and cow costumes. They leave the porch light on after sunset so a neighbor with a just-deployed spouse knows it's all right to call if she's lonely. They write mailboxes full of thank-you notes. They befriended me, no questions asked, before I knew how to give anything at all back.

And here they are—here we are, because I have become one of them—at the end of deployment. The jets are deafening in their urgent desire to land and make families whole again. Scores of military wives squint into the sun, waving with one hand at the Prowlers tearing through the clouds overhead and covering a toddler's ear with the other hand.

As I waited at the hangar bay, joy pulsed through my veins. The roar of the four jets wiped away the possibility of words, tossed thoughts to the wind. Finally, the planes landed, taxied to their places on the flight line, and shut down. For all their unholy power, it was as simple an act as moving a lever that stopped fuel flowing to the engines. A moment of silence pulsed the air, not sacred but disbelieving.

Ethan and Esther looked up at me. They were pure and pitiful in their innocent beauty, in their hope. They were baby birds, faces upturned, waiting for food.

Now? their eyes asked.

"Now," I said pushing them forward onto the flight line. "Run to Daddy. Go!"

Scott climbed out of the cockpit. He kneeled down on the asphalt with outstretched arms, and Ethan and Esther flung themselves into his embrace. I remained at the entrance to the hangar bay, watching as if it were a movie or someone else's life. Then Scott stood triumphant against the marbled sky, a child aloft in each arm. Our eyes met. I didn't run, but by the time we hugged my heart beat faster than a sprinter's. I'm not sure how long we held each other, body to body, cheek to cheek. We were like territories on a map: unfamiliar and misshapen when pried apart, recognizable and whole only once fitted together again, ready to chart the way forward. I'd worried for so many months over that map and where to push the pin called home. Was it east or west, this Washington or the other Washington? Was it "wherever the Navy sends you"?

Fretting over these questions since I'd married into the military provided no useful answers. But standing by Scott, as Ethan and Esther pulled on our legs and begged to be held, I suddenly understood that our family is its own territory, a place fixed forever in time. In fact, we are one tiny but powerful nation, indivisible by anyone's calculations. And in that moment, I was finally home.

Afterword

"You know what's still so hard to believe?" I asked Martina as we wound our way through an art gallery in the Old Town neighborhood of Alexandria, Virginia. It was the summer of 2012, three years exactly since Scott's tour in Washington state ended and we relocated to the Washington, D.C., area. Martina's husband had also received orders to D.C. after his last tour, and she and I met every couple of months for a girls' night out.

She stopped in front of a colorblock painting, the graduated shades of lavender as subtle as Anacortes's summer sunset. Her eyes were question marks, waiting.

"Everything we went through together out West is behind us," I said. "From here, it seems like someone else's life."

"We didn't think we could survive it, but we did," Martina said with a nod.

Such stark terms, as if we ourselves, our own little band of sisters, had experienced combat. And here we were to tell the tale—clear across the country, families thriving, as it if had never even happened.

Life certainly looked different in every way, post–NAS Whidbey Island. Martina enrolled in a graduate program she'd always hoped to pursue. I had become a communications consultant for an international development organization, grateful to reclaim a professional persona so far removed from the Navy. It didn't matter to my colleagues whether I was married or what my husband did for a living.

Did I deliver good work? Did I get to the office on time and meet my deadlines? That's what they cared about. It was liberating—a welcome respite from the experience of living and working in a tight-knit military community, where the personal and the professional had been so intimately intertwined. I was more comfortable at work than I had ever been in my volunteer role as the CO's wife because the rules were simpler. Office politics and hierarchies may exist, but personal relationships are not freighted with baggage like whose husband is senior to whom. As a result, I could interact with my new colleagues and friends authentically—not as spouses-of-other-people-whose-later-actions-might-impact-my-husband's-career-so-I-better-not-say-too-much.

Martina felt the same way in her graduate program, and she seemed inspired and relaxed. We shared other sighs of relief, too: Though both of our husbands were still active-duty military officers and worked long hours, these were desk jobs, not deployments; the men might not be home in time for dinner, but they made it back to quiz the kids on spelling homework, listen to violin practice, and answer a few dozen questions about the mysteries of the universe. The same was true for Millie's husband, Leo, who was midway through a staff tour. (Millie had also gone back to work, and loved it.)

But despite my new job and Scott's smiling presence at the kids' back-to-school nights, we were the same military family we'd been for all those years that deployments defined us. Nothing thrilled Ethan (now nine years old, in fourth grade) more than escorting a flight-suited Scott to his classroom for career day. Esther (now seven years old, in second grade) proudly plastered the door of her bedroom with the black-and-white oval "IRQ—I served" bumper stickers that are ubiquitous on cars at military bases.

Thankfully, our children's lives no longer revolved around squadron cruise calendars and video teleconferences. Instead, Scott introduced Ethan to Monty Python, *Star Trek*, racquetball, ropes courses, fossil hunting, and the graphic novels our son now pored over every night in bed. In the process, this once moody child matured into a thoughtful, funny boy—calm, centered, and at peace. Esther still crawled into bed with us every morning, but not out of anxiety because Scott had just returned from a deployment or was preparing for another one. It was just part of her sweetness, transformed into our family's regular routine, and that made the experience even more delicious. As part of this wonderful new "regular routine"—just the thought of it thrilled me—she and Scott played *Legend of Zelda* on the Wii for entire weekend afternoons, and he combed the tangles out of her long, wet hair after her bath, just as he had done in Anacortes when she was a toddler.

As for me, in the three years since *Standing By* was published I still received e-mails from military spouses who told me that my book put words to feelings they'd never been able to express, and helped them feel less alone. I became involved in groups like Blue Star Families, which shares my goal of bridging America's civilian-military divide, and I occasionally accepted invitations to represent military spouses on panels for cultural events like the *Theater of War* performance, which presents readings from Sophocles' plays to forge a common vocabulary for openly discussing the impact of war on individuals, families, and communities.

The real war was the opposite of theater, of course, and even with Scott home it was always on my mind. Sixty-eight thousand troops still fought in Afghanistan, and on some days the headlines held me hostage—as on one sad morning in the fall of 2012, when I read that the number of American troop casualties in Afghanistan reached 2,000, and I spent the rest of the day in a fog of anger and sadness. (This terrible number doesn't even take into account the rising suicide rate among veterans, which that fall eclipsed the number of troops dying in battle. The one-suicide-per-day average marched statistics toward a record annual high since the start of the wars in Iraq and Afghanistan.)

My thoughts that day, and any time I heard casualty counts, were with the families of the dead. But I had equal empathy for the wives and parents of currently deployed service members listening to that statistic and fearing the next knock on the door. It's a dread that rises like nausea, overpowering the senses and stifling every other thought. I felt it as soon as we moved back to the Washington, D.C., area in the summer of 2009, when Scott was tapped for an unexpected year-long assignment in Iraq.

Scott's return from deployment, in the last chapter of *Standing By*, was supposed to end sea duty with a welcome break on shore duty, likely a staff tour in Washington, D.C. But the Navy had other plans for us, and again the phrase "Orders are not options" whirled around my brain like a siren passing much too close. This time, the orders materialized into a one-year tour in Iraq—not a cruise on an aircraft carrier, like all of Scott's previous deployments, but a job on the ground at Camp Victory, the sprawling U.S. base in Baghdad. At that time, it was a new kind of assignment called an Individual Augmentee, or IA, where service members from one branch were tapped to help round out units of other U.S. military branches overseas.

Translation? Barely a year after the squadron's homecoming, we left Washington state and moved back into the house we owned in the D.C. suburbs so that Ethan, Esther, and I could be close to family. Scott immediately traded his flight suit for two-piece Army camouflage. He spent six weeks in training stateside in a sort of remedial boot camp for naval aviators, learning Army skills like how to throw a grenade, administer an IV, and crawl on his belly. Then he strapped a backpack onto to his shoulders. With that and two weapons padlocked into what looked like a cello case, he reported to his new Army unit in Baghdad, one of two million U.S.

service members deployed to Iraq or Afghanistan since the start of the war.

It was our turn. Again.

Back in our new/old home, I noticed Ethan drawing at the kitchen table one summer morning. He was quiet, so I left him alone. He found me upstairs, unpacking boxes, and handed me a piece of paper full of stick figures calling out "Welcome home, Daddy" in cartoonish word bubbles. Scott had only been gone a few days. There were literally fifty-one more weeks to go until his return.

"You know Dad won't be back for a while, right?" I asked him cautiously.

"I want him to know we're waiting for him," Ethan answered.

That afternoon, to avoid slitting open yet another box of knick-knacks, I wrote an essay about Ethan's "Welcome home" sign for a Slate.com blog on women's issues. The editor e-mailed me back immediately, offering me a monthly column chronicling my time on my own. I named it "Deployment Diary." For the next year, with Scott on the ground in Iraq, my religion was writing and my prayers were public.

I'm glad I have those monthly deployment diaries to reflect back on now, because I didn't keep any other records of Scott's time in Iraq. Even now, I try not to think too much about it. My family and friends helped me through what turned out to be the darkest period of my life, cooking meals and babysitting children and even returning phone calls on my behalf when I couldn't face that small task. My mother-in-law came by several afternoons a week with crafts and games for Ethan and Esther, and she happily hauled them off to every G-rated movie that opened that year. Most weekends, my dad did my grocery shopping for me, and some nights my mom tucked me into my bed and my kids into theirs at the same time. All I wanted was an end to each day, and if that end came at eight p.m., I thought, even better.

Why was my response to the IA different from Scott's previous deployments? I was away from any type of squadron support, but that wasn't it: my parents, my psychiatrist, and a prescription for Prozac provided the moral and chemical backup I needed. I missed my husband terribly, but I'd lived through that emotion before. Maybe it was Ethan's trouble transitioning to a new place. He made friends following the move, but his nightmares had returned, and he cried as much in his sleep as he did when he thought of his dad during the day. He stormed around the house, ignored people who spoke to him, berated me for leaving Anacortes. Esther was quiet, which was almost worse, since I wasn't sure what she was thinking. I spent extra time with her to try to make up for Scott's being away, but I feared I was as blank and drained with her as I felt inside.

I knew, deep down, that the kids' troubles had nothing to do with my overwhelming need to climb under the covers. What was different was me. I had surpassed some internal quota for stress and was exhausted from the emotional roller coaster of the last few years. I was angry that the military had sent Scott away so soon after his last deployment. I was scared that the coming years would unfold in exactly the same way because our future was in someone else's hands, and I longed to be able to control our own destiny as a family, especially as the children got older. Being a bystander to my own life left me feeling hopeless—despite my pride in Scott, despite my certainty that his work in Iraq helped save other American troops.

Yet another failure as a Navy wife. I continued reminding myself that others had it worse—longer deployments, scarier locations, fewer options. But I no longer wondered how they did it; I just knew I couldn't do it anymore.

Still, looking back on the "Deployment Diary" columns I wrote that year for Slate, I see someone who was trying to make the best of it, and it gives me hope that this classic (and admirable) Navy wife characteristic filtered down to me after all. When our guinea pigs provided the children with a hilarious impromptu sex ed class, I wrote about that. When two county sheriffs knocked on the door asking for charitable contributions, and I hid because I thought they were military officers informing me of my husband's death, I wrote about that. When Ethan got swine flu for two weeks, and I was so tired from being up all night with him that I fell asleep while walking up the stairs—then fell down the stairs, breaking my foot—I wrote about that. Each column yanked me out of that month's pity party by forcing me to appreciate the absurdity of my own situation. Best of all, with the publication of each "Deployment Diary" I flipped over one more page of the kitchen calendar. That was all I could do to speed us toward a reunion.

Unlike Scott's homecomings from his squadron deployments and detachments, which have a hazy, observer-like quality in my memory, Scott's return from Iraq still feels intense and immediate, as if we were the only two individuals on Earth at that moment.

The clapping, the hooting, and the whistling were all very familiar. But just as the IA was markedly different from the squadron deployments so familiar to us during Operation Iraqi Freedom, Scott's welcome home was a new breed of welcome back for the two of us.

As I hurried toward the terminal at Baltimore-Washington International Airport, where U.S. troops land after serving overseas, I spotted the cheerful retirees from Operation Welcome Home who applaud each service member returning from deployment. These greeters, clad in American flag T-shirts and carrying handmade signs thanking the troops, organize themselves to be present for every incoming military flight, even ones landing at two a.m.

But after endless planning for the day, I feared I had missed Scott's flight. There was no unit representative for family members of IAs who could update us on timing, and when the military airline's schedule changed, as this one had, service members were usually in transit and couldn't call or send e-mail. I ran from the escalator to the gate, half expecting to see Scott leaning against his duffel bag, bored and waiting. A few of the greeters, looking sympathetic, approached and assured me that that no one had walked through the double doors yet. I stationed myself off to the side and scanned the terminal.

Unlike the celebratory, crowded homecomings for military squadrons and units, there were very few other families present that day because many of these returning service members were IAs like Scott. And although Scott was home, the terminal at BWI was only the first point of entry into the United States for many of them before boarding a series of connecting flights to their local airports across the country. The BWI affair was for most a not-quite-home-yet homecoming, low-key and deflating. That's why Operation Welcome Home had organized itself, creating a memorable event in place of a solitary meander to another gate.

"Come closer," one of the Operation Welcome Home greeters urged me, pulling my elbow forward. He had a camera in his hand and his patriotic T-shirt was tucked neatly into his chinos. But I was rattled after convincing myself that I was late, and when I tried to talk, it came out as a sob. I covered my mouth. The greeter seemed sympathetic to emotions he couldn't understand. He returned to his spot, leaving me alone, which was exactly what I wanted.

The past year of Scott's Iraq deployment played in my mind like a film, and I let myself watch it because I knew the movie was finally ending: scenes from winter's record snowstorms and multiple power outages, from the kids' long illnesses, from my broken foot and a concussion following an accident on black ice. There was a scar over my eye from that same accident, and I touched it often to test the tenderness. Sometimes that eye wept, and I wasn't sure whether I was really crying. This time, I was.

Service members in camouflage stepped through the double doors, blinking in the bright light of the terminal. The greeters cheered and clapped. Soldiers, sailors, and Marines navigated the gauntlet of outstretched hands, some reaching back eagerly, most nodding politely and smiling, a few staring straight ahead, acknowledging no one. They carried little, and they looked exhausted. "Thank you for your service," the greeters called out over and over. But it never sounded rote.

What does service really mean? After America's eleven years of war in Iraq and Afghanistan, and my eleven years as a military spouse, I have a better understanding of what it entails—not just in the military, but in any field that demands similar sacrifice and devotion. I'm still not sure where the obligation of service ends. I'm not sure if thinking of service as an obligation negates the authenticity of that service. Clearly, the greeters set out to serve their country each time they met these flights, vowing that no veteran will return to the United States unappreciated. If they consider it an obligation, it is one they fulfill joyfully, which is more than I can say for how I felt about our family's commitment to the military when Scott was deployed.

My eyes were still on the double doors. As Scott walked through, I heard myself gasp. He looked exactly the same as he does in the photos hanging throughout our house, but he was smiling back at me. I ran to him, thinking: *We made it.* I heard applause as we embraced. I don't know how long we stood there, but when we pulled apart and made our way toward the exit, dozens of greeters reached toward Scott. He tried to shake every hand and return every hug.

"Thank you for your service," a female greeter said, but I didn't look up. "Thank you for your service," I heard again, insistently. The same voice. I searched her out in the crowd. The woman had close-cropped gray hair and was so small that she barely peeked out among the others in the group. When I found her, she was already looking into my eyes. I realized she was talking to me, and not to my husband. I appreciated the sentiment, but I wasn't used to hearing it and I didn't know what to say in return. She disappeared into the throng. I held Scott's hand tightly and we started home, this time for good.

October 2012
Potomac, Maryland

Reader's Guide

The author says in the introduction that the intensity of life as a military spouse has transformed her into a warrior on behalf of her children. Is there something inherent about mothering in the midst of crisis that causes this reaction in parents everywhere?

Millie and Martina have dramatically different approaches to how to live life as a military spouse, and their attitudes are strikingly different. Explore and discuss the two outlooks. How do these attitudes help each woman cope with life during deployment? How might those attitudes ultimately be helpful or destructive?

Many families must relocate because of one partner's job. In what ways are there differences between a civilian family that moves to a new location because of a new career opportunity, and a military family that relocates because of a new posting?

The author speaks of the first civics lesson she gives her children, when the three of them are watching the flag come down during "retreat," and how she answers her son when he asks why they must remain quiet and still. Do you think her explanation about the significance of the flag is appropriate? How would you explain an abstraction like patriotism to a young person?

Families of some officers—in this case, a squadron commander— live in a fishbowl environment where their behavior is scrutinized

by many. Other families, such as those of religious ministers or political figures, describe their lives the same way. Is it fair to bring
children up in this way? Might this sort of attention to a family's
actions cause them to act one way in public and differently in private?

Are military wives today more likely to make decisions for themselves in the same way that economic empowerment has given
women the freedom to make their own choices in life? If so, what is
the source of military wives' empowerment? If you think that the
position of military wives has remained unchanged throughout
the decades, why is that the case?

Was there a particular character with whom you felt closest (one
with a similar educational background, socioeconomic status, family makeup, and so on)? What was it about her story that you most
identified with?

The author describes the military as a "secular faith" and "working
man's religion," stating that it draws people with a belief in something bigger than themselves. Does this "secular faith" inspire a
feeling of alienation or admiration? Discuss the author's assessment
of religion in *Standing By*, and how it affects her outlook after the
family moves to Washington state.

Has the integration of women in the military changed how we
look at service members? Is there still a sense of the military as a
boys' club?

What did you find surprising about the facts about children who
experience the deployment of a parent?

How has reading this book changed your opinion of or interest in
military families?

Resources

IAVA (Iraq and Afghanistan Veterans of America): www.iava.org
The first and largest nonprofit, nonpartisan organization for Iraq
and Afghanistan veterans.

Blue Star Families: www.bluestarfam.org
Founded by a group of military spouses to raise awareness in civilian
communities and leaders of the challenges of military family life.

Code of Support: www.codeofsupport.org
Seeks to ensure that all Americans understand and appreciate the
service and sacrifice of the 1 percent who serve in uniform, are
committed to sharing responsibility for our national defense, and
are actively involved in supporting troops, veterans, and military
families.

**Tragedy Assistance Program for Survivors (TAPS): 1.800.959.
TAPS (8277) or www.taps.org**
A resource for those grieving someone who died while serving
in the military, providing safe and confidential support for the
bereaved.

**Veterans Crisis Line/National Suicide Prevention Lifeline:
1.800.273.8255 (press 1) or www.veteranscrisisline.net**
Connects veterans in crisis and their families and friends with qualified, caring Department of Veterans Affairs responders. Veterans

and their loved ones can call, chat online, or send a text message to **838255**.

The Legacy Project: www.warletters.com
A national, all-volunteer initiative that encourages Americans to seek out and preserve the personal correspondence of our nation's veterans, active-duty troops, and their loved ones.

Acknowledgments

Learning about the experience of military families throughout American history has been awe-inspiring and humbling. I have often felt that I had no business writing about a world in which I have passed only a half-dozen years, when so many military wives have devoted their entire adulthood to supporting the cause. I wish they would write their own books, because their stories are electrifying. I respect and admire these women immensely, and I stand a little straighter knowing that they have welcomed me into their ranks. Although I can't thank them individually, I am grateful to the spouses of VAQ-130 and the women of NAS Whidbey Island who spoke openly to me about their experiences. I could not have written this book without them.

I write often of my involvement with our squadron, but Theresa Chelberg and Lisa Rouse were on the front line; they are the heroes of our squadron's families. Their selflessness and devotion to military families taught me more about Navy life on the home front than any book I've read.

Here in town, the intelligent and kind employees of the Anacortes Public Library, where I wrote large chunks of this book, always knew what to say, how to help, and where I could find a quiet spot to work. The families of Fidalgo Bay Montessori School were unfailingly caring and solicitous, and I am especially grateful to school director Charmaine Johannes and to fellow parents Lisa Jackson and John Lunsford and Janna and Todd Young for their support. The friendship of K. C. Pohtilla, Nadia Garrick, Karen and

Jack McDonald, and Allan Redstone and Marie Christenson helped me surmount obstacles large and small.

Outside this community, Sue Hoppin of the Military Officers Association of America provided many valuable insights into the world of military spouses and pointed me toward important sources of information. Vianne Newell opened my eyes to so many things, especially the ways nomadic, father-deprived military kids become successful adolescents and adults with loving families of their own. Joe Perpich reached out when our family experienced a deployment-related crisis, and held my hand until we crossed to the other side. Marilyn Brilliant, Ellen Steinberg, Cathy Sulzberger, Joan Nathan, Debbie Kessler, and Linda Lingle advised with exactly the right touch. Greg Ashe, Mark Ermi, and Diana Ermi retrieved old memories of growing up as military brats on bases across the country and around the world. Alan Buckholtz, T. J. Williams, Milton Cooper, and the late Howard Goldstein reached back to long-ago scenes from their own military service. Mady Wechsler Segal and Donald Zillman graciously shared their scholarly research. Pamela Elbe of the National Museum of American Jewish Military History unearthed facts and figures that I was unable to track down on my own. Laurence Kotler-Berkowitz helped me make sense of statistics and thought through the numbers with me.

Dan Jones understood immediately that the phrase "Flat Daddy" revealed a truth far deeper than a cardboard cutout. The seed of this book was planted in *The New York Times'* "Modern Love" column on a Sunday morning that would change my life, and Dan's careful reading and thoughtful editing is the reason why.

Andrew Carroll's Legacy Project, his books, and his tireless efforts on behalf of American military families have permanently altered the way American service members are recognized and remembered. His enthusiasm energized my efforts to give voice to the life of at least one military spouse. Similarly, Da Chen's belief that this book was inevitable gave me the confidence to think so myself, and his ongoing dedication to this project inspired me to maintain faith during dispiriting moments.

My colleagues at SPARC (the Scholarly Publishing and Academic Resources Coalition) acted as if my taking an indefinite leave of absence to write a book was a completely rational request. I am fortunate to count Heather Joseph, Rick Johnson, and Jennifer McLennan as much more than just coworkers.

For resources provided to Scott and me in our role as lay leaders, sincere thanks to Lieutenant Commander Philip D. King, USN, and the NAS Whidbey Island Department of Religious Ministries, as well as Captain Gerral David and Anne David. Rabbi Barry Baron and Rabbi Nathan Landman of the JWB Jewish Chaplains Council, have provided ongoing assistance and support. Rabbi Menachem M. Katz and the Aleph Institute helped our family and our community mark every holiday. Rabbi Yossi Mandel and Chaya Sara Mandel, formerly of Chabad of Snohomish County, and Rabbi Levi and Hadassah Backman of Chabad of Bellingham, reached out on numerous occasions. Captain Irving Elson, USN, has been there for us since this journey began.

Alisa Kotler-Berkowitz, my first reader, should have earned frequent flyer miles by the word, because she'd have traveled the globe twice by now. Monique Dull and Eric Miller's sensitive translation of Penelope's words made her come alive for me and helped me appreciate *The Odyssey*'s purpose and depth. Gadi Karmi, who listened with great gentleness, was always just one e-mail or phone call away. Tamara Shepard, Christa Degnan Manning, Sabine Durier, and Sandy Trupp read and responded with care. Julia Serebrinsky has been steady, patient, and loyal throughout this entire process.

My skilled, savvy, and thoughtful agent, Joëlle Delbourgo, helped me achieve a dream I have nurtured since I was six years old. My editor, Sara Carder, worked closely with me while giving me the freedom to fly, and I will always appreciate her confidence in me and her dedication to this book. Kat Obertance helped me meet important deadlines. Gary Mailman spent hours on the phone with me, asking hard, important questions. Thanks as well to Brianna Yamashita for her excellent publicity campaign for the book.

My mother-in-law, Susan Moran, has celebrated the good times with us and mourned when circumstances warranted. I am grateful every day that she and my sister-in-law, Lindsay Moran Kegley, steered Scott my way. My aunt Eileen Buckholtz has provided valuable counsel from the moment I began my career as a writer. My uncle Edward Weidenfeld and my aunt Sheila Rabb Weidenfeld made the time early on to guarantee that this project was on the right track.

I am wordlessly, tearfully, and eternally grateful to my siblings, Charlie Buckholtz, Joshua and Ashley Buckholtz, and Hillary Buckholtz. Their frequent visits calmed me when panic set in. My grandmother Beatrice Weidenfeld dispenses wisdom with great intelligence and tact, and I feel lucky every day that I can pick up the phone and call her for advice.

My parents, Marjorie and Neil Buckholtz, were my first friends, and through word and deed they have always demonstrated to me how to stand by those you treasure. Their take-no-prisoners approach to love has multiplied the joys and divided the sorrows. They have made everything possible for me, and taught me everything I know—especially the rewards of being bold, original, and honest. As my brother says, thanking them is like breathing.

Writing about my children, Ethan and Esther, forced me to see past the sleep deprivation their nutty habits imposed on me. Once that happened, I was stunned by their bravery and resilience. I respect them tremendously. It will be many years until they read this book, but I hope they eventually understand how the process of writing it made me a better mother (though at times a very distracted one).

My husband, Scott, is a very private person, but he has never wavered in his commitment to this project. He urged me to speak in my own voice at all times. His open heart and generous spirit leave me breathless; his encouragement and support make our life together the purest, easiest joy I have ever known. There are a lot of words in this book, but none of them portrays the depth of what we have together, or how thankful I am for him. Miracles happen, and finding him was mine.

Selected Bibliography

This is by no means a comprehensive record of sources detailing the experience of American military spouses, but I have listed below the books and articles that resonated with me most deeply, and may provide useful background for readers wishing to learn more. I am deeply grateful to the authors of these works, which helped shape my perspective and understanding of military life.

Ageton, Arthur. A., with William P. Mack, *The Naval Officer's Guide*. Annapolis, MD: Naval Institute Press, 1972.

Ali, Lorraine, and Raina Kelley. "The Curious Lives of Surrogates," *Newsweek*, April 7, 2008.

Alt, Betty Sowers, and Betty L. Alt. *Following the Flag: Marriage and the Modern Military*. New York: Praeger, 2006.

Alt, Betty Sowers, and Bonnie Domrose Stone. *Campfollowing: A History of the Military Wife*. New York: Praeger, 1991.

Alvah, Donna. *Unofficial Ambassadors: American Military Families Overseas and the Cold War, 1946–1965*. New York: New York University Press, 2007.

Biank, Tanya. *Under the Sabers: The Unwritten Code of Army Wives*. New York: St. Martin's Press, 2006. (Reissued as *Army Wives: The Unwritten Code of Military Marriage*.)

Bleser, Carol K., and Lesley J. Gordon, eds. *Intimate Strategies of the Civil War: Military Commanders and Their Wives*. New York: Oxford University Press, 2001.

Carroll, Andrew, ed. *Grace Under Fire: Letters of Faith in Times of War*. New York: Doubleday, 2007.

Carroll, Andrew, ed. *Operation Homecoming: Iraq, Afghanistan, and the Home Front, in the Words of U.S. Troops and Their Families*. New York: Random House, 2006.

Carroll, Andrew, ed. *War Letters: Extraordinary Correspondence from American Wars*. New York: Washington Square Press, 2001.

Carson, Ann Baker, and Mary Clarke. *The Memoirs of the Celebrated and Beautiful Mrs. Ann Carson: Daughter of an Officer of the U.S. Navy, and Wife of Another, Whose Life Terminated in the Philadelphia Prison* (1838; orig. from the New York Public Library). Digitized by Google Books, July 19, 2007.

Chesnut, Mary. *A Diary from Dixie: The Civil War's Most Celebrated Journal, Written During the Conflict by the Wife of Confederate General James Chesnut, Jr.* New York: Gramercy Books, 1997. (Facsimile of the 1905 edition edited by Isabella D. Martin and Myrta Lockett Avary.)

Cline, Lydia Sloan. *Today's Military Wife: Meeting the Challenges of Service Life*. Mechanicsburg, PA: Stackpole Books, 1995.

Conroy, Pat. *The Great Santini*. New York: Dial Press, 2002.

Custer, Elizabeth B. *Boots and Saddles, or Life in Dakota with General Custer*. Norman: University of Oklahoma Press, 1961.

Estes, Mary Belle. *With Powder on My Nose: Adventures of a Military Wife*. Kenton, TN: Write Up the Road, 2005.

Garrett, Sheryl, and Sue Hoppin. *A Family's Guide to the Military for Dummies*. Hoboken, NJ: Wiley/For Dummies, 2008.

Harrell, Margaret C., Nelson Lim, Laura Werber Castaneda, and Daniela Golinelli. *Working Around the Military: Challenges to Military Spouse Employment and Education*. Santa Monica, CA: RAND Corporation, 2004.

Henderson, Kristin. *While They're at War: The True Stories of American Families on the Homefront*. New York: Houghton Mifflin, 2006.

Hightower, Kathie, and Holly Scherer. *Help: I'm a Military Spouse. I Get a Life Too: How to Craft a Life for You As You Move with the Military.* Washington, DC: Potomac Books, 2007.

Holmes, Kenneth L., ed. *Covered Wagon Women: Diaries & Letters from the Western Trails, 1850,* vol. 2. Lincoln: University of Nebraska Press, 1983.

Hosek, James, Beth Asch, C. Christine Fair, Craig Martin, and Michael Mattock. *Married to the Military: The Employment and Earnings of Military Wives Compared with Those of Civilian Wives.* Santa Monica, CA: RAND Corporation, 2002.

Houppert, Karen. *Home Fires Burning: Married to the Military— For Better or for Worse.* New York: Ballantine Books, 2005.

Krajeski, Marna A. *Household Baggage: The Moving Life of a Soldier's Wife.* Deadwood, OR: Wyatt-MacKenzie, 2006.

Leckie, Shirley Anne, ed. *The Colonel's Lady on the Western Frontier: The Correspondence of Alice Kirk Grierson.* Lincoln: University of Nebraska Press, 1989.

Lehr, Doreen. "Do Real Women Wear Uniforms? Invisibility and the Consequences for the U.S. Military Wife," *Minerva* 14, no. 3 (December 1996).

Levya, Meredith. *Married to the Military: A Survival Guide for Military Wives, Girlfriends, and Women in Uniform.* New York: Fireside, 2003.

McCandless, Bruce, Brooks J. Harral, and Oretha D. Swartz. *Service Etiquette: Correct Social Usage for Service Men on Official and Unofficial Occasions.* Annapolis, MD: Naval Institute Press, 1959.

McGrath, Lissa. *The Complete Idiot's Guide to Life as a Military Spouse.* New York: Alpha Books, 2008.

Moreau, Donna. *Waiting Wives: The Story of Schilling Manor, Home Front to the Vietnam War.* New York: Atria Books, 2005.

Potter, Jane Grey. "A Lass Who Loved a Sailor." *Scribner's Magazine* 67 (January–June 1920). Digitized by Google Books.

Pye, Anne Briscoe, and Nancy Shea. *The Navy Wife: What She Ought to Know About the Customs of the Service and the Management of a Navy Household*. New York: Harper & Brothers, 1942.

Richey, Frances. *The Warrior: A Mother's Story of a Son at War*. New York: Viking, 2008.

Roth-Douquet, Kathy, and Frank Schaeffer. *AWOL: The Unexcused Absence of America's Upper Classes from Military Service—and How It Hurts Our Country*. New York: HarperCollins, 2006.

Segal, Mady Wechsler. "The Military and the Family as Greedy Institutions," *Armed Forces & Society* 13, no. 1 (1986): 9–38.

Smiley, Sarah. *Going Overboard: The Misadventures of a Military Wife*. New York: New American Library, 2005.

Stallard, Patricia Y. *Glittering Misery: Dependents of the Indian Fighting Army*. Norman: University of Oklahoma Press, 1992.

Stavridis, Laura Hall. *Navy Spouse's Guide*. Annapolis, MD: Naval Institute Press, 2002.

Steen, Joanne M., and M. Regina Asaro. *Military Widow*. Annapolis, MD: Naval Institute Press, 2006.

Stockdale, Jim and Sybil. *In Love and War*. Annapolis, MD: Naval Institute Press, 1990.

Summerhayes, Martha. *Vanished Arizona: Recollections of My Army Life*. Ed. Milo Milton Quaife. Chicago: The Lakeside Press, 1939.

Tillery, Carolyn Quick. *At Freedom's Table: More than 200 Years of Receipts and Remembrances from Military Wives*. Nashville: Cumberland House, 2001.

Wertsch, Mary Edwards. *Military Brats: Legacies of Childhood Inside the Fortress*. New York: Harmony Books, 1991.

The author gratefully acknowledges permission to quote from the following:

The Navy Wife by Anne Briscoe Pye and Nancy Shea. Excerpt from pages 24, 25, 192, 290 of the fourth edition. Copyright 1942, 1945, 1949, 1955, 1965 by Harper & Brothers. Copyright renewed © 1970, 1973 by Philander B. Briscoe and Margaret B. Pegg. Reprinted by permission of HarperCollins Publishers.

"Meditation at Lagunitas," from *Praise*, copyright © 1979 by Robert Hass. Reprinted by permission of HarperCollins Publishers.

"Night in Blue," from *Here, Bullet*, copyright © 2005 by Brian Turner. Reprinted with the permission of Alice James Books, www.alicejamesbooks.org.

Sincere thanks to Pat Conroy for permission to reprint selections from his introduction to Mary Edwards Wertsch's *Military Brats: Legacies of Childhood Inside the Fortress*.

Lines from *The Odyssey* are quoted from an original translation by Monique Dull and Eric Miller.

Portions of this book appeared, in different form, in the following: *The New York Times, Real Simple, Seattle Metropolitan, World Jew-*

ish Digest, and the *Forward.* The author gratefully acknowledges these publications and their editors.

Portions of the afterword appeared in the "Deployment Diary" column that Alison Buckholtz wrote for Slate.com. The author would like to thank her editor, Hanna Rosin.

ABOUT THE AUTHOR

Alison Buckholtz wrote Slate.com's "Deployment Diary" column, and her articles and essays have been published in *The New York Times, The Washington Post, Real Simple,* and many other publications. As an advocate for military families, she has appeared on *NBC Nightly News,* NPR, and in national news stories. Her *L.A. Times* op-ed, "An 'It Gets Better' for the Troops," was the inspiration for a national public service announcement campaign drawing attention to the fast-growing rate of military suicides. She lives in the Washington, D.C., area with her husband, an active-duty Naval officer, and two children.